ETHICS AND AIRPOWER
IN WORLD WAR II

Also by Stephen A. Garrett

Bangkok Journal

From Potsdam to Poland: American Policy toward Eastern Europe

Ideals and Reality: An Analysis of the Debate over Vietnam

ETHICS AND AIRPOWER IN WORLD WAR II

The British Bombing of German Cities

Stephen A. Garrett

St. Martin's Press
New York

ISBN 0-312-16453-X (paperback)

Library of Congress Cataloging-in-Publication Data

Garrett, Stephen A., 1939-
    Ethics and airpower in World War II: the British bombing of
    German cities / Stephen A. Garrett.
        p. cm.
    Includes bibliographical references and index.
    ISBN 0-312-08683-0 (cloth)—ISBN 0-312-16453-X (pbk.)
       1. World War, 1939-1945—Aerial operations, British—Moral and
ethical aspects. 3. World War, 1939-1945—Germany—Moral
    and ethical aspects. 4. Great Britain—Military policy—Moral
    and ethical aspects. I. Title.

    D786.G36 1993
    940.54'4941—dc20   92-37119
                                           CIP

First published in hardcover in the United States of America in 1993
10 9 8 7 6 5 4 3 2 1

*For Marta, as before and as always,
and for Crister, Karolina, and Eric as well,
for whose generation this cautionary tale
may hopefully lead to its not being repeated.*

CONTENTS

Preface

The origins of this book may be at least partly traced to two experiences I had during a trip to Europe several years ago.

The first occurred during a visit to the Franconian city of Würzberg in Germany. Located along the river Main and founded in the eighth century, Würzberg has been called a rococo jewel box. It is also sometimes referred to as "the town of Madonnas," based on the numerous replications of the city's patron saint found in niches of old homes. The university at Würzberg is some 400 years old, and is today one of Germany's leading educational institutions. The city perhaps achieved its greatest prominence during the 18th century, by which time the prince-bishops who governed Franconia had established their presence in the famed *Residenz*. This town palace constituted one of the most ornate and extravagant Baroque creations of the period and was visited by all the leading personalities of Europe.

Built over a period of 24 years by the famed court architect Balthazar Neumann, the *Residenz* is set amid extensive gardens and is a virtual fairyland of marble busts, columned vestibules, glittering chandeliers, white and gold stucco work and statuary, and gold-encased mirrors. Numerous murals are to be found in the spacious rooms spread throughout the structure. Particularly notable is the ceiling fresco by the Venetian painter Giovanni Battista Tiepolo entitled *The Four Continents,* depicting hundreds of men, women, children, angels, and animals as well as a good part of the history and geography of the world. When I observed to a docent at the *Residenz* that all this seemed to be in a remarkable state of preservation, he commented evenly that actually much of it was a restoration. Most of the *Residenz,* he said, had been destroyed in a British bombing raid on the night of March 16, 1945.

On that particular night (I later discovered) a force of some 225 Lancasters, the main British heavy bomber during World War II, appeared over Würzberg and dropped 1,127 tons of bombs with great accuracy in a period of 17 minutes. About 90 percent of the built-up area of the city was destroyed and estimates of the number of dead varied between four and five thousand.[1] It was possible to restore the *Residenz* primarily because much of the outer shell of the building survived the fire caused by the bombing. Other major structures in Würzberg were also reconstructed, a painstaking process that often involved using the original stones to create an approximation of the original walls.

A German fighter pilot, Wilhelm Johnen, offered his recollections of the raid on Würzberg. He remembered his co-pilot growling that "they're not even going to respect the hospital city of Würzburg. There really aren't any armaments factories there." Johnen went on to describe how

> bomber crews opened their bays and rained incendiaries on to the city below. The phosphorus ignited as soon as it hit the air and joined into a huge burning cloud which slowly settled on the city. It was a Dantesque and terrible sight. . . . This fiery cloud knew no pity. It sank on churches and houses, palaces and citadels, broad avenues and narrow streets. At the outset burning drops spurted from the cloud causing isolated fires, then the burning veil enveloped Würzburg. In a few moments a gigantic path of flame lit up the dark night and turned the clouds to scarlet. Würzberg was burning.[2]

Würzberg, at the time of its ordeal, evidently did contain very little industry, particularly of military significance, and given the fact that Germany was virtually prostrate before Allied military forces at this point (the final surrender came only seven weeks later), it was hard to imagine by what calculation it could have been considered fit for destruction.

Some weeks later I was in London and paid a visit to the Imperial War Museum. This is a magnificent collection of information and artifacts on military history, and in particular the British experience with war in the 20th century. Overall, it celebrates the British success in waging war and is at times a self-congratulatory account of Britain's ability to endure and prevail during wartime. There was, for example, a particularly interesting exhibit of the courage of the British people during the German blitz of London in 1940-1941. In all of the exhibits in the Imperial War Museum, only one struck a discordant note. This had to do with British bombing of Germany in World War II.

One of the pictures in this display carried a caption stating that the "strategic bombing offensive played a major but by no means decisive role in victory in World War II." There were several references to how "controversial" British bombing of Germany had been and a particular comment on Dresden, "where thousands of civilians died." Remarkably for a museum that generally was a testament to British aptitude (and fair play) in war, there was a frank statistic to the effect that "between 300,000 and 600,000 German civilians died in the British bombing offensive." Overall the impression seemed to be of some embarrassment at the efforts of Bomber Command in World War II, particularly when this exhibit was compared to the rest of the museum and its tributes to British arms.

These encounters with Würzberg and the Imperial War Museum aroused in me more than the normal curiosity about the circumstances behind British strategic bombing of Germany in World War II. I already had some familiarity with the general details of that policy (who has not heard of Dresden?), but I began to read into the literature concerning British air policy in a more systematic fashion. In doing so I noticed that there were consistent references to the moral issues involved, but that these were generally offered only as asides or as a small part of the overall analysis. Given the fact that the British assault on German cities seemed a pretty important event in the evolution of ideas concerning ethics in wartime, this seemed to be a surprisingly casual and/or at least incomplete way of approaching the matter. Indeed there didn't seem to be any single study that tried to address the moral questions raised by the bombing as a topic in itself.

Thus the genesis of what is offered here: certainly not a full history of British air policy in World War II, but an attempt at systematically examining the moral issues presented by the British bombing offensive against German cities in the period 1939-1945. It should be clear from the outset that this is a basically critical look at Bomber Command, at least insofar as the ethical implications of its work are concerned. Yet the spirit of the enterprise is not so much prosecutorial, the simple levying of moral condemnation, as it is an attempt to let both the supporters and the opponents of British strategy speak for themselves and to arrive at a reasonably fair assessment of the viewpoints presented. A particular point of concern is to establish why apparently humane individuals agreed to the systematic destruction of hundreds of thousands of German civilians and what lessons we may draw from this fact.

There are a few preliminary observations about British policy at the time that may be appropriate in establishing a sense of the issues involved. During the first few months of the war, British long-range bombers did little more than make occasional forays over the Ruhr valley dropping propaganda leaflets (although there were a few strikes against German naval facilities on the Baltic). The atmosphere at this point was perhaps reflected in the astonished reaction of one high-ranking British official to the idea that German industrial facilities should be attacked. Quite out of the question, he insisted, since after all these facilities were private property. British restraint during this period may be accounted for in part by her relatively limited technical capability for massive air strikes against Germany. There was also concern about German retaliation in kind if the informal proscription against large-scale city strikes was abandoned. Also important, however, was the principle that civilized states were bound, even in wartime, to observe the crucial distinction between combatant and non-combatant. The indiscriminate bombing of German cities evidently would represent a total rejection of this traditional credo.

Having considered the initial British stance on strategic bombing against Germany, it is instructive to consider the events of the night of July 27, 1943. That evening 787 British bombers attacked the center of the German city of Hamburg with a combination of explosive and incendiary bombs. It had been a hot and dry summer in northern Germany, and this fact, combined with the unusually tight concentration of the bombs on the working class districts of the city, produced a firestorm that eventually covered an area of about four square miles. Temperatures at the center of the firestorm reached about 1,800 degrees Fahrenheit, accompanied by winds of hurricane force. One British pilot described the scene: "It was as if I was looking into what I imagined to be an active volcano. . . . Our actual bombing was like putting another shovelful of coal into the furnace." Over 40,000 people died on that evening in Hamburg within a period of about two hours.[3]

The transition in British policy from a rejection of "indiscriminate bombing" to an apparent embrace of precisely this concept resulted over the course of the war in the progressive destruction of large areas of almost every major city in Germany. In view of the odious character of the Nazi regime, and the normal tendency in wartime for public opinion to accept their government's definition of "military necessity," it might be supposed that the change in British bombing policy would have aroused relatively little comment or protest, at least within Britain itself. It is true that only a small minority actively opposed the new strategy, yet one is also struck by the fact that the activities of Bomber Command did become increasingly controversial as the war progressed, not only among segments of the general public but within the British government itself, including individuals from both the civilian and military establishments.

Moreover, there has been a much wider debate over the appropriateness of British air strategy in the years since, and the fact that feelings still run high on the matter was reflected in the recent controversy over the erection of a statue in honor of Bomber Command's chief, Sir Arthur Harris, on the grounds of a chapel dedicated to the Royal Air Force. Under the auspices of the Bomber Command Association, this memorial to Harris and the aircrew of Bomber Command was unveiled on May 31, 1992, by Queen Elizabeth, the Queen Mother. The current German major of Dresden declared that the memorial did not belong in the Europe of 1992. His counterpart in Würzburg even appealed to the British ambassador to Germany to use his influence to stop the construction of the memorial "in the name of countless victims of bombing attacks against civilians." Within Britain itself a heated debate also arose over the notion of paying tribute to Sir Arthur Harris. The press was filled with letters and articles either defending the area offensive as a military necessity or denouncing the inhumanity of Britain's assault on German cities. Nine protesters were arrested during the dedication ceremony, and during her speech, the Queen Mother was frequently interrupted and heckled by those condemning the work of Bomber Command.[4]

This book concentrates on British strategic bombing in World War II, but in doing so I am not suggesting or implying that some very important moral questions might not be raised as well about the American use of airpower in that struggle. As it happens, there is a study that considers the American side of things in considerable detail, and that is one reason for my focusing on the British experience in this particular essay.[5] It does need emphasizing, in any case, that general attacks on population centers were hardly the exclusive preserve of Bomber Command in World War II. To be sure, American doctrine generally stressed "precision" bombing of specific military and industrial targets such as airfields, petroleum installations, defense factories, and the German transportation system. As the war progressed, there was an increasingly ill-concealed American disdain for the supposedly crude and ineffective British obsession with simply devastating large urban areas. General Ira Eaker, commander of the Eighth Air Force, asserted that "we should never allow the history of this war to convict us of throwing the strategic bomber at the man in the street."[6]

Despite this pious stance, however, the United States, particularly in the last year of the war, did engage in general area attacks on German cities. American aircraft participated, for example, in the destruction of Dresden in February 1945. They also staged a series of area attacks on the Ruhr (or what was left of it). Berlin was bombed on February 3 in an assault that may have taken as many as 25,000 lives. Under Operation Clarion, American planes sought out targets in smaller German towns and villages whose populations had so far been spared air attacks. Such raids were justified as likely to produce a "stupefying effect" on the morale of those attacked.[7]

And, of course, there was the American fire-bombing of Japanese cities, notably the March 9, 1945 raid on Tokyo (in which 300 B-29s destroyed over 16 square miles of the city), as well as the atomic devastation of Hiroshima and Nagasaki.

I would suggest, then, that American readers have a good deal to reflect on themselves as they consider this study of the moral issues involved in British bombing in World War II. This is even more the case given various controversies that have arisen over the use of American airpower in the years since 1945. There was the debate that developed in this country, for example, about the use of American air strikes in Vietnam. More recently there has been some heated discussion about the number of Iraqi civilian casualties in the 1991 Gulf War as a consequence of American bombing attacks. There was also the increasing furor in the 1980's over the morality of American nuclear targeting doctrine, in particular the American strategy of putting millions of Soviet citizens at risk as part of the concept of deterrence.

In suggesting that these debates (and others) were in many ways reflective of the one waged over British bombing policy in World War II, it is important to identify the similarities. One obvious parallel is that both British society and American society have long prided themselves on their adherence to relatively humane values and civilized standards of conduct. Both countries conceive that they traditionally have been in the forefront of the struggle to establish higher norms of behavior for others in the world community to emulate. The British during World War II, and the Americans for most of the period after 1945, were similar in that both saw themselves as opposing a particularly virulent threat to these very standards. In both instances there was the notion of the "supreme national emergency," which, many argued, justified the adoption of measures that might be rejected in the absence of such a fundamental challenge. To what extent each nation should compromise some of its basic values in meeting the threat was a basic point of contention.

British decisions concerning the bombing of Germany, and American use of airpower as well, may also be seen as a response to certain basic technical factors. In each instance the British and Americans developed devastating new capabilities for wreaking havoc on the enemy, and there was an inevitable pressure to employ (or threaten to employ) these new capabilities in the national defense. Moreover, each set of decisions was made in an atmosphere in which previous moral constraints on the use of violence by states had come under severe pressure. The British turn toward area bombing was in a sense only a logical extension of methods used in World War I, in particular the German use of submarine warfare against civilian shipping and the British *de facto* policy of trying to starve the German people into surrender by instituting a naval blockade of Germany. In the American case, the use of atomic weapons against Hiroshima and Nagasaki (which, ironically, might be regarded as a logical extension of British area bombing) presumably conditioned American opinion to the notion of using—or threatening to use—airpower as a fundamental ingredient of national strategy, no matter what its implications in terms of traditional standards of civilian immunity in wartime.

This book is divided into three sections. Part I briefly discusses some of the developments in the use of airpower, and theories as to its use, prior to World War II. This is followed by a summary description of the British strategic air offensive during the conflict itself. Part II focuses on the reactions of various individuals and groups in British society to the bombing campaign against German cities. Part III attempts to offer a general moral critique of the area offensive and concludes with some general observations about what British air policy in World War II may have ultimately signified. I make no claim here that this is an exercise in primary research on the details of British bombing. There are a number of fairly exhaustive studies that have plumbed the relevant data to the extent that it is unlikely any genuinely new or startling information will come to light at this point on the subject. Nor is this a formal essay in moral philosophy on the relationship between ethics and violence. There is a literature in its own right on that topic. Instead what I have tried to do here is something in between: to take the standard evidence that does exist on the British strategic air offensive in World War II and to subject it to a special form of inquiry using some basic propositions in ethical discourse.

As I have already suggested, an important focus of this essay will be on the arguments, values, and perspectives of those who either opposed or approved of British strategy at the time it was unfolding. I want to give special attention to the way in which various individuals confronted their own humanity in dealing with the issues raised by the bombing of German cities. Perhaps more than anything else this essay seeks to depict and analyze a daunting type of moral dilemma, in which there were perhaps few if any complete villains or complete heros. Indeed the drama to be presented here might be regarded without exaggeration as a type of classical tragedy, in which even the strongest and most praiseworthy of individuals feel themselves overwhelmed by circumstances. A British scientist working in operational research for Bomber Command referred to these lines from *Macbeth* to express the "emptiness of the soul which allowed me to go on killing without hatred and without remorse":

. . . I am in blood
Stepp'd in so far that, should I wade no more,
Returning were as tedious as go o'er.

This is strong language and perhaps too strong. Yet one of the political and philosophical conundrums to be examined here is how a sensitive humanity in the modern era can meet challenges to basic civilized values without at the same time undermining those very values in the process of defending them.

PART I

BACKGROUND

1

The Crescendo of Bombing

"Then rose the seed of Chaos, and of Night
To blot out order and extinguish light."

—Alexander Pope

This is a book about the evolution of an idea: the use of airpower by one country to impose its will on another. We might begin with two historical references.

On June 23, 1812, Emperor Napoleon Bonaparte invaded Russia. In the ensuing weeks his soldiers routed all the opposition that the regime of Alexander I offered to them. As Napoleon approached the outskirts of Moscow, the Russians tried an entirely novel tactic to slow the inexorable march of the Grand Army. They attempted to use a balloon filled with explosives to stem the advance of the French forces. There is no record of this innovation having produced any noticeable results. Napoleon occupied the Russian capital a few days later.

A little over 132 years later, British and American military planners proposed the following scheme, codenamed Thunderclap, for bringing the war against Germany to a successful conclusion. Thunderclap envisioned a joint assault by several thousand British and American bombers on the German capital of Berlin; there would be round-the-clock bombing over a period of four days and nights. The explicit military premise behind Thunderclap was that much if not most of Berlin would be reduced to smoking rubble. The expectation was that this type of cataclysmic assault would totally shatter the German people's will to continue the war.

For a variety of reasons Thunderclap was never fully implemented. However the distance that warring powers had traveled from the first abortive use of "airpower" by the Russians in 1812 to the awesome deployment of armadas of strategic bombers in World War II represents perhaps one of the most striking developments in the history of armed conflict. It is instructive to consider how all this came about, both in terms of the march of technology and even more in terms of the march of ideas as to how war could success-fully—and legitimately—be waged.

THE PAST AS PROLOGUE

The experiment by Imperial Russia with airborne bombing was to find little further reflection in military tactics for almost a hundred years, save for an equally fruitless effort by the Austrians to use balloons to drop explosives on Venice in 1849. The first generally recognized use of bombing from the air in the modern period came only with a fairly haphazard use of Italian aircraft in the Italo-Turkish war of 1911-1912 (the bombs were flung over the side of the aircraft after the pilot had pulled their pins with his teeth.) In this instance the Italians launched several air strikes against Arab villages in Libya as part of their campaign to liberate that country from the Ottomans.[1]

It was not until World War I that the application of aerial attacks on an enemy's homeland was introduced as a regular part of the strategy of the warring powers. Aircraft specifically designed for such missions came under development, including the necessary bombsights and directional devices as well as bomb racks themselves with ordnance designed to fit them. Beginning in 1916, French aircraft launched strikes against several German cities in retaliation for enemy assaults on Paris and other French towns. The British undertook a series of raids on zeppelin factories and other military targets in Germany in the area of the Saarland, Mannheim, and Stuttgart. It was the Germans, however, who led the way in demonstrating how aircraft could be used against the enemy's own territory.

From January 1915 to November 1916, zeppelins were employed to attack targets in the north of England and the Midlands as well as in the British capital. Beginning in May 1917, the so-called Gotha raids against London and other cities were initiated. These involved genuine bombers rather than airships, and their employment served to reinforce the earlier impression of a basic threshold having been crossed in the means of modern war. Overall there was a total of 208 airship and 435 airplane sorties undertaken against England by the German air force. About 300 tons of bombs were dropped, killing around 1,400 people and wounding another 3,400.[2]

Compared to the figures that were to be produced by the next great war, these may have been relatively modest results, but they established an ominous precedent. The notion that civilians could be a legitimate and even important target of air strikes seemed to have acquired at least a tentative acceptance. As one authority on the use of airpower in World War I wrote, "One principle seems to have been followed [which was] that military objectives could be bombed wherever found, regardless of their location, and, it seems, regardless of the injury to non-combatants and private property."[3] The fact that an expanded utilization of airpower was now an accepted item on the agenda of defense planners in Great Britain as well as elsewhere was reflected in the establishment of an independent British bombing force in April 1918, and even more in the amalgamation of the Royal Flying Corps and the Royal Naval Air Service into the Royal Air Force in the same month. By the end of the war, the new service could claim some 300,000 officers and enlisted personnel, which represented a 150-fold increase of its strength as of 1914. Even more impressive was the fact that in the period 1914-1918 Britain built almost 50,000 flying machines of all types.[4]

In the interwar period a heated and generally rather abstract debate developed over what the experience of World War I had to say about the potential of strategic bombing. In the generic sense the strategic application of airpower simply meant the use of aircraft for direct assaults on the enemy's homeland and his fundamental capacity to make war (as distinguished, for example, from the use of aircraft in tactical support of ground forces). The discussion remained somewhat abstract because there was, after all, a rather slim body of actual evidence on which to base conclusions. This did not prevent such distinguished voices as that of the military historian Sir Basil Liddell Hart from arguing that strategic bombing might prove the decisive weapon in a new war. Liddell Hart was persuaded of the merits of such bombing in part because of his desire to develop a military alternative that would avoid the mindless slaughter of the trenches in World War I. He argued somewhat plaintively that when it was realized that strategic bombing would inflict "a total of injury far less than when [a war was] spread over a number of years, the common sense of mankind will show that the ethical objection to this form of war is at least not greater than to the cannon-fodder wars of the past."[5]

From an operational point of view, Liddell Hart based his support of strategic bombing on the supposed fragility of civilian morale in wartime. Drawing in part on his analysis of the effects of the limited German bombing campaign against British cities in World War I, he focused on the spirit and will of societies as a whole in supporting the military in the field. Defeat in war, he claimed, "is the result not of loss of life, save, at the most, indirectly and partially, but by loss of morale."[6] The quickest way to undermine or destroy this morale, he claimed, would be by a sustained campaign of strategic bombing. This was an argument that was to prove critical to the subsequent British bombing offensive against Germany in World War II, and it was elaborated on at the time by the famous Italian airpower theorist, General Giulio Douhet.

Douhet's approach to the significance of the bomber offensive may be taken as a particularly unvarnished summary of the view of many bombing advocates before World War II. His essential proposition was that a massive air attack by a fully-developed strategic bomber force at the outbreak of hostilities would prove decisive to the outcome of any war.

> A complete breakdown of the social structure cannot but take place in a country subjected to this kind of merciless pounding from the air. The time would soon come when, to put an end to horror and suffering, the people themselves, driven by the instinct of self-preservation, would rise up and demand an end to the war—this before their army and navy had time to mobilize at all![7]

Douhet impatiently dismissed any notion that such an attack might be regarded as unduly harsh. Indeed he echoed Liddell Hart in arguing that "mercifully, the decision will be quick in this kind of war, since the decisive blows will be directed at civilians, that element of the countries at war least able to sustain them." Thus a conflict fought in these terms might yet "prove to be more humane than wars in the past in spite of all, because they may in the long run shed less blood."[8]

Within British official circles the leading voice in the interwar years arguing for the primacy of a strategic bombing capability for Britain was undoubtedly that of Sir Hugh Trenchard, the first chief of the Air Staff for the RAF. Trenchard waged an untiring campaign to obtain what he considered adequate support for his airmen and even more to fight off the doubts of the more senior services about the necessity of their being a continued independent British air force. Trenchard's views were perhaps best summarized in a memorandum to the other service chiefs in May 1928.[9] He put his case directly: "It is not necessary for an air force, in order to defeat the enemy nation, to defeat its armed forces first. Air power can dispense with that intermediate step . . . and attack directly the centres of production, transportation and communication from which the enemy war effort is maintained." Trenchard envisioned his bombing campaign as actually having two fundamental purposes: to destroy the enemy's technical capacity for continuing the war effort, and to undermine his will for doing so. On the latter point, he put the "moral" effects of bombing as more important than the physical effects by a factor of 20:1.

Trenchard did accept that it was "contrary to the dictates of humanity [to engage in] the indiscriminate bombing of a city for the sole purpose of terrorizing the civilian population." On the other hand, he regarded it as entirely legitimate to terrorize munitions workers into ceasing their work or stevedores to stop loading arms onto ships. "Moral effect," he said, "is created by the bombing in such circumstances but it is the inevitable result of a lawful operation of war—the bombing of a military objective." Put in this way, many later critics of British bombing policy in World War II would have been forced to nod assent. The question was to be, however, how the concept of a military objective was subject to elaboration and expansion as the air offensive evolved.

Sir Hugh Trenchard's confident predictions about the effect of a modern strategic bombing campaign was hardly translated into a commitment of resources to the RAF at the time by his superiors in the British government. Between 1920 and 1938, the RAF received on average only 17 percent of extremely limited defense expenditures of less than $1 billion. Even so, both the Government and the British people in general tended to nurse rather apocalyptic images concerning the probable effect of air strikes during the first days of a new war with Germany. The widely held belief was that the Germans would initiate hostilities with massive bombing of vulnerable British cities. Winston Churchill himself estimated that under a continuous air assault on London at least three or four million people would be driven out into the surrounding countryside. On the eve of war in 1939, the government was prepared for about a quarter of a million casualties in the capital alone for the first three weeks of air attack, along with three million psychiatric cases, an equivalent number of refugees, and up to 50 percent destruction of property. Upon the declaration of war, the Ministry of Health issued a million burial forms to local authorities.[10] Ironically, it seems that at the same time as the RAF was denied the resources to build itself up, the essential arguments of Liddell Hart, Douhet, and Trenchard concerning the potential of airpower had received wide acceptance.

The fears expressed were given a certain degree of impetus by the scattered examples of air strikes against cities that had taken place in the years after 1918. The Italians bombed the Ethiopian capital of Addis Ababa in 1936, the Japanese devastated Nanking in China in 1937, and in the same year there was the attack of the German Condor Legion on the undefended Basque town of Guernica, in which about 1,000 people were killed and 70 percent of the buildings destroyed. To be sure, each of these attacks took place against relatively primitive or even non-existent air defenses, but they seemed to cast a sinister shadow nonetheless. It was against this background that the British government was finally led to make some firm decisions on the future strength of the RAF as the prospect of war with Germany steadily increased in the late 1930s.

On the basis of a report from a Joint Planning Committee submitted to the cabinet and the Committee of Imperial Defence in the spring of 1937, the decision was to give primary emphasis to building up British fighter defenses in order to blunt the anticipated German aerial assault on Britain should war come. The British bomber force during this period was expected to concentrate its efforts largely on attacking German airfields and giving support to ground operations in Western Europe. There was, however, some guarded language in the decision suggesting that Bomber Command (established as a separate unit of the RAF in 1936) would also have responsibility for a broader campaign of strategic bombing of Germany as the war progressed.[11]

This may have provided some satisfaction to Trenchard and his supporters, but the essential fact was that Bomber Command at this point hardly had a significant capacity for undertaking any kind of sustained strategic air offensive. It is true that in 1936 the Air Ministry authorized plans for the development of a fleet of large four-engined bombers, and designs were approved for aircraft that later evolved into the Stirling, Halifax, and Lancaster. As of 1939, however, only 17 of the 33 operational squadrons scheduled for Bomber Command were equipped with aircraft even theoretically capable of strikes against European targets from England. Aircraft based on the 1936 designs (notably the Lancaster) were not expected to be available until 1943.[12]

Given this situation, a subcommittee of the Committee on Imperial Defence seriously considered a proposal in which Britain would publicly offer not only to refrain from any attacks on German industries in the Ruhr but even to eschew imposing a naval blockade on Germany as well. The Government rejected the idea, but there is no question that at this point, given her weaknesses in strategic airpower, British officials were of the opinion that mutually agreed-upon restrictions on bombing would be an advantage. The guidelines issued to the RAF were that they were "to do nothing that might be construed as an attack on civilians and so give the enemy an excuse to do likewise."[13]

Despite this supposed commitment to using air strikes against only traditional and essentially tactical military targets, the siren call of a decisive strategic air offensive against Germany still had its adherents in Great

Britain, both within and outside government. The alluring image of a short-cut to victory through airpower may not have received a specific imprimatur in the late 1930s, but it wasn't totally rejected either. Given an as yet unforeseeable combination of circumstances, there was certainly a strong possibility that Bomber Command would eventually get a chance to show what it could do to make Trenchard's arguments come to life. In the event, this was precisely what happened.

THE COMING OF THE STRATEGIC AIR OFFENSIVE

At precisely eleven o'clock (European summer time) on the morning of September 3, 1939, the government of Great Britain declared war on Germany in response to Hitler's invasion of Poland. Later that evening, some ten British Whitley bombers rolled down the runways at Linton-on-Ouse airbase in Northern England, bound for Germany. Their targets were a half-dozen cities in the Ruhr valley and the Baltic ports of Bremen and Hamburg. Shortly before daybreak, nine of the ten bombers returned to base (one aircraft landed in France). Their 13-ton payload had consisted of nothing more lethal than some 5.4 million propaganda leaflets, meant to impress on the German people that victory by the Allies was inevitable and inviting them to overthrow the Hitler regime.[14]

Given the extensive attention paid to the possibilities of strategic bombing prior to 1939, it was rather bizarre and certainly ironic that the first assault on Germany in World War II by British Bomber Command should have consisted of nothing more than a shower of paper. Sir Arthur Harris, who was later to achieve fame (and notoriety) as head of Bomber Command, spoke for many British airmen when he dismissed such efforts as essentially frivolous. "The only thing achieved," Harris commented, concerning this and later leaflet exercises, "was largely to supply the continent's requirements of toilet paper for the five long years of war." He was presumably just as dismissive of another operation of Bomber Command at this time, which involved dropping huge quantities of teabags over Holland to demonstrate that beleaguered Britain still possessed sufficient comforts to be generous with them.

From early September to about the middle of May 1940, Bomber Command divided its time between dropping still more leaflets over the German Reich, occasional attacks on naval and other "precise" military targets, and a distinct concern about avoiding any unnecessary harm to enemy civilians. For example, in November 1939, the War Cabinet secretly considered a plan for bombing targets in the Ruhr in response to a German invasion of Belgium, but there was great reluctance to do so because of the expected effect on the civilian population.[15]

The factors in this self-restraint were varied. As already mentioned, Bomber Command hardly had the resources at this point to undertake a major strategic bombing effort against Germany. There was also concern about the reaction of the rest of the world, and especially of the United States, to a major aerial assault on Germany that would put civilians at risk. On September 1, 1939, President Roosevelt had addressed an appeal to all the belligerent powers calling for a restriction of aerial warfare to specifically military targets. The French and British announced their acceptance of this standard on the following day, and the Germans added their assent as well on September 18th.[16] The Nazi motivation in doing so was clear enough: their concern that in an unrestrained contest of strategic bombing, Germany might well be at a disadvantage. As Hitler himself said, "the guiding principle must be not to provoke the initiation of aerial warfare by any action on the part of Germany" (a somewhat striking statement in view of the prewar fears in Great Britain about the German threat to British cities).[17]

What may be regarded as a period of innocence for Bomber Command during the first eight months of the war came to a close on May 15, 1940, when in a directive signed by Winston Churchill, who had replaced Neville Chamberlain a few days earlier, the RAF was now authorized to attack land targets east of the Rhine. The spur to this decision was evidently a reduced concern about the possibilities of German retaliation on British cities as well as the fact that at least some strategic bombing of the enemy seemed at this point to be one of the few ways in which the British could carry the war to the enemy, a consideration that acquired particular currency after the evacuation at Dunkirk.

For approximately the next two years Bomber Command undertook a steadily widening series of strikes against the German homeland. At the official level the stated emphasis was on what were called precision or selective attacks against carefully defined military and industrial objectives (the German oil industry, communications, and aircraft plants, for example). There were further references to the necessity of sparing civilians as much as possible. An instruction from the War Cabinet to the Air Ministry in early June 1940, for example, stressed that air attacks "must be made with reasonable care to avoid undue loss of civil life in the vicinity of the target."[18] At the same time, what would come to be called "area bombing," or generalized assaults on urban targets, was, like Banquo's ghost, never very far from the proceedings. As early as October 1940, the Air Staff issued a new directive that oil targets should be attacked on clear nights but that whole cities could at least be considered as alternative targets in less favorable weather. In December 1940, what is generally considered the first open British effort at area bombing came with an attack on the city of Mannheim, a raid specifically described as a retaliation for the earlier German assault on Coventry.

Perhaps the principal voice calling for a less restrained approach to Bomber Command's activities was that of the Prime Minister himself. As far back as July 1940, he had written to Lord Beaverbrook, Minister for Aircraft Production, that there was only one thing that would bring Hitler down, and that was "an absolutely devastating exterminating attack by very heavy bombers from this country upon the Nazi homeland."[19] Several months later Churchill expanded on this theme in a statement to the War Cabinet, which suggested that "whilst we should adhere to the rule that our objectives should be military targets, at the same time the civilian population around the target areas must be made to feel the weight of war."[20] Churchill's chief of the Air Staff, Sir Charles Portal, also was increasingly persuaded of the merits of area bombing. Portal suggested that 20 to 30 towns and cities should be selected as potential targets for Bomber Command, with the primary aim being the deliverance of very heavy material destruction and a demonstration to the enemy of the expanding power and severity of air bombardment from Britain. As one individual privy to the discussion on bombing policy at this point put it, "the moral scruples of the Cabinet on this subject have been overcome."[21]

The government's wavering between an ostensible program of precision bombing and an increasing tendency toward area bombing was resolved finally in a policy statement of February 14, 1942. The bomber offensive, according to Directive No. 22 issued to Bomber Command, was now to be "focused on the morale of the enemy civil population and in particular of the industrial workers." In case there was any doubt at Bomber Command headquarters about what was now intended, the chief of the Air Staff sent a follow-on communication the next day: "Ref the new bombing directive: I suppose it is clear that the aiming points are to be the built-up areas, not, for instance, the dockyards or aircraft factories. . . . This must be made quite clear if it is not already understood."[22] Sir Arthur Harris, who was to become head of Bomber Command on February 23, indicated that he, at least, had no misunderstanding on this point.

The decision by the British to adopt a straightforward strategy of area or indiscriminate bombing of Germany (in other words, the systematic devastation of German cities) after 1942 was obviously a landmark in the evolution of warfare and more particularly the concept of total war. Over the next three years, about three-quarters of the bombs dropped on Germany by Great

Britain were against area targets. How to account for the adoption of such a momentous course of action?

A rather curious mix of emotional, political, technical, and theoretical considerations seems to have been involved. For some there was clearly the feeling that the Germans had after all initiated city attacks—first with the bombing of Warsaw, then the assault on Rotterdam in May 1940 (which was said to have caused 30,000 fatalities), and finally with the blitz on Britain itself. Extending in its most intense form from the fall of 1940 to the spring of 1941, the Blitz eventually resulted in some 50,000 tons of bombs being dropped on British cities, which led to about 40,000 civilian deaths. Given this record of events, it was not hard to argue that after all the Germans had indeed sowed the wind and now were to reap the whirlwind. The Prime Minister himself sometimes seemed to suggest that even though he personally had little desire as such for revenge, the British people did expect retaliation in kind. In a flight of hyperbole he commented that the people now demanded that all Germans should be massacred or castrated. He told the House of Commons that "on every side is the cry, 'We can take it,' but with it is also the cry, 'Give it them back.'"[23] In effect, Churchill's argument seemed to be that in order to sustain the nation's morale, it was necessary to do unto others as they were doing to Britain.

It is hard to gauge how significant a factor the calls for pure retribution were in the February 14 directive to Bomber Command. As it happens, however, there was a key operational factor confronting the government in early 1942 that may be seen as pushing the RAF toward a strategy of area bombing quite on its own. It became apparent early in the war that the lack of sufficient fighter support, and the growing effectiveness of German air defenses, presented the RAF with the prospect of prohibitive losses if it attempted to attack German targets in daylight. As a matter of policy, then, Bomber Command by the spring of 1940 had come to concentrate almost entirely on nighttime bombing of the enemy.

Could such raids achieve a sufficient accuracy to allow the targeting of precise military objectives? For a time, the analysts at Bomber Command attempted to maintain the fiction that such was possible, but the evidence as it accumulated seriously undermined their case and was dealt a particular blow by the so-called Butt Report of August 1941. At the behest of Lord Cherwell, Churchill's principal scientific adviser, Mr. D. M. Butt of the Cabinet Secretariat undertook a systematic study of the efforts of Bomber Command to date. His analysis revealed that in British air strikes against specific targets in the Ruhr, only one-tenth of the bombers even found their way to within five miles of the assigned target. For other areas the figure was a still depressing one in three.[24] The conclusion seemed to be, then, that if Great Britain were to continue its strategic bombing offensive against Germany, the only feasible targets were large urban areas, where the problems of inaccuracy would be much less compelling. Since few, if any, of the major figures in the Government were inclined simply to call a halt to the bombing offensive—particularly as it was the only major evidence at the time of Britain's determination to carry on the war effort—the turn to indiscriminate bombing followed almost as a matter of course.

Still, it would be somewhat misleading to suggest that those involved simply, and rather mindlessly, adopted area bombing without thought as to its practical military utility and only because it was the one thing Bomber Command could do. There were in fact attempts by those in authority to develop a broader strategic rationale for area bombing beyond simply the limitations that Bomber Command then confronted. Lord Cherwell was a particular contributor to this process, and his ideas reflected one of the standard themes of the prewar airpower theorists. In a famous minute to the Prime Minister on March 30, 1942, Cherwell concentrated on the impact on German morale of a major British area bombing campaign. Based on his analysis of the German bombing of British cities, he argued that "having one's house demolished is most damaging to morale. People seem to mind it more than having their friends or even relatives killed." He went on from there to estimate that with adequate resources and by concentrating on the 58 major German population centers, Bomber Command could by 1943 render a third of the German people homeless. "There seems little doubt that this would break the spirit of the people." The concept of the shattering of the German people's morale, and thus of Germany's will or ability to continue the war, was enshrined henceforth as one of the guiding premises of British bombing policy. As the official history of Bomber Command puts it, "Because of the position which he occupied and the time at which he submitted his minute, Lord Cherwell's intervention was of great importance. It did much to insure the concept of strategic bombing in its hour of crisis."[25]

There were, to be sure, other rationales brought forward to justify the bombing of German cities aside from its putative effect on morale. One of these was that it would help to divert German resources from the Russian campaign and the Middle East in order to provide for the air defense of the Reich. Moreover, since German industry was naturally concentrated in and around the major German cities, even so-called indiscriminate attacks on these places was bound to damage or destroy some of the relevant factories. Such attacks would also lead to a shattering of the whole fabric of German civil life, which in turn would create a basic dislocation in war production and the German home front's ability to support the Reich military machine. Sir Arthur Harris was particular ardent in advancing these propositions. He even went so far as to suggest that if the British government gave its full support to the bomber offensive, Germany could essentially be defeated by airpower alone.[26]

THE AREA BOMBING OF GERMANY: THE FIRST PHASE

Sir Arthur Harris did not wait long after assuming leadership of Bomber Command before he began his long campaign to demonstrate that the theory of area bombing could be translated into a productive reality. The Baltic port city of Lübeck provided a convenient early test case. An old medieval town constructed largely of wood ("built more like a fire-lighter than a human habitation," as Harris observed), Lübeck was attacked on the night of March 28 by 234 RAF bombers. Some 200 acres, or about half the city, was leveled, the German estimate being that over 15,000 people had their homes destroyed as a consequence of the raid. Another old Hanseatic city, Rostock, was given similar treatment later in April. Over 100,000 civilians were forced to evacuate the city as a result of this attack. At this point Bomber Command had in its raids on Lübeck, Rostock and other places destroyed a total of about 780 acres, which was roughly equal to the damage visited on Great Britain during the Blitz. As Harris laconically recorded, we had now "about squared our account with Germany."[27] The war—and the area bombing of Germany—was to continue for three more years.

Despite these early successes, Harris was acutely aware that the credibility of Bomber Command as a major, perhaps the major, focus of the British war effort was hardly accepted by everyone in authority. The February 14th decision had authorized a policy of area bombing of Germany, but a number of important individuals continued to question the wisdom of committing really substantial resources to the bombing campaign when other needs (for example, in the Middle East) were also pressing. Doubts also continued to exist as to whether Bomber Command, even if given all that it asked for, could really produce results commensurate with such an outlay of men and materiel. Even the Prime Minister seemed to have his doubts. Earlier he had been an enthusiastic supporter of the bombing campaign, but by the fall of 1941 he reacted to a plan from the RAF for the building of a total force of 4,000 bombers by saying that "it is very disputable whether bombing by itself will be a decisive factor in the present war. On the contrary, all that we have learnt since the war began shows that its effects, both physical and moral, are greatly exaggerated."[28]

In a rather striking admission of the situation in which he now found himself, Harris recalled that he "had to regard the operations of the next few months as a commercial traveller's samples which I could show to the War Cabinet." He decided that there was a need for a truly spectacular operation that hopefully would lay to rest the doubts of his critics and in particular ensure support for Bomber Command from the Prime Minister. It was thus that the plan for Millenium, the first thousand-bomber raid of the war, was conceived. The target chosen was Cologne, and the results were impressive indeed. Approximately 600 acres of the city were devastated on the night of May 30, 1942, and as the final wave of bombers approached, the city was burning with such ferocity that the light from the flames could be seen from 150 miles away. More than 45,000 people were rendered homeless, and the roads out of Cologne were clogged with a massive exodus of refugees. When Harris reported the results of Millenium to Churchill, he was gratified by the Prime Minister's reaction. "I knew at once that he was satisfied then. . . . he wanted above all to get on with the war and no one understood better than he the vast strategic consequences of this operation."[29] Thus the continuation of a full-fledged area bombing offensive, together with the necessary commitment of resources, had apparently ben accepted by the one person whose opinion was decisive.

Even so there was to be a period of some months before Bomber Command actually entered into a sustained campaign of destroying German cities. One problem was the lack of sufficient numbers of aircraft to sustain such a campaign. Despite the thousand-bomber raid against Cologne (achieved by using every available aircraft at Harris's disposal, including even training units), Bomber Command on an average daily basis had at its disposal only 261 bombers as of the end of 1942. Equally important was the slow introduction of the Lancaster, perhaps the best heavy bomber on all sides in the war, but not available in any quantity until early in 1943. There was also the challenge of developing adequate guidance systems for Bomber Command's attacks against the German heartland. Even given the less stringent standards of accuracy required for area bombing, it was not until the end of the year, with the arrival of Oboe and H2S as navigational aids, that the British could feel a renewed confidence about hitting their aiming points in the areas being attacked.[30] Also important in supplementing the new navigational technology was the development of the Pathfinder Force, which consisted of elite Bomber Command crews whose task it was to identify and mark the target for the bombers that followed. One of the most successful innovations of the air war, the Pathfinders, together with the other developments in equipment and navigation, now made a full area offensive conceivable.[31]

In January 1943, the British Prime Minister and the American President, together with their principal advisers, met in Casablanca to consider the future of the strategic bombing of Germany. The Casablanca Conference, and the subsequent Washington Conference in May of the same year, provided an overall framework for a Combined Bombing Offensive (codenamed Pointblank) against Germany. The directives that issued from these meetings were regarded by Bomber Command as final authorization for a general assault against German cities. In actuality, the wording of the decisions on Pointblank seemed to place primary emphasis on attacking relatively precise targets in Germany such as submarine construction yards, the German aircraft industry, and oil and transportation facilities. At the same time, there was a built-in ambiguity in the instructions, caused basically by differing American and British theories on the strategic air offensive, that allowed or encouraged Arthur Harris to pursue a strategy that he was resolved on in any case.

The British area bombing offensive against Germany over the next 12 months involved a host of different operations but can be summarized by reference to three important episodes in that campaign. After the war, the United States Strategic Bombing Survey offered a rather clinical description of how Bomber Command generally went about its business.

> In determining the aiming point for city attacks, Bomber Command prepared a zone map of the city based on aerial photographs. Administrative and residential areas between 70 and 100 per cent built-up were outlined in red. Similar areas between 40 and 70 per cent built-up were outlined in green. Major railroad facilities were outlined in buff and industrial areas in black. In most German cities the black areas lay largely on the perimeter. Area attacks on a previously unbombed city were aimed at the center of the red area, while subsequent attacks on the same city were usually directed against the center of the most heavily built-up areas which remained undestroyed.[32]

The first major application of this technique was in the Ruhr valley, where over the period March–July 1943, there were a total of 43 major raids. Virtually all the major urban centers of the Ruhr suffered badly as a result, with the city of Barmen-Wuppertal, for example experiencing the destruction of almost 90 percent of its built-up area during a raid on May 29. Bomber Command's efforts during the so-called Battle of the Ruhr amply demonstrated that it had developed a raw striking power greater than that heretofore displayed by any of the world's major air forces. The pilots themselves seemed to view with some awe the nature of the enterprise on which they were embarked. On looking down upon the burning spectacle of the Ruhr one night, one man commented that "the clouds were like cottonwool soaked in blood."[33] Such emotions were presumably also in evidence during the second major event of the area offensive during this period, the Battle of Hamburg.

Hamburg was the recipient of 33 major air attacks (code-named Operational Gomorrah) from July to November 1943. The night raids on July 24, July 27, and July 29 represented the apex of the assault on Hamburg. In each instance well over 700 bombers from the RAF rained a combination of incendiary and explosive bombs on the central city area of Hamburg. Approximately 74 percent of the most densely populated area of the city was destroyed. About 50,000 people were killed in these attacks, and around one million refugees fled to safer outlying areas.[34] Perhaps the most noted aspect of the Hamburg raids was the phenomenon of the firestorm, which produced hurricane-type winds of 150 MPH and sucked people, trees, even whole buildings into the center of the flames. The Police President of Hamburg summarized the fate of his city this way:

> Its horror is revealed in the howling and raging of the firestorms, the hellish noise of exploding bombs and the death cries of martyred human beings as well as in the big silence after the raids. Speech is impotent to portray the measure of the horror, which shook the people for ten days and nights and the traces of which were written indelibly on the face of the city and its inhabitants.[35]

The devastation of Hamburg was henceforward referred to by the Germans simply as *Die Katastrophe.*

The final significant event in the first phase of the area offensive against Germany was the Battle of Berlin. This began on the night of November 18 and continued for four months until the end of the following March. During this period some 35 raids of more than 500 bombers each were launched against the German capital as well as other cities. Sixteen of the missions were directed at Berlin itself, which represented the greatest single focusing of Bomber Command's efforts since the beginning of the war.[36] Arthur Harris had begun the Battle of Berlin with high hopes. In a typically self-confident communication to the Prime Minister, he had asserted that "we can wreck Berlin from end to end if the US Army Air Forces will come in on it. It will cost between us 400 and 500 aircraft. It will cost Germany the war."[37] As it happened there was only marginal American participation in this enterprise, and the results of Bomber Command's own efforts proved to be a great disappointment. For various reasons far less devastation was delivered on Berlin than in the raids against Hamburg (only about one-third of the acreage destroyed as compared to the earlier attacks). Moreover these results had to be balanced against the increasing losses that Bomber Command was now suffering in its campaign against Berlin and other major cities. The potency of the German night-fighter force, as well as of their anti-aircraft defenses, was reflected in an average loss rate for British bombers on the order of about 5.0 percent. Sometimes it was even more severe: in an attack on Nuremberg in March 1944, some 94 bombers were lost and another 71 damaged out of a total force of 795 employed.[38]

This level of attrition could not be long sustained, and in view of the rather problematical effect that area bombing seemed to be having on the German ability to maintain her war effort, something of a crisis of confidence developed at Bomber Command and amongst others in authority about the future of the air offensive. As it happened, however, the doubts that had now arisen became submerged in the planning for D-Day, the Allied invasion of Europe. In what, under the circumstances, may be regarded as a blessing in disguise for Bomber Command, Harris was now ordered to divert virtually all his aircraft from the bombing of Germany to more direct support for the coming landings in Normandy. Over the next several months, Bomber Command devoted the brunt of its operations to attacks on the German rail system in France and the Low Countries in order to disrupt German transport of reinforcements and materiel to the front after D-Day. They did so with admirable success, and the evidence in fact suggests that the combined British and American assault on these targets played a critical role in the successful Allied invasion. By late May, traffic on the railway network in France had declined to 55 percent of the January figure, and by D-Day itself had fallen to only 30 percent of the earlier figure.[39]

THE AREA BOMBING OF GERMANY: THE SECOND PHASE

By September 1944, Allied forces had not only firmly established themselves in France but were making rapid progress against the increasingly shattered German defenses. At this point, the debate resumed over strategy for Bomber Command in its attacks on Germany itself. There was a clear consensus on the part of the Combined Chiefs of Staff as well as most other informed observers that Bomber Command would do best at this point to concentrate on German oil facilities as well as the enemy's communications network. The prospects that Harris's forces could now carry out this sort of precision bombing campaign, moreover, seemed almost beyond dispute. Earlier limited strikes by the British and Americans against petroleum targets in Germany had proved a great success.

By September, the Luftwaffe's fuel supply had been reduced to ten thousand tons of octane, whereas a monthly minimum of around 160,000 tons was needed. Bomber Command's ability to hit oil targets, as well as its efficiency in attacking the German transportation system, demonstrated prior to D-Day, suggested that it was indeed capable now of a general precision bombing campaign.

That this was within its reach was indicated even more by the severe deterioration in German air defenses by this stage of the war. The Luftwaffe's lack of fuel, the severe attrition inflicted on the German fighter force by introduction of the American P-51 Mustang, and the steady loss of German radar and ground control stations in France made the skies over Germany increasingly comfortable for Allied aircraft. From September onward, in fact, the Allies came to enjoy what the British official history termed "virtual operational omnipotence" in the air, at night, and even during the day. The latter point was a key one: daylight bombing, with relatively modest losses, promised a degree of accuracy in hitting targets that was crucial to any precision bombing campaign. In pondering all this, however, Arthur Harris saw no need to abandon his long-held belief in the essential correctness of the area bombing strategy. As he put it, "I strongly objected to stopping the [area] offensive for which we had worked for five years." He dismissed the earlier success of Allied bombers in attacking oil targets by saying that "what the Allied strategists did was to bet on an outsider and it happened to win the race."[40] He remained skeptical of what he called "panacea targets," that is, supposed chokepoints in German war industry whose destruction could be decisive.

In the months that followed, the chief of the Air Staff, Sir Charles Portal, repeatedly urged Harris to join with the Americans in a precision bombing campaign against Germany. Harris strongly implied that he would resign rather than accept any significant limitations on his renewal of the area offensive, and he stubbornly continued to stress his own priorities. In the last three months of 1944, the British dropped more bombs on Germany than in the whole of 1943, and some 53 percent of these were delivered on cities compared to 14 percent directed at oil facilities and about 15 percent on transportation targets. Earlier Harris had established a list of 60 German cities that he intended to destroy, the accomplishment of which, he believed, would effectively end the war. By December, Harris's list of cities ripe for destruction had been pretty well translated into reality. Bomber Command had devastated or seriously damaged 80 percent of all German urban areas with populations of more than 100,000. This exercise in destruction continued even into the spring of 1945, with almost 40 percent of British bombing being directed at city targets.[41]

The most famous (or notorious) of these attacks was undoubtedly the raid on Dresden on the night of February 13. It has already been remarked how

Arthur Harris insisted on continuing his area offensive despite pressure from higher authority to focus on more precise targets. It is thus more than a little ironic that perhaps the most dramatic single bombing attack of the war was spurred on by direct instructions from the British War Cabinet itself. The ostensible rationale for the raid on Dresden had much to do with the Russians. The attack would help to relieve German pressure on the Eastern front and convince Stalin that despite some recent Allied difficulties, in particular the Battle of the Bulge, his Western partners were still doing their fair share in defeating the Nazis. Dresden was attacked by two waves of approximately 800 Lancasters (the Americans delivered their own strikes on the following two days), and as a result burned for a week. Estimates on casualties vary widely, from a minimal guess of about 35,000 to a more drastic figure of over 200,000. In order to prevent the spread of disease, the authorities cordoned off the center of the city and constructed 25-foot-long grills where thousands of the victims were cremated.[42]

The British official history describes the Dresden raid as "the crowning achievement in the long, arduous and relentless development of a principle of bombing [the area offensive]"[43] At this point Prime Minister Churchill evidently decided that Bomber Command's "crowning achievement" should be left to speak for itself, and in perhaps the most controversial reference to the area offensive that he offered during the war, he wrote to the chief of the Air Staff along the following lines:

> It seems to me that the moment has come when the question of bombing of German cities simply for the sake of increasing the terror, *though under other pretexts,* should be reviewed. Otherwise we shall come into control of an utterly ruined land. We shall not, for instance, be able to get housing materials out of Germany for our own needs because some temporary provision would have to be made for the Germans themselves. The destruction of Dresden remains a serious query against the conduct of Allied bombing. I am of the opinion that military objectives must henceforward be more strictly studied in our own interests rather than that of the enemy.

> The Foreign Secretary has spoken to me on this subject, and I feel the need for more precise concentration upon military objectives such as oil and communications behind the immediate battle-zone, *rather than on mere acts of terror and wanton destruction, however impressive.*[44]

Sir Charles Portal was greatly offended by Churchill's reference to "terror" as a previous goal of British strategy, and in response the Prime

Minister delivered a revised minute that dropped such sensitive references and instead concentrated on the pragmatic benefits to be obtained from a cessation of the area offensive. Having said this, it is striking that whatever qualms were now being felt did not prevent area attacks on German targets being continued virtually to the last days of World War II. Thus Würzberg was devastated on March 16, 1945, two days later the city of Witten was two-thirds destroyed, and a month later there was a further raid on the Berlin suburb of Potsdam by 500 Lancasters, resulting in about 5,000 civilian fatalities.[45] In a sense all this could be considered as simply reflexive actions of the vast machine of destruction that Bomber Command had become by this point. At long last, however, the RAF Air Staff issued a directive on April 16 that officially ended Bomber Command's strategic air offensive against Germany. Harris accepted this directive on the practical grounds that there were essentially no more area targets to be attacked in Germany.

OVERVIEW

In all Bomber Command launched some 390,000 sorties against Germany in the entire course of the war, with area attacks accounting for about 70 percent of the total effort. Some 8,900 British aircraft were destroyed in the conflict, and approximately one million tons of bombs were dropped on the enemy. During the war, about 125,000 men and women joined Bomber Command, either as aircrew or ground support personnel. Of this number about 56,000 (almost all officers and NCOs) lost their lives, about half that were injured, and more than 11,000 taken prisoner, for an overall casualty rate of about 76 percent. The sacrifice in officers alone was greater than what the British suffered in the whole of World War I.[46] As to the destruction visited on Germany, it is estimated that over 500,000 German civilians lost their lives to Allied bombing. Perhaps another 1,000,000 received serious injury. Around three million homes were destroyed. And, of course, Germany lost the war.

The connection between the last sentence and the preceding statistics is a matter that requires some careful consideration. As Albert Einstein once commented, "Not everything that counts can be counted, and not everything that can be counted counts." One recalls Robert Southey's famous lines about an earlier application of military power, the Battle of Blenheim in 1704. Winston Churchill's esteemed ancestor, the Duke of Marlborough (John Churchill), defeated the French on a field in Bavaria at a cost of 12,500 dead and wounded (about a quarter of the victorious army). The French suffered some 40,000 casualties (almost half of their army). The issue giving rise to this bloodletting was the question of who would assume the Spanish throne following the death of Charles II. In "After Blenheim," Southey described a scene in which a Bavarian peasant, many years later, tried to explain to his grandchildren (notably the young Peterkin) what the battle had all meant:

> 'My father lived at Blenheim then,
>   Yon little stream hard by;
> They burnt his dwelling to the ground,
>   And he was forced to fly;
> So with his wife and child he fled,
> Nor had he where to rest his head.

> 'With fire and sword the country round
>   Was wasted far and wide
> And many a childing mother then
>   And newborn baby died;
> But things like that, you know, must be
> At every famous victory.

> 'And everybody praised the Duke
>   Who this great fight did win.'
> 'But what good came of it at last?'
>   Quoth little Peterkin:—
> 'Why that I cannot tell,' said he,
> 'But 'twas a famous victory.'

Trying to sort out what the area bombing offensive really amounted to, whether it was indeed a "famous victory" or not, and what—to cite young Peterkin—it ultimately meant, must be a crucial part of any moral critique that may be offered of it. In beginning that critique, it is instructive in the first instance to consider how various individuals and groups in British society reacted to the unfolding of the area offensive and what combination of ideas, character, and values shaped their thinking on this method of warfare.

PART II

REACTIONS

2

The Masters of the Realm

"I learn a good deal by merely observing you,
and letting you talk as long as you please,
and taking note of what you do not say."

—T.S. Eliot

When technical developments first introduced the possibility of using airpower on a large scale to undertake direct attacks on an enemy's homeland in wartime, the international community was perforce confronted with a compelling question: would such attacks be in accordance with the traditional laws of warfare and, even more, would they be consonant with accepted standards of moral and humanitarian restraint by civilized nations concerning the tools of violence?

As early as 1899, the Hague Peace Conference had unanimously adopted a declaration to prohibit "for a period of five years . . . the discharge of projectiles or explosives from balloons or by other new methods of a similar nature."[1] Article 25 of the 1907 Hague Convention "forbade any attack on undefended towns, villages, residential places or buildings by any means whatsoever." This stipulation reflected a fairly elementary moral consideration in that it was hardly necessary to attack an undefended town except for reasons of pure revenge or reprisal. However, the notion of "undefended" created a host of ambiguities. Did this literally mean that there must be no anti-aircraft gun in the vicinity, no air or army base in the region, not even some semblance of civil defence? Under the circumstances, Article 25 seemed to hold out few protections for any but the smallest village or hamlet. The principle of the undefended town also produced another difficulty, although of quite an opposite character. In theory, the enemy could protect his most vital industrial targets simply by declaring that they lay in "open" (i.e., undefended) cities. Moreover, Article 25 seemed to be mostly relevant to situations in which a city was under siege by land armies and subject to capture (with or without the use of ground artillery). What about cities that were far to the rear of the front lines and might contain important military defenses but were beyond the range of artillery and not subject to actual seizure? In this instance the only applicable threat that could be levied against them was from the air, but the purpose could hardly be the traditional one of investing the city itself.

The introduction of genuine strategic bombing in World War I, and in particular fairly indiscriminate attacks on urban areas, led to renewed pressures for defining more precisely the laws of war as they applied to aerial combat. At the Washington Naval Conference in 1921-1922 an Aviation Subcommittee considered ways of limiting the actual type and quantity of aircraft suitable for strategic bombing as an indirect means to controlling indiscriminate air warfare, but no agreement was possible, primarily because of concern about the effect of such steps on the burgeoning civilian aviation industry. The issue of city bombing was then referred to a special Commission of Jurists, which met at the Hague from December 1922 to February 1923. The Commission consisted of legal experts from the United States, Great Britain, France, Italy, Japan and the Netherlands, and they were assisted by various military and naval advisors in their deliberations. At the outset the Commission decided to avoid any attempt to set limits on types or numbers of aircraft and instead concentrated on the way they were used in war. They also determined not to be hamstrung by a continuation of the "undefended town" doctrine. The Hague Draft Rules that emerged out of this conference established for the first time a body of principles specifically related to the exercise of strategic air power.[2]

The jurists did not bother to conceal their feeling that the introduction of aerial attacks on cities was an abhorrent development in war. "The conscience of mankind revolts against this form of making war outside the actual theatre of military operations, and the feeling is universal that limitations ought to be imposed." The Hague conferees eventually agreed on a set of Rules of Aerial Warfare, comprising 62 articles, of which five related specifically to air attacks on cities. Article 22 stated that

> Aerial bombardment for the purpose of terrorizing the civilian population, of destroying or damaging private property not of a military character, or of injuring non-combatants, is prohibited.

The critical part of the Hague Draft Rules, however, could be found in Article 24, which contained, *inter alia,* the following provisions:

> Aerial bombardment is legitimate only when directed at a military objective, that is to say, an object of which the destruction or injury would constitute a distinct military advantage to the belligerent.

> The bombardment of cities, towns, villages, dwellings or buildings not in the immediate neighbourhood of the operation of land forces is prohibited. In cases where [legitimate military] objectives are so situated that they cannot be bombarded without the indiscriminate bombardment of the civilian population, the aircraft must abstain from bombardment.[4]

The Hague Draft Rules, when published, met with a good of hostility from various circles, especially concerning the definition of a genuine military objective and the supposed impracticality of attempting to restrain technical developments in airpower. For these reasons, among others, the participating governments at the Hague drew back from formal ratification of the Hague principles. As of 1939, they remained simply Draft Rules and thus not technically binding on any of the belligerents. Even so, the deliberations at the Hague had set out a code of aerial warfare that represented a combined juridical and military judgment from representatives of the most important air powers of the day. From this perspective they had considerable influence, even if not officially ratified, and as one leading authority put it, constituted "an authoritative attempt to clarify and formulate rules of law governing the use of aircraft in war."[5]

The other major international attempt during the interwar years to deal with the issue of permissible conduct in air operations came at the Geneva Disarmament Conference in 1932. In this instance there was a renewed emphasis on limiting the capabilities of the powers for city bombing rather than on trying to hold them to legal standards of discrimination, even though the conference did state that air attacks on civilian populations were in violation of the laws of war. Discussion thus focused on restricting the size, bombload, and range of operation of aircraft and there was even serious consideration given to the total abolition of long-range bombers, except for a residual force to be under the direct control of the League of Nations to enforce sanctions against aggression.

This received surprising political support in Great Britain, save for the Air Ministry, who favored retention of a bombing force for policing the Empire. A spokesman for the Royal Navy, however, supported a total ban on bombers, saying that "only the Air Ministry want to retain these weapons for use against towns, a method of warfare which is revolting and un-English."[6] Ironically (in view of later events), Winston Churchill was one of those who voiced support for the abolition of aircraft designed for strategic bombing. Hitler's coming to power in Germany, however, undermined whatever chance there was at Geneva for a fundamental agreement on airpower restrictions. He withdrew Germany from the conference in October 1933, although the Nazi government did propose in March of 1936 that a general prohibition be established against "the dropping of bombs on open towns and other inhabited places."[7]

What we are left here with, then, seems clear enough. Prior to World War II, there was no convention that was legally binding on Great Britain forbidding her from indiscriminate air attacks on German cities. At the same time, the whole direction and substance of international discussion on the parameters of strategic bombing suggested that what Michael Walzer calls the "war convention" did proscribe such attacks. As defined by Walzer, the war convention composes "the set of articulated norms, customs, professional codes, legal precepts, religious and philosophical principles, and reciprocal arrangements that shape our judgments of military conduct."[8] Described in this way, the concept of the war convention combines both formal (or positive) stipulations as to how war legally *must* be fought and customary (or normative) standards as to how war *should* be fought, and as such it provides a fundamental framework for all our subsequent analysis.

What has to be emphasized for purposes of the present discussion is that the British government prior to World War II seemed clearly to accept that area bombing as such was prohibited by the war convention. More specifically, the British announced that they would adhere to the Hague Draft Rules, even though they were not formally binding, as long as others did so. Thus Prime Minister Neville Chamberlain issued the following guidelines to Bomber Command in June 1938:

1. It is against international law to bomb civilians as such and to make deliberate attacks on the civilian population.
2. Targets which are aimed at from the air must be legitimate military objectives and must be capable of identification.
3. Reasonable care must be taken in attacking those military objectives so that by carelessness a civilian population in the neighbourhood is not bombed.[9]

In the same month, he observed publicly in the House of Commons that even though there was no "international code of law with respect to aerial warfare which was the subject of general agreement," there was at the same time "rules of international law which had been established for sea and land warfare. These rules, or the principles which underlay them, were applicable to aerial warfare, and were not only admitted but insisted upon by his Government." Most important of these was the illegitimacy of any policy "to bomb civilians as such and to make deliberate attacks on the civilian population." Chamberlain went on to summarize the case against area bombing with admirable directness.

> We can strongly condemn any declaration on the part of anybody, wherever it may be made, that it should be part of a deliberate policy to try to win a war by the demoralization of the civilian population through the process of bombing from the air. This is absolutely contrary to international law, and I would add that, in my opinion, it is a mistaken policy from the point of view of those who adopt it, but I do not believe that the deliberate attacks upon a civilian population will ever win a war for those who make them.[10]

What is interesting about Chamberlain's stance on airpower is his commingling of both a legal/moral argument and a practical one. In the time-honored phrase, area bombing, from Chamberlain's point of view, was more than a crime, it was also a mistake. The Prime Minister reiterated his position on the matter even after war had broken out. "Whatever be the lengths to which others may go, his Majesty's government will never resort to the deliberate attack on women and children, and other civilians for purposes of mere terrorism."[11]

The only fair conclusion to be drawn from the discussion in the previous chapter is that, as things turned out, the British government did indeed resort to a policy of area bombing in World War II that had as at least one major objective the "mere terrorism" of the German civilian population. Some might want to dispute the notion that such a goal was inherent in the new policy, but it seems hard to mistake that the concept of undermining German morale depended basically on terrorizing the population into abandoning their support for the war effort. Churchill himself admitted as much in his famous minute after the bombing of Dresden, when he referred to the "bombing of German cities simply for the sake of increasing the terror, though under other pretexts." If the basic proposition is accepted, then, a rather momentous question presents itself. Given the existing strictures of the war convention and, perhaps even more, the stated policy of the British government prior to and even during the early days of World War II, how did the principal figures involved in organizing and carrying out the area offensive confront the evident contradiction between what had been said and accepted prior to the conflict and what actually was undertaken during the course of the struggle?

RETREAT FROM RESPONSIBILITY

There is a famous passage in one of the Sherlock Holmes adventures in which the great detective comments to Watson that the key to solving his case lay in the behavior of a certain dog at the scene of the crime. Watson, in his typical confusion, questioned the logic of this, saying that the dog hadn't even barked during the commission of the murder. "That is precisely the point," Holmes suavely replied.

What strikes one initially about the British government's public stance on Bomber Command's activities over Germany is that for the most part, "the dog didn't bark." In other words, given all the resources assigned to Bomber Command, and the sometimes elaborate projections as to how area bombing could prove critical to the war effort, one might have expected that the Government would openly and unashamedly describe the progressive devastation of German cities. This would have involved not just a recitation of the punishment being visited on the German population but a detailed presentation as well of the whole theory behind area bombing, including the notion of breaking German morale and the progressive dislocation of the enemy's social and economic infrastructure. In case such discussion might prove too arcane for some of the citizenry, there was Churchill's personal assessment that the British people insisted that "the German people taste and gulp each month a sharper dose of the miseries they have showered upon mankind."[12] A candid description of how such medicine was being administered to the German nation presumably would have proved a tonic to a great many in Britain.

In the event, very little of the above was attempted. On the contrary, there was a steady and concerted effort throughout the war to deny or at least not to admit to the reality of area bombing. One of the most astute and fair-minded historians of the area offensive summarizes governmental policy this way:

> In some ways, area bombing was a three-year period of deceit practised upon the British public and on world opinion. It was felt to be necessary that the exact nature of R.A.F. bombing should not be revealed. . . . the impression was usually given that industry was the main target and that any bombing of workers' housing areas was an unavoidable necessity. Charges of 'indiscriminate bombing' were

consistently denied. The deceit lay in the concealment of the fact that the areas being mostly heavily bombed were nearly always either city centres or densely populated residential areas, which rarely contained any industry.[13]

To be sure there were occasional statements from the government that suggested the reality of what was being done over Germany. Thus in early June 1942, the Prime Minister openly boasted "that as the year advances, German cities . . . will be subjected to an ordeal the like of which has never been experienced by a country in continuity, severity and magnitude."[14] A year later he candidly admitted that "to achieve this end [defeat of the Nazis] there are no lengths of violence to which we will not go."[15] As a general matter, however, spokesmen for the government seemed to feel that they had a somewhat delicate problem on their hands: how to encourage the morale of the British people by suggesting that Bomber Command was doing real damage to the German war effort without at the same time admitting that this effort was somewhat ambiguous in terms of traditional British standards of respect for the war convention. The decision, in most cases, was to emphasize the former and obscure the latter.

Thus after the early raids against Lübeck and Rostock in the spring of 1942, Secretary of State for Air Archibald Sinclair insisted that the attacks had been directed at "armament factories" rather than simply "dwelling houses," although he conceded that "it is impossible to distinguish in night bombing between the factories and the dwellings which surround them."[16] A year later he continued to adhere to this position, saying that Bomber Command had been given no leave to engage in area bombing and that its targets "are always military."[17] Sinclair was far from being the only governmental spokesman to take this tack with Parliament. For example, Lord Robert Cecil, the Secretary of State for Dominion Affairs, assured the House of Lords in February 1944 that the "Royal Air Force has never indulged in pure terror raids . . . of the kind which the Luftwaffe indulged in at one time on this country."[18]

This effort to disguise reality found its way even into the realm of private correspondence. On November 26, 1943, the Marquess of Salisbury—head of one of the most distinguished families in Britain and a principal supporter of the RAF before the war—sent a handwritten and confidential communication to Sinclair in which he referred to Air Marshal Harris's boast about continuing to bomb Germany until "the heart of Nazi Germany ceases to beat."

This would seem to bring us up short against the repeated Government declaration that we are bombing only military and industrial targets. . . . there is a great deal of evidence that makes some of us afraid that we are losing moral superiority to the Germans. . . . Of course the Germans began it, but we do not take the devil as our example. Of course all these criticisms may be groundless, but if not, issue fresh confidential orders, I hope.

In a rather significant afterword, Salisbury cautioned, "Please remember that we can say nothing in public for obvious reasons."[19]

Sinclair needed no convincing that the matter had best be kept from the public, and even though Salisbury had pledged discretion, the Secretary for Air cast about for a way to reply to his letter in a way that sustained the public fiction about Bomber Command's strategy. He sought the advice of the Deputy Chief of Air Staff, Sir Norman Bottomley, in this effort. Bottomley replied as follows:

> To be strictly accurate, our primary object is the progressive destruction and dislocation of the German military, industrial and economic system and *the undermining of the morale of the German people.* There is no need to inform Lord Salisbury of the underlined phrase, since it will follow on success of the first part of the stated aim.[20]

Sinclair responded to Salisbury's letter on November 29, taking Bottomley's cue in omitting any reference to the destruction of German morale and going out of his way to suggest that the Air Staff actually were resisting the calls of some for a policy of reprisals against German towns. Sinclair stressed that no responsible governmental spokesman had ever gloated over the destruction of German homes and he reiterated that Bomber Command "adhered fully to the principle that we would attack none but military targets." If Sinclair adopted this sort of stance in private correspondence with one of the most distinguished men in Britain, it is hardly surprising that he was no more forthcoming in his presentations for general public consumption.

It is interesting that Arthur Harris himself was uneasy about the government's dissimulation, saying that "in the House of Commons he [Archibald Sinclair] should have been far more forthright than he was. . . . I personally thought this was asking for trouble; there was nothing to be ashamed of."[21] In fact, Harris took the trouble to write the Air Ministry on October 25, 1943, urging them to stop their public denials that the bombing campaign was focused on "the obliteration of German cities and their inhabitants as such." Instead, Harris urged, "the aim of the Combined Bomber Offensive . . . should be unambiguously stated [as] the destruction of German cities, the killing of German workers and the disruption of civilized life throughout Germany."

Archibald Sinclair was evidently rather alarmed by this plea for candor, and he emphasized to his aides that in drafting a reply to Harris there was a need not to "provoke the leaders of religious and humanitarian opinion to protest." What followed was a rather bizarre exchange of memoranda in which the Air Ministry denied to Harris that any of the confidential directives to Bomber Command actually targeted German cities and civilians as such. It was admitted that in pursuit of military objectives some cities might become prime targets but, the Air Ministry claimed, this was very different from a general policy of attacking all urban areas. "This distinction is in fact one of great importance in the presentation to the public of the aim and achievements of the bomber offensive." For Harris, this was a distinction without a difference, and at least in this instance one is compelled to admire his logic. He argued that since his primary directive was to destroy the German social and economic infrastructure and undermine German morale, he perforce had to target cities. What stands out in this exchange is that the Air Ministry, in its continuing concern about how to present the "facts" about the bomber offensive, rather astonishingly assumed that Harris himself could be persuaded to accept the fiction that was being presented to the general public.[22]

Air Marshall Harris may have thought there was nothing to be ashamed of with respect to the area bombing offensive, but the only reasonable conclusion is that for many in authority there was a considerably greater reluctance to submit the details of the offensive for general public inspection. This may suggest that at least some within the government themselves had doubts about the legitimacy of what Bomber Command was doing, and thus they chose to obscure what was indeed being done. For the great majority of those involved in directing the area offensive, however, the issue was not any personal moral qualms they may have felt about the bombing of German cities but their perception that the British people would have such qualms if they knew the full details of the area offensive. In order to avoid unpleasant and possibly disruptive questioning of the government's air strategy, therefore, it was best from their point of view simply to conceal the essentials of the bombing of Germany. What is particularly interesting in this regard is the assumption on the part of leading figures that the public was morally sensitive to indiscriminate air attacks on Germany and would protest if their existence were revealed. Whether this would generally have been the case is a matter perhaps open to debate, but one is reminded of the famous French sage La Rochefoucauld's aphorism that "hypocrisy is the tribute that vice pays to virtue." The British people seemed to have been credited with considerable virtue, and the government's hypocrisy paid tribute to it.

If deception was indeed prevalent throughout the war in the British government's discussion of its bombing policy, this does lead in a curious sense to a somewhat positive conclusion. The existence of hypocrisy is *prima facie* an acceptance of the fact that "virtue" does exist and that as a general matter it "should" be adhered to. Otherwise, why engage in hypocrisy? This consideration is critical in reacting to the spurious commonplace that there are no really legitimately binding limits to violence in wartime. If this were indeed the way in which most people (including the typical statesman or even the military professional) actually regarded his society's conduct of hostilities, there would be no need for disguising the character of various military activities if they seemed to be efficient in gaining victory. Since British policy-makers in World War II did feel the need for disguise, this substantiates the argument that the war convention, specifically as it applies to aerial combat, did (and does) exist and can be identified, at least in broad stroke.

The Campaign of Forgetting

There is another body of evidence that can be introduced in support of this proposition, and it concerns the behavior of British authorities after the end of hostilities in 1945. If the standard operating mode of the government during the war was to dissemble on the facts of area bombing, following the surrender of Germany there was a seeming effort to discourage any further detailed examination of Bomber Command's activities by interested parties. This effort was likely spurred on in part by the fact that a good deal of new information on these activities was now emerging unfettered by the strictures of wartime security.[23]

Churchill's famous memorandum on Dresden, even though it was meant only for official eyes, has to be interpreted as one of the earliest steps in this direction. It seems unmistakable that, with victory in sight, the Prime Minister—in not his finest hour—was attempting to put some distance between himself and the enthusiasts of area bombing. Churchill, after all, knew full well what area bombing had meant for Germany, even if most of his countrymen had not, and one day the actual historical record would be open for inspection. Churchill, with his historian's instincts, presumably was preparing for this eventuality.

His Foreign Secretary seemed to have some of the same concerns. The original Dresden minute indicated that Anthony Eden had spoken to the

Prime Minister about his "concerns" with respect to the continuation of bombing merely for purposes of increasing the terror. Yet this was the same man who on April 15, 1942, had written to the Secretary of State for Air along the following lines:

> The psychological effects of bombing have little connexion with the military or economic importance of the target; they are determined solely by the amount of destruction and dislocation caused. . . . I wish to recommend therefore that in the selection of targets in Germany, the claims of smaller towns of under 150,000 inhabitants which are not too heavily defended, should be considered, even though those towns contain only targets of secondary importance.[24]

There was at the least a somewhat doubtful consistency between this stance and the expression of doubt about terror bombing delivered by Eden to Churchill following the Dresden raid.

It is of interest in this connection that Churchill expressed his firm opposition to Britain's undertaking a systematic postwar study of the effects of strategic bombing similar to that which the United States had organized (the United States Strategic Bombing Survey, or USSBS). When the British Bombing Survey Unit was finally established over his objections, it was granted few resources, and its final report was withheld from public inspection, even though the USSBS's findings became available almost at once. As one fervent supporter of Arthur Harris put it, "One can only conclude that there was a desire on the part of the Government to deny to the British public, firstly, the truth about the contribution of Bomber Command to victory and, secondly, any knowledge of the greatness as a commander of Sir Arthur Harris."[25]

There does indeed seem to have been a reluctance at the time to consider these matters in any detail. Even when there was some attention given to the contribution of Bomber Command by governmental figures in the postwar period, the tone of the analysis was remarkably elliptic. A representative example was a presentation by the Under-Secretary of State for Air, Mr. John Strachey, to the House of Commons on March 12, 1946. His remarks consisted in part of a general survey of the role of Bomber Command in World War II, and in this connection it is remarkable how Bomber Command's emphasis on area bombing was virtually ignored. Instead, the stress was on their success in undertaking *precision* air strikes against oil and transportation targets in the latter stages of the war (the sort of panacea targets that Arthur Harris had always deprecated). The success that greeted these efforts, Strachey enthused, "I shall always regard . . . as the very greatest achievement which Bomber Command made in the whole course of the war."

Seemingly oblivious to the irony of Bomber Command's having resisted a precision bombing strategy for much of the conflict, Strachey went out of his way to quote German officials such as Albert Speer to the effect that "the war would have ended much sooner if precision bombing attacks had begun earlier than they did."[26] The suggestion seemed to be that Bomber Command's "greatest achievement" rested on the degree to which it allowed itself to be diverted from the basic premise of its air campaign through virtually the entire war.

Aside from these attempts to reinterpret Bomber Command's activities in what was evidently regarded as a more palatable fashion, the most dramatic evidence of the government's disinclination to have the reality of British strategic bombing policy become a matter of extended public debate lay in its treatment of Bomber Command personnel after the war and the attention (or, more properly, non-attention) given to its famous wartime commander. In the glow of victory, various honors were showered on the units of the British armed forces that had contributed to the defeat of the Nazis, but as it turned out some of these units were more equal than others. For example the British Eighth Army, famous for its defeat of Rommel's Afrika Korps, received a campaign medal in recognition of its achievements. So did the RAF's Fighter Command, in particular for its role in the Battle of Britain. Arthur Harris had strongly urged that Bomber Command be equally honored, but in vain. His pilots and ground crew had to be satisfied with the relatively innocuous "defense" medal, which, as Harris sourly observed, was "among the people concerned . . . the subject of much bitter comment. Every clerk, butcher or baker in the rear of the armies overseas had a 'campaign' medal."[27] In Westminster Abbey there is a plaque honoring the pilots of Fighter Command who died in service, listing them all by name. The much heavier losses incurred by Bomber Command resulted in no such plaque nor any other recording of individuals who made the supreme sacrifice.

Then there is the treatment of Harris himself. Given the fact that he was one of the half-dozen principal commanders of British forces in the war, it might have been expected that he would have received honors equal to those bestowed on other famous captains in the great struggle, such as Montgomery, Alanbrooke, and Alexander. In the event, Harris was unique in not receiving such recognition from the British government. On the occasion of Harris's death some thirty years later, an obituary in a leading British newspaper commented on "the sad truth . . . that when the war ended and bombing turned out no longer to be a political asset, those who had decided upon the strategy of heavy bombing and had chosen him as the man to carry it out now turned their backs on him."[28] It is true that Churchill recommended that Harris be given a Peerage for his service as head of Bomber Command, but the Labour government of Clement Atlee rejected this proposal. Harris remained in Britain for a time after the war, but when he was offered no continuing employment in the RAF he left for South Africa at the end of 1945 in a not surprising mood of bitterness and feeling of betrayal. It was not until 1953 (when Churchill was back in power) that he finally received a baronetcy, a relatively minor honor usually bestowed on obscure luminaries such as long-serving members of Parliament. Even at this late date there was evidently controversy over even such a modest recognition of Harris's role in the war. Churchill's Principal Private Secretary recorded that "some of the P.M.'s wishes [concerning the honours list] cause consternation—especially baronetcies for 'Bomber Harris' and Louis Spears.[29]

The stance taken by the British government toward Harris is further illustrated by the fact that his final Official Dispatch, unlike others, was never published, and only introduced into a very limited circulation some three years after it was written. Even then it was available only when accompanied by a long, written rebuttal from the Air Ministry of much of what he had written, particularly concerning his claims about Bomber Command's success in reducing German war production. The Air Ministry's critique also strongly suggested that Harris's superiors in the war had always regarded area bombing as only a temporary measure until precision bombing was technically feasible, but that Harris's obstinacy had prevented such a change in strategy being introduced when the possibility existed. Undoubtedly sensitive to the treatment being meted out to him and to Bomber Command generally, Harris rushed into print in 1947 with the first published account by a senior British commander of one part of the nation's war effort. *Bomber Offensive* received decidedly mixed notices, and the Royal United Services Institute (RUSI), the premier defense institute in Great Britain, declined even to review it.[30]

All of the above seems to admit of only one conclusion: after the war there was at a minimum considerable embarrassment in official circles about the conduct of Bomber Command. The uneasiness that was felt resulted in a calculated effort not to bring attention to either Bomber Command itself or to its former chief in the form of honors and recognition, since this would have the effect of focusing and perhaps intensifying public debate on the activities of the organization and the man.[31] What we had here, in effect, was a tacit admission that Britain had seriously violated the war convention and that those in authority knew she had done so.

THE MEN OF ACTION

These efforts at obliterating, or at least obscuring, the past do raise the rather tricky matter of responsibility. However one may feel about Harris and the strategy of area bombing, it remains that he was hardly a free agent during the war (nor was his aircrew). In a system in which civil authority was acknowledged to be supreme over the military, there always existed the possibility—some might say, the duty—for the former to assert its power over the latter and simply order the end of area bombing. In the event, such instructions were never issued, or at least never enforced, and the spectacle of officialdom, once victory had been achieved, basically washing its hands of Harris and all that he had wrought is not a particularly redeeming one. The question of responsibility is so important to any critique of the area offensive, in fact, that it merits a good deal more detailed consideration. We do so here by taking a closer look at the principal players in the formulation and conduct of British bombing policy, the relationships that existed among them, and the roles that they adopted in the formulation of strategy.

The True Believer: Arthur Harris

Air Marshal Sir Arthur Travers Harris was one of those men who seemed almost determined to provide a continually fresh list of reasons for disliking or even detesting him. He pursued the strategy of area bombing with an almost religious fervor and with a contemptuous disregard for even marginal quibbles about the pragmatic or moral correctness of such a strategy. The Official History of Bomber Command ironically offers one of the most compelling warts-and-all descriptions of Harris's character:

> Sir Arthur Harris made a habit of seeing only one side of a question and then exaggerating it. He had a tendency to confuse advice with interference, criticism with sabotage, and evidence with propaganda. He resisted innovations and he was seldom open to persuasion. He was skeptical of the Air Staff in general and of many officers who served upon it he was openly contemptuous. Seeing all issues in terms of black and white, he was impatient of any other possibility, and having taken upon himself tremendous responsibilities, he expected similar powers to be conferred.[32]

Added to this was a personality that in its daily manifestations was a model of crudeness, rudeness, and insensitivity to elementary human values. He was once pulled over by a motorcycle policeman for driving with excessive speed. "You might have killed someone, sir," the policeman cautioned. Harris imperiously responded, "Young man, I kill thousands of people every night."[33]

His peers called him "Bert," but for many others outside his hearing he was "Bomber Harris" or often "Butcher Harris," a title favored even by his aircrew (not, it might be said, because of the Germans that his bombers had killed, but because of the high rate of casualties amongst the aircrew). A fair description of his intellectual horizons would be that he knew little of the world outside his headquarters at High Wycombe and that what he did know he didn't like. Foreigners of all types were subject to his sarcasm. He dismissed the French High Command as being "really quite incapable of directing any bomber force at all." The Germans, he opined, "can always be relied upon to make all the imaginable large and catastrophic mistakes, together with a good many that only a German would think out."

His aversion toward countries and peoples not British was matched by an equally robust dismissal of many within his own government, both civilian and military. In speaking of those at the British Treasury, he mused that "it is perhaps an exaggeration to speak of the Treasury as having sense; they are purely opportunist and have no qualms whatsoever about grinding the faces of the poor, that is, of the serving officer." He asserted that Bomber Command would have been far more effective "if the armament and production authorities had not bungled everything they did." His operational problems, in his view, indeed could have been solved expeditiously by a few bombs on the appropriate government departments.[34] His attitude toward the Ministry of Economic Warfare, a particular *bête noire* for its insistence on Bomber Command's attacking economic chokepoints in Germany, could be seen in the following comment:

> They come along and tell me now you bomb this factory and that factory; they make all the shoestrings for the army. All right, I bomb them and lose some good men in the bargain. But the German army's still fighting. I ask why and some bloody civil servant says, 'Oh, they're using strings for shoelaces.'"[35]

These outbursts directed at civilian authority were matched by an equal venom toward the other military services. Despite the enormous resources assigned to Bomber Command during the war, he could never escape a feeling of bitterness that the navy and army had received an undue proportion of the materiel and personnel available. Assessing the interwar period, he commented that "for nearly twenty years, I watched the army and navy, both singly and in concert, engineer one deliberate attempt after another to destroy the Royal Air Force." If they had succeeded, "the Nazis would have ruled Europe—if not the world—for centuries."[36] To the end he was convinced that it was only Bomber Command that had made it possible for British and American armies to invade Europe successfully and defeat the *Wehrmacht.*

This description of Harris's personal qualities has a significance far greater than simply conveying the fact that he was a difficult man to work for and an even more difficult man with whom to debate large strategic issues. Since Harris was in so many ways such an unattractive individual, opponents of British area bombing in World War II have not unnaturally tended to make a close connection between Harris as Air Marshal and the strategy itself. The suggestion has been that Harris's unfortunate personality led directly into a policy that was unfortunate (or worse), and that the ugly side of Harris found its outlet in an equally ugly willingness to kill large numbers of women and children in the cities of Germany. In short, Harris was not just the prime actor in the drama, he was admirably suited in all respects to be the villain of the piece as well.

To concentrate on Harris's persona this way may be intuitively satisfying and may in fact have some explanatory merit, but there are difficulties with such an approach as well. For one thing, the demonization of Arthur Harris tends to turn him into something of a cardboard figure that ignores any contribution he may have made to the British struggle against the Nazis. A more balanced perspective would have to concede that, particularly in the earlier years of the war, he managed to galvanize the dispirited ranks of Bomber Command in a way a more judicious leader might not have been capable of doing. As a general matter, his aircrew were drawn from the British lower-middle class, and Harris's willingness, even enthusiasm, for slaying sacred cows of the British establishment right and left contributed to his popularity. His personal clerk (perhaps not an unbiased witness) commented that "we would have crawled on our hands and knees from High Wycombe to London had he asked us."[37]

Moreover Harris's unqualified insistence that Bomber Command was performing a critical role in the war effort went a long way toward convincing his men that their lives were not being put at risk in vain. Also essential to the sustaining of Bomber Command morale was the perception by most of its personnel that Harris was genuinely concerned about their fate and that he would do all in his power to provide the best equipment to insure their survival. On one occasion at the Ministry of Aircraft Production, he furiously demanded the rapid replacement of the Stirling bomber by the more effective Lancaster, saying "it's murder, plain murder to send my young men out to die in an aircraft like that [the Stirling]."[38] There is considerable irony in this emotional umbilical cord between Harris and his flyers, for he was on a day-to-day basis a quite remote figure who virtually never left High Wycombe to mingle with ordinary aircrew. If the test of wartime leadership, however, is the ability to inspire men to the importance of their actions and to suggest a common bonding of purpose and spirit between the ranks and their commander, then Harris deserves some praise for his performance.

Harris may not have been a man of outstanding intellectual gifts, and he could be maddeningly obtuse at times, yet he wasn't totally insensible of the charges of immorality levelled against him both during and after the war. Even though they comprise only a tiny part of his memoir of Bomber Command, ethical issues are addressed by Harris in a few places in an obvious attempt to deflect the notion that he was a totally unfeeling mechanic of destruction. As a general matter he denounced the idea that he or any military man was drawn to war. It was "nonsense" to assert that the career military person was a militarist "in the sense that he desires and encourages war in order to serve his own interests." Indeed the successful general frequently was ignored after the conflict while the losing one often faced an even more drastic fate.[39]

Harris also offered a few reflections on the relationship between morality and war when he discussed the firebombing of Hamburg. "In spite of all that happened at Hamburg," he argued, "bombing proved a comparatively humane method." For one thing it avoided the mass slaughter of British youth that had occurred in World War I. Moreover, the number of German civilians killed by Bomber Command hardly exceeded—and in fact was greatly less than—the number effected by the British naval blockade in the previous war, which led to a "death-rate much in excess of the ambition of even the most ruthless exponents of air frightfulness."[40]

The one other passage in *Bomber Offensive* that touches at least obliquely on the moral issue concerns the devastation of Dresden. Harris doesn't offer any formal defense of the ethics of the Dresden raid, but once again he does indicate an awareness at least that the issue exists.

I know that the destruction of so large and splendid a city at this late stage of the war was considered unnecessary even by a good many people who admit that our earlier attacks were as fully justified as any other operation of war. Here I will only say that the attack on Dresden was at the time considered a military necessity by much more important people than myself, and that if their judgment was right the same arguments must apply that I have set out in an earlier chapter in which I said what I think about the ethics of bombing as a whole.[41]

His comments on Hamburg, to be sure, may not be very convincing to critics of area bombing. Its basic thrust is that an earlier outrage against a civilian population makes subsequent outrages—provided that they are no greater in scope—justifiable. One is also struck by the fact that after these moral ruminations, which comprise a total of three paragraphs, Harris without further ado resumes a discussion of technical details in German air defenses following Hamburg. Moreover, in the immediate aftermath of the Dresden bombing, Harris was somewhat less careful in his remarks. In responding to criticism about the destruction of the city, he offered the following: "The feeling, such as there is, over Dresden could be easily explained by any psychiatrist. It is connected with German bands and Dresden shepherdesses." Sir John Colville, an aide to Churchill, recalls as well that when he met Harris at a dinner party at Chequers shortly after the Dresden attack, and asked him about the effects of the raid, Harris responded: "Dresden? There is no place such as Dresden."

Clearly Harris was not very comfortable with disquisitions on the subtleties of moral philosophy. Yet to expect such a sensitivity in a wartime operational commander is expecting a lot, and perhaps expecting too much. Moreover, there is a question whether one would really want a major military figure to have such a mindset. It is hard to envision someone being able, on a daily basis, to make the sort of brutal decisions involving life and death that Harris was charged with if at the same time he constantly was agonizing over the moral parameters of his actions.

Perhaps one way in which to assess Harris properly is to draw an analogy between him and another famous air force commander, the American Curtis LeMay. The latter achieved fame as head of the Twenty-First Bomber Command in the Pacific during World War II; it was he who ordered the devastating firebombings of Tokyo in March 1945, in which more than 100,000 people died. When asked later by an Air Force cadet about his moral feelings on this occasion, he replied calmly: "Killing Japanese didn't bother me at that time. It was getting the war over with that bothered me. So I wasn't particularly worried about how many people we killed in getting the job done."[42]

After the war LeMay rose to become chief of staff of the Air Force, and a man noted for his unvarnished views on airpower stated in unsentimental terms (in the late 1960s he advocated a strategy of "victory" in Vietnam by "bombing North Vietnam back into the Stone Age.") LeMay was head of the Air Force during the Kennedy administration, and the President was asked by one of his aides why he kept on a man whose views seemed so primitive and out of touch with the spirit of the New Frontier. Kennedy's response was that he didn't intend to ask LeMay for his advice on American foreign policy, but that if it ever became necessary to use American airpower in a war situation he wanted LeMay in operational command because of his professional expertise.

This seems like a reasonable attitude to take toward Harris, yet even in its own terms it leaves us with a highly troubling issue, which has to do with Harris's "professional expertise." Accept for the moment that we can't have expected Harris—or, perhaps more strongly, wanted Harris—to worry about the ethics of area bombing. What essentially pragmatic judgment can we make about his strategic and tactical abilities? After all, this was the man who defiantly resisted every attempt to switch Bomber Command from area to precision bombing, who argued against the formation of the Pathfinder Force on the grounds of its impracticality (although it proved to be one of the most successful innovations of the air war), and who expressed astonishment at the fact that his bomb crews enjoyed a huge success in attacking transportation targets in Western Europe prior to D-Day. It is at the very least a troubling record, and out of it comes a moral judgment that can reasonably be applied to this man of action rather than thought.

There is a considerable body of evidence that the area offensive hardly produced results comparable to those that could have been achieved by another strategy. This point will be elaborated on in due course. If we do accept for the sake of argument that the area offensive was ill-advised from a pragmatic point of view—particularly in the last year of the war—then the violations of the war convention that the offensive entailed become especially indefensible. And to the extent that it was Harris's professional failings, in particular his refusal to admit that there were viable alternatives to the area offensive, that kept the strategy going, then he has to assume a share of the moral condemnation. The point is not that Harris was an evil man in any commonly understood sense of the term. The point is that his fatal lack of imagination, his mulish confidence in his own judgment, and his inability or unwillingness to change produced evil.

The Commander-In-Chief: Winston Churchill

We have painted Sir Arthur Harris as a distinctly limited and rather unpleasant individual. He was all too glad to be given a loose leash to undertake the progressive devastation of German cities, and of course his professional judgment as to the effect of such a campaign on the German war effort had to influence the calculations of civilian policy-makers. But what about those who held the end of the leash? If their overall power of decision was supreme, so perhaps was their moral responsibility, and for none more than Britain's wartime Prime Minister.

In assessing Winston Churchill's role in and attitude toward the area bombing of Germany, one is confronted with a curious package of ambiguities and seeming contradictions. By selecting certain statements from Churchill over a long period of time, it can be demonstrated that he was a fervent believer in strategic air power generally; by selecting others, it can be shown that he was skeptical about the actual potential of bombing to defeat a formidable enemy. Perhaps one key to the Churchillian attitude toward Bomber Command's activities was his love of the dramatic if risky military venture. As one distinguished military historian put it, "Winston Churchill felt intense exhilaration in the sense of battle, and the sounds of battle—more, indeed, than most professional soldiers." As Churchill himself said, "I love the bangs."[43]

Did Churchill ever feel any moral compunctions about the area bombing of Germany? Given certain statements he made before the war broke out, one might suppose that at least some doubts might have existed. Even prior to World War I, he had written in a letter to the First Lord of the Admiralty that he did not believe civilized nations would ever resort to submarine warfare (that is, unprovoked attacks on civilian ships). In 1935 he expressed his outrage that "it is only in the twentieth century that this hateful condition of inducing nations to surrender by massacring the women and children has gained acceptance."[44] He continued to denounce the concept of "terror" bombing in an article for the American magazine *Colliers* in June 1939.

Even after hostilities had broken out, Churchill seemed at times to hesitate about the indiscriminate bombing of enemy civilians. An interesting incident in this regard came on October 17, 1940, when a Conservative MP for Eccles (Robert Cary) confronted him in the smoking-room of the House of Commons and demanded that the Prime Minister authorize full-scale city bombing of Germany in retaliation for German attacks on Britain. Churchill's reply: "My dear sir, this is a military and not a civilian war. You and others may desire to kill women and children. We desire (and have succeeded in our desire) to destroy German military objectives." This was an admirable defense of standards of discrimination in wartime, and Churchill appears admirable for having offered it.

Unfortunately, he didn't stop there. He went on to say to Cary, "I quite appreciate your point. But my motto is 'Business before Pleasure.'"[45] This last sentence, considering the issue at hand, was a coarse and rather unpleasantly flip remark that can be taken as an early indicator of the increasingly unfeeling attitude that Churchill seemed to adopt toward area bombing as the war progressed. Indeed, during the main period of the area offensive against Germany, from February 1942 to the spring of 1945, there is one constant in the body of Churchill's speeches and writings on the matter, and that is the general absence of any hint of concern with the moral implications of area bombing. Even one of his close aides and unalloyed admirers admits that "as time went on, and the accumulated horrors of the war hardened all our hearts, he grew indifferent to the sufferings of the German cities."[46] Indeed Churchill is on record as saying that "it is absurd to consider morality on this topic. . . . In the last war the bombing of open cities was regarded as forbidden. Now everybody does it as a matter of course. It is simply a question of fashion changing as she does between long and short skirts for women."[47] One exception to this insouciant attitude might be the famous minute after the attack on Dresden, with its reference to "terror" as the object of British bombing policy. But even here Churchill, as already noted, agreed to delete such references in his revision of the original memorandum. Perhaps his attitude can best be summarized by a comment he made to a former staff officer of Bomber Command after the war. "We should never allow ourselves," he said, "to apologize for what we did to Germany."[48]

The famous British historian A. J. P. Taylor offers a somewhat different verdict on this matter of Churchill's moral sensibilities, which stands in contrast to Taylor's typical iconoclasm concerning the behavior of famous politicians. Taylor observes that

> bombing strategy involved a moral judgment for which Churchill later was sometimes condemned. . . . Churchill himself was often uneasy, particularly as he did not share Bomber Command's wholehearted conviction of success. Rulers in other countries . . . were ready to use methods equally destructive and equally barbarous. Churchill at least had the redeeming quality of disliking what he was compelled to do. Though he, too, waged war destructively, he remained a humane man.[49]

It is hard to know what this really means, for example, that Churchill remained a "humane man" and disliked "what he was compelled to do." The reality is that the Prime Minister not only condoned the area offensive but was an active spur to it. Even assuming that he may have occasionally had some passing qualms during the war years about the suffering of German civilians, this hardly stands as a solid defense against the burden of his actions.

If Churchill's approach to the question of area bombing can be seen as basically utilitarian, that is, dependent almost entirely on whether such a strategy would be efficient in defeating the enemy, his military judgment concerning the air offensive still has certain ethical implications. If one can establish that he was unconvinced of the efficiency of area bombing, yet allowed it to go forward nonetheless, his moral responsibility for the suffering inflicted by the area offensive seems rather more pronounced than if he sincerely believed in the military efficacy of such a strategy. It may be that he personally was impatient with the ethical arguments against area bombing, but he could hardly have been unaware of their existence. Under these circumstances to allow a policy to proceed unimpeded even when he was dubious of its practical returns would constitute a rather arrogant indifference to the concerns expressed by many.

A fair conclusion about Churchill's attitude toward the military rationale of the strategic air offensive is in any case difficult to arrive at, as we have already observed. Consider the following analysis, which he offered as Minister of Munitions as far back as 1917:

> It is improbable that any terrorization of the civil population which could be achieved by air attack would compel the Government of a great nation to surrender. . . . In our own case, we have seen the combative spirit of the people roused, and not quelled, by the German air raids. Nothing that we have learned of the capacity of the Germany population to endure suffering justifies us in assuming that they could be cowed into submission by such methods, or indeed, that they would not be rendered more desperately resolved by them. Therefore our air offensive should consistently be directed at striking at the bases and communications upon whose structure the fighting power of his armies and his fleets of the sea and of the air depends. Any injury which comes to the civil population from this process of attack must be regarded as incidental and inevitable.[50]

This deprecation of the "morale" thesis behind the strategic air offensive, together with the emphasis on what later would be called precision bombing, rather surprisingly anticipated the very criticisms that would be levied against Bomber Command by a good many during World War II. To be sure, the technical capabilities that Britain used in 1917 for air attacks against Germany paled before those available in the later struggle, and one might simply conclude that Churchill's views changed in response to these developments. Certainly there is evidence to support such a conclusion. Thus in the grim days following the fall of France, when Britain stood alone against the might of the German war machine, Churchill seemed to feel that there was only one possibility of reversing the fortunes of war. He wrote to Beaverbrook at the Ministry of War Production on July 8, 1940 (in a minute to which we have already referred), that

when I look around to see how we can win the war I see that there is only one sure
path. We have no Continental Army which can defeat the German military power.
The blockade is broken and Hitler has Asia and probably Africa to draw from.
Should he be repulsed here or not try invasion, he will recoil eastward, and we have
nothing to stop him. But there is one thing that will bring him back and bring him
down, and that is an absolutely devastating, *exterminating* attack by very heavy
bombers from this country upon the Nazi homeland. We must be able to overwhelm
him by this means, without which I do not see a way through.[51]

Such a drastic analysis, particularly its reference to "exterminating"
attacks on Germany, would seem to represent a full conversion of Churchill
from his earlier skepticism to a full-fledged acceptance of the Trenchard
doctrine of the strategic air offensive. Yet some considerable confusion about
Churchill's real position remains. It is important to emphasize that the above
analysis was offered at a time when, as Churchill noted, there was literally
no other military alternative apparently available for prosecuting the war
effort. To downplay the potential of British air power would be, in effect, to
admit that there was no possibility of defeating the Germans. That Churchill
at this point was rather desperately searching for ways to carry on the war
effort is also reflected in the fact that he issued authorization for the
widespread use of mustard gas and other toxins against German troops on
the beaches should they attempt an invasion of Great Britain.

By the fall of 1941, however, the overall strategic situation had changed
appreciably. The threat of a German invasion of Britain had evidently
ended and instead the German armed forces were now embroiled in a titanic
struggle with the Russians in the East. Moreover, the United States, while
still ostensibly a neutral, was providing major assistance to Britain through
Lend Lease as well as in the patrolling of the sea lanes in the North Atlantic.
Within a few months, Washington would become a formal belligerent in
the struggle against Germany. Under these circumstances Churchill's
views on the strategic bombing offensive seemed to take yet another turn.
As he dryly noted in his recollection of this period, "I was forced to cool
down the claims which some of our most trusted officers, especially Air
Marshal Harris, the head of Bomber Command, put forward in their natural
ardour." In "cooling down" Arthur Harris and other bombing enthusiasts,
Churchill was nothing if not blunt. He wrote to Sir Charles Portal on
October 7 along the following lines:

We all hope that the air offensive against Germany will realize the expectations
of the Air Staff. . . . I deprecate however placing unbounded confidence in this

means of attack, and still more expressing that confidence in terms of arithmetic. . . . Even if all the towns of Germany were rendered largely uninhabitable, it does not follow that the military control would be weakened or even that war industry could not be carried on. . . .The Air Staff would make a mistake to put their claim too high. Before the war we were greatly misled by the pictures they painted of the destruction that would be wrought by air raids. . . . It may well be that German morale will crack, and that our bombing will play a very important part in bring the result about. But all things are always on the move simultaneously, and it is quite possible that the Nazi warmaking power in 1943 will be so widely spread throughout Europe as to be a large extent independent of the actual buildings in the homeland. A different picture would be presented if the enemy's Air Force were so far reduced as to enable heavy accurate daylight bombing of factories to take place. This however cannot be done outside the radius of fighter protection, according to what I am at present told. One has to do the best one can, but he is an unwise man who thinks there is any *certain* method of winning this war, or indeed any other war between equals in strength.[52]

The skepticism reflected in these communications was undoubtedly fueled in part by the completion of the Butt Report, which had so effectively undermined Bomber Command's claims concerning the accuracy of its air strikes and which had been given to Churchill the previous August. The greatly changed military situation also played an important part, since it seemed to open up alternatives for crushing the Nazis that were quite different from the gloomy circumstances facing the British in the summer of 1940. The real interest of the October 7 minute, however, lies in two seeming contradictions it seems to contain when we place it within the context of the overall British war effort.

There is, first of all, the apparent anomaly of Churchill's expressing skepticism about the bomber offensive while at the same time he was issuing instructions that an enormous proportion of Britain's available resources be given to Bomber Command. In July 1942, for example, he commented that "we must observe with sorrow and alarm the woeful shrinkage of our plans for Bomber expansion. . . . Renewed, intense efforts should be made by the Allies to develop during the winter and onwards ever-growing, ever more accurate and ever more far-ranging bomber attacks on Germany."[53] As of January 1943, there were 31 heavy bomber squadrons with some 338 aircraft available to Arthur Harris. Quarterly heavy bomber production was about 232 machines. Two years later, Bomber Command had 80 heavy squadrons with over 1,300 aircraft, and quarterly heavy bomber production was approximately 450 machines.[54]

There is some dispute over how best to calculate the share of the national output that Bomber Command received in comparison to the other services, but one estimate is that about one-third of Britain's total war effort was devoted to the bombing offensive. Bomber Command absorbed resources roughly equal to those given to all British land forces, and received as well the cream of British wartime high technology. The degree to which the needs—or demands—of Sir Arthur Harris received priority over other claimants is reflected in the fact that during the war Britain was forced to buy all of its transport aircraft, most of its landing craft, a high percentage of its tanks, and huge quantities of ammunition from the United States. The reality, then, is that right up to the closing days of the war Bomber Command—despite Harris's constant complaints about lack of men and materiel—received what can be considered a quite disproportionate share of Britain's wartime output.

How to account for Churchill's acceptance of this policy? Three possibilities suggest themselves. We have seen how, in the dark days after the fall of France, Churchill viewed the bombing offensive as the only visible alternative for carrying the war to Germany and potentially achieving victory. Decisions on research and development as well as procurement were taken at the time that reflected this belief, and given the relatively long lead-time necessary to bring new bombers and equipment on line, the effect of the earlier judgments on resource allocation began to be heavily felt only toward the end of 1942 and beginning of 1943. Even though Churchill had acquired new doubts about the effectiveness of Bomber Command by this point, the fact is that he may have been in some measure a prisoner of the earlier decision to give priority to the bombers. To reverse course at this stage of the war, to preside over a fundamental reallocation of resources away from Bomber Command, would have called into question the legitimacy and even rationality of his previous strategic judgments. Under the circumstances, it may have seemed best to Churchill not to open a Pandora's box by altering the course previously chosen. His concern about protecting his (and his government's) reputation for effective prosecution of the war effort is reflected in a memorandum he wrote to the Secretary for Air in April 1942:

> We are placing great hopes on our bomber offensive against Germany next winter, and we must spare no pains to justify the large proportion of the national effort devoted to it. The Air Ministry's responsibility is to make sure that the maximum weight of the best type of bombs is dropped on the German cities by the aircraft placed at their disposal. Unless we can insure that most of our bombs

really do some damage, it will be difficult to justify the pre-eminence we are according to this form of attack.[55]

There is also the fact that, for much of the war, the efforts of Bomber Command were by far the most visible evidence to the British public of the government's resolute prosecution of the war effort. This concern about public morale has to be distinguished from satisfying the putative calls for revenge against Germany described earlier. Aside from Montgomery's defeat of Rommel in the African desert, and the gradual move up the Italian peninsula, there was not much to sustain the spirit of the country and confidence in its arms until the success of the D-Day invasion. Night after night, however, Bomber Command provided a demonstration that Britain was indeed carrying the war to the Nazis and supposedly with ever-increasing effect. Presumably this played an important part in maintaining national morale, and, even more, in convincing the public that the continuing war effort was worthwhile. Whether justified or not, Churchill and others were quite concerned at various times about the British people's susceptibility to war-weariness, which in turn could lead to pressures for a compromise peace with the Germans.

Finally, there seems little question but that Churchill, like many other Englishmen of his generation, was obsessed by his memories of World War I and in particular by the mindless slaughter of the trenches. It will be recalled that it was precisely in hopes of avoiding a repetition of this carnage that the whole concept of strategic bombing received a powerful impetus in the interwar years. The Prime Minister was under constant pressure from both the American and Russian Allies to commit British ground forces to an invasion of the Continent as soon as possible. Washington, for example, had initially suggested a landing in France as early as 1942, and Stalin never tired of pointing out to Churchill—at least prior to D-Day—that the Red Army was engaging the vast bulk of the German armed forces while there was relatively little contact between British units and the *Wehrmacht,* except in Africa and subsequently in Sicily and Italy.

Against this background, a steadily expanding bomber offensive served several critical functions. It was a testimonial to the Americans that even though London might be loath to undertake an early invasion of Europe, she was still committed to a vigorous pursuit of the war effort against Germany. This was an important consideration, since there were some fears in the British Government that the United States would turn its major efforts to the war against Japan—particularly given the outrage occasioned by the attack on Pearl Harbor—if the British were seen as laggard in the campaign against the Nazis. It was also necessary to convince Stalin that Great Britain was making a serious contribution to the war effort, all the more so since there were continuing concerns about Moscow's willingness to sign a separate peace with Germany should she perceive that her Allies were content to have her do the bulk of the fighting with Hitler. The key fact was that a Second Front against the Germans in Western Europe was not established until June 1944, some three years after the Nazi invasion of the Soviet Union. As early as March 1942, Churchill pushed for the bombing of Germany as a way of "taking the weight off Russia by the heaviest air offensive against Germany which can be produced, having regard to other calls on our air power." In his meeting with Stalin in August 1942, the Prime Minister proclaimed that Britain "hoped to shatter almost every dwelling in almost every German city." Stalin laconically replied that "that would not be bad."[56]

Moreover, the massive bombing of Germany, even if it was unlikely to achieve the aims posited by its most enthusiastic supporters, was bound to soften up the enemy sufficiently that British casualties in the eventual invasion of Europe would be measurably lessened. In effect, Churchill was willing to accept the progressive devastation of German cities if it would limit in any way British losses after D-Day. A. J. P. Taylor, in a (perhaps) more supportable argument concerning Churchill and area bombing, suggested that the bombing was only a new version of the so-called insular strategy in which Churchill had always believed. "British industrial power was to produce the bombers needed for victory, as in earlier times it had produced the Royal Navy. . . . The mass army of the First World War would not be needed. The British Army would enter the continent only to restore order when Germany had already collapsed."[57] One can argue about principles of proportionality here, to wit, how many German civilians was it legitimate to kill in order to save an indeterminate number of British lives? Yet the basic concern was not in itself ignoble or hard to understand.

There is another aspect of Churchill's minute of October 7, 1941, that deserves consideration, however. The Prime Minister suggested that Bomber Command might prove to be an even more significant force in the war should the enemy's air defenses be so shattered that precision daylight bombing of arms factories became a real possibility. In the event, this is precisely what happened during the spring of 1944, particularly with the introduction of long-range fighter escorts such as the Mustang. Following the success of the D-Day operation, German air defenses became even more enfeebled. Yet Bomber Command was allowed in September 1944 to resume much of its massive area offensive against Germany instead of being forced to concentrate entirely on precision daylight strikes against specific military targets such as the German arms industry, petroleum facilities, and the transportation network. The critical question becomes why Churchill did not implement his earlier judgment and simply order Arthur Harris to alter his strategy along the indicated lines. In arriving at an answer to this question, it is necessary to consider Harris's relationship with Churchill as well as with other of his superiors. Such an examination says a good deal in its own right about the fundamental issue of moral responsibility for the British bombing of German cities.

The Choices and the Choosers

There are two matters that require special attention here: (1) To what degree was Harris simply carrying out directives on the area offensive from higher authority? (2) If he (at least occasionally) seemed to defy or ignore such directives, to what extent did his nominal superiors attempt to rein him in or even hold out the threat of dismissal?

In arriving at a judgment on these questions, it has already been suggested that it is necessary to focus not only on the relationship between Harris and Churchill, but also on the interaction between Harris and several other major players in the drama of the strategic air offensive, notably Sir Charles Portal, who for most of the war was chief of the Air Staff, and Sir Archibald Sinclair, Secretary of State for Air. The former was the main military superior to Harris and the latter his ostensible civilian chief. For a considerable period of time after Harris assumed control of Bomber Command, he could hardly be accused of simply ignoring or defying the basic strategic premises handed down to him by these men. Indeed, the basic theory of the area offensive was settled on at the highest levels of command—notably the directive of February 14, 1942—and passed on to Harris in his capacity as head of Bomber Command. We have seen how Churchill, at least in the early years of the conflict, seemed to be committed to strategic air power, and both Portal and Sinclair also paid ritualistic obeisance on various occasions to the potential of the area offensive. Naturally Harris found these views entirely congenial to his own thinking, but the point is that during a major part of the war there was at least a broad area of agreement between Harris and higher authority on basic strategy.

Having said this, it is also apparent that Harris consistently interpreted his orders in a manner that accorded with his own views on the *details* of strategy. Even given the overall posture of the British government in favor of the area bombing offensive, there was always a good deal of ambiguity and even disagreement in various quarters about targeting and allocation of Bomber Command's resources. In every instance Harris exploited this ambiguity in a way that, not surprisingly, reinforced his own predilections. In effect he simply chose to ignore those directives, or portions of such directives, that he found objectionable. A prime example of this *modus operandi* was his reaction to the decisions reached at the Casablanca Conference.

It will be recalled that the meeting of Allied leaders at Casablanca established the framework for a combined bombing offensive against Germany and resulted in the following instructions to Harris and his American counterpart, General Ira Eaker:

> Your primary object will be the progressive destruction and dislocation of the German military, industrial and economic system, and the undermining of morale of the German people to a point where their capacity for armed resistance is fatally weakened.

Within these general terms, the directive said, the primary objectives of strategic bombing should be, in order of priority, "the German submarine construction yards, the German aircraft industry, transportation, oil plants and other targets in enemy war industry."[58]

The above wording represented basically a compromise between British and American theories as to the strategic air offensive, but examined in their own terms they clearly implied that future bombing should concentrate on specific targets of special importance to the German war effort. Harris, however, chose to put quite a different interpretation on their meaning. In a letter to the Air Ministry one month after he had received the Casablanca directive, the head of Bomber Command rephrased his instructions to read that he had been "categorically" ordered to undertake "the progressive destruction and dislocation of the German military, industrial and economic system *aimed at undermining the morale of the German people to a point where their capacity of armed resistance is fatally weakened.*"[59]

This represented at the very least a somewhat creative analysis of the Casablanca directive. In fact, it was quite misleading in its use of the term "categorical" and even more in describing the "undermining of morale" as the supreme objective of the air offensive instead of being simply one (and a relatively subordinate) objective of British bombing of Germany. What basically happened here was that Harris took the Casablanca directions to discover a mandate for pursuing the policy upon which he was in any case resolved. One writer summarizes the point by saying that Harris treated the directive "as a harmless plaything for the Ministry of Economic Warfare and the Air Staff."[60] In his memoirs, Harris was even more disingenuous about the intent of the Casablanca instructions. He says that "the subject of morale had been dropped, and I was now required to proceed with the general 'disorganization' of German industry . . . which gave me a very wide range of choice and allowed me to attack pretty well any German industrial city of 100,000 inhabitants and above."[61]

It was in the last year of the war, however, that the gap between Harris's interpretation of his orders and the evident intent behind those orders became strikingly apparent. The crucial fact was that by the spring of 1944—particularly after the doubtful results of the Battle of Berlin—there was a growing body of opinion within the Air Staff and other relevant quarters that questioned whether a general area offensive was the most efficient application of Bomber Command's resources. At this point it wasn't just a question of Harris's tailoring rather vague instructions to suit his own purpose. Instead there was a seemingly flat contradiction between Harris's own ideas on the employment of Bomber Command and the new consensus that was developing within higher authority on the matter. Harris seemed unconcerned about this anomaly. As Anthony Verrier suggests, "Who ran the show ostensibly was of little moment [to him] since he believed that he ran a large chunk of it in reality."[62] The basic political strategy of the head of Bomber Command at this point seemed to be to keep his superiors sullen but not mutinous.

The climax in this struggle of wills came in the fall of 1944. We have already described the virtual collapse of German air defenses by this time, the availability of long-range fighter escorts, and the indubitable success that Bomber Command had had in attacking precision targets both before and after D-Day. Given these factors, the prevailing view within the British government was that Harris's aircrew could now make a truly decisive contribution to victory by focusing their efforts on certain critical chokepoints in the German war effort. The Chiefs of Staff, in their directive of September 25 to Bomber Command, stressed that oil was to be the sole first priority, with transportation links and tank and vehicle production as a second priority. Gone was the equivocation of the Casablanca instructions, and it seemed as if even Harris could hardly fail to respond to this very specific set of orders.

In actuality, Bomber Command continued to put primary stress on general area attacks against German cities, leaving it to the Americans to undertake the majority of the effort against oil and transportation. In attempting to deal with this rather bizarre situation in which Bomber Command was being ordered to do one thing and in reality did another, the chief of the British Air

Staff, Sir Charles Portal, alternated between polite requests that Harris adhere to policy, somewhat sterner reminders that he was not doing so, and finally rather abject pleading that Harris follow his instructions.

On November 5, 1944 (in response to a protest from Harris about the suggested "diversion" of his resources to precision targets and the abandonment of the area offensive "just as it nears completion"), Portal wrote the head of Bomber Command that "at the risk of your dubbing me 'another panacea merchant,' I believe the air offensive against oil gives us by far the best hope of complete victory in the next few months." Harris paid dutiful lip service to this observation even while giving no indication that he planned to change his operational orders to his aircrew. A week later Portal responded with some further gentle nudging:

> You refer to a plan for the destruction of the sixty leading German cities, and to your efforts to . . . exceed your average of two and a half such cities devastated each month; I know that you have long felt such a plan to be the most effective way of bringing about the collapse of Germany. Knowing this, I have, I must confess, at times wondered whether the magnetism of the remaining German cities has not in the past tended as much to deflect our bombers from their primary objectives as the tactical and weather difficulties which you described so fully in your letter of 1 November. I would like you to reassure me that this is not so. If I knew you to be as wholehearted in the attack on oil as in the past you have been in the matter of attacking cities, I would have little to worry about.[63]

A month later Harris, seemingly oblivious of Portal's efforts to rein him in, wrote again expressing skepticism about the value of the oil offensive and referring, as always, to the illusion of attacking panacea targets. Portal answered by saying that he was "profoundly disappointed that you still appear to feel that the oil plan is just another 'panacea' . . . Naturally, while you hold this view you will be unable to put your heart into the attack on oil." Harris responded with asperity that "I am sorry that you should doubt [my willingness to follow orders], and surprised indeed if you can point to any precedent in support of your statement. I can certainly quote precedent in the opposite sense." In a subsequent communication, Harris threw down the gauntlet quite directly, saying that he had no faith in precision bombing "and none whatever in this present oil policy." He then played his final card.

> I will not willingly lay myself open again to the charge that the lack of a success of a policy which I have declared at the outset [does] not contain the seeds of success is, after the event, due to my not having tried. That situation is simply

one of heads I lose, tails you win, and it is an intolerable situation. I therefore ask you to consider whether it is best for the prosecution of the war and the success of our arms, which alone matters, that I should remain in this situation.

Portal, in his wartime memoirs, recalled that this offer of resignation was by no means the only one he had had from Harris, and he didn't regard it as being seriously offered. In any event, he took pains at the time to assuage Harris's evident umbrage at being asked to follow instructions.

I willingly accept your assurance that you will continue to do your utmost to ensure the successful execution of the policy laid down [*sic*]. I am very sorry that you do not believe in it, but it is no use my craving for what is evidently unattainable. We must wait until after the end of the war before we can know for certain who was right, and I sincerely hope that until then you will continue in command of the force which has done so much toward defeating the enemy, and has brought such credit and renown to yourself and to the Royal Air Force.

In explaining the reason for this rather abject submission to Harris's defiance, Portal commented that "his good qualities as a commander far outweighed his defects, and it would have been monstrously unjust to him and to his command to have tried to have him replaced on the ground while assuring me of his intention to carry out his orders, he persisted in trying to convince me that different orders would have produced better results."[64] This of course was not the issue at all: Harris was not engaged in trying to convince Portal of the merits of a different strategy, he was *carrying out* a different strategy, despite his superior's specific instructions to the contrary. One fact previously cited conveys the essence of Harris's triumph: of the 181,000 tons of bombs dropped on Germany by Bomber Command in the last four months of the war, cities continued to represent the largest single category of target.

The Sources of Harris's Independence

How can we account for the charmed life that Harris seemed to lead as head of Bomber Command? He was seemingly invulnerable to criticism or pressure. Dissenting views from peers or subordinates were dismissed with a shrug; those from higher authority received a somewhat politer response but were ultimately defeated as well by Harris's stubborn resolve. In trying to sort out this puzzle, we need first to consider Harris's relationship with Churchill. Their association has been a matter of continuing controversy.

Harris, not unnaturally, stressed that he always had a very good working partnership with the Prime Minister, and that there was general agreement between them on the activities of Bomber Command. "I was never pressed by Mr. Churchill to do anything at his dictation, or anything with which I was not personally satisfied."[65] Others have presented a more mixed picture of Churchill's attitude toward Harris. General Paget thought that "Bert Harris was the sort of buccaneer whom Churchill particularly liked," a straightforward personality who saw his duty and did it. Major Desmond Morton, on the other hand, an officer in British intelligence who was one of Churchill's inner circle, believed that "he never cared for Harris as a person," perhaps because of Harris's rather narrow personality and lack of intellectual interests outside technical problems of bombing German cities.[66] One seemingly trivial factor that may have helped to maintain Churchill's support for Harris was the circumstance of High Wycombe's being quite near to the Prime Minister's country retreat at Chequers. This meant that Harris could easily visit Churchill in order to press his views on bombing policy in person.

Whatever the Prime Minister's personal feelings toward Harris, one is left with the impression that removing Harris from Bomber Command was never seriously on Churchill's agenda simply because he saw relatively little benefit and considerable cost in doing so. Even though Churchill became increasingly skeptical about area bombing's proving a decisive factor in the defeat of Germany, he admired Harris's qualities of leadership and was persuaded that Bomber Command was doing at least some considerable harm to the German war effort. Even more important was the fact that Harris had been built up as one of the great captains of Britain's war effort—a role very much assigned to and created for him by Churchill himself. To dismiss Harris would thus reflect on Churchill's own judgment and perhaps erode public confidence in the competence of Britain's wartime leadership.

There is a suggestion that in this regard Churchill may have been heavily influenced by his disastrous experience with the Gallipoli expedition in World War I. As First Lord of the Admiralty Churchill had personally taken the lead in pushing the Gallipoli scheme, against the advice of more experienced hands within the government. When it failed, his political career suffered a drastic reverse (he was in fact dismissed from office). As Prime Minister, then, he was inclined to operate within a general military consensus and avoid any dramatic conflict with the major figures around him. Once, when urged to dismiss a certain general, he replied plaintively, "It is not so easy as that. Lloyd George did not trust Haig in the last war—yet he could not sack him." It may well be that Churchill simply wanted a prominent group of decision-makers as permanent fixtures to diffuse responsibility for controversial policy judgments.[67] Under the circumstances, then, there was much to recommend having Harris stay in place, even though he became increasingly difficult as the war progressed.

The gingerly relationship between Churchill and Harris is perhaps best reflected in Harris's response to the Prime Minister's minute about terror bombing in the aftermath of the Dresden attack. This was as close as Harris ever came to a direct attack on Churchill.

> To suggest that we have bombed German cities 'simply for the sake of increasing the terror though under other pretexts' and to speak of our offensive as including 'mere acts of terror and wanton destruction' is an insult both to the bombing policy of the Air Ministry and to the manner in which that policy has been executed by Bomber Command. This sort of thing, if it deserves an answer, will certainly receive none from me after three years of implementing official policy. We have never gone in for terror bombing.[68]

Even at this late stage of the war, the Prime Minister, by amending his original memorandum so as to delete any reference to terror bombing, showed a concern with not ruffling the feathers of the man whom he had appointed to oversee the strategic air offensive against Germany.

Sir Charles Portal was a man in whom Churchill reposited a great deal of trust and confidence; moreover, Portal had served as head of Bomber Command himself. Given this background, Portal was perhaps uniquely placed to deal with Harris's vagaries and, when it came to that, to ask for Harris's resignation, most notably when he effectively defied the Combined Joint Chiefs' directives on the air offensive in the fall of 1944. In the event, as we have detailed, Portal never felt compelled—or perhaps able—to force a showdown with his ostensible subordinate. That Portal would shrink from an ultimate confrontation with Harris might have been anticipated from his passive performance at the time of the Casablanca affair, in which Harris quite clearly "misinterpreted" his instructions from the Combined Chiefs of Staff. At that time, Portal simply allowed Harris to proceed without offering any amending of the record, gentle or otherwise. As one writer puts it, "Portal's position was anomalous; through his own Air Staff he could theoretically issue guide-lines for the prosecution of the offensive but he never chose or saw any need to do so." An even more blunt assessment was that "Harris's strength lay in his ability to defy Portal, the principal channel of communication with High Wycombe."[69]

In accounting for this seeming withdrawal in the face of Harris's insubordination, it would appear that Portal was moved by several of the same considerations as the Prime Minister. He regarded the chief of Bomber Command as extremely effective in inspiring the efforts of the aircrew. Portal also was hardly immune to the political considerations that swayed Churchill. Harris had assumed an almost mythical reputation with much of British public opinion by 1943, although any objective evaluation would have suggested that this reputation hardly rested on concrete achievements by Bomber Command. Very few people at the time, however, had any clear sense of the actual results of the area offensive, and the constant barrage of publicity given to the aircrew of Bomber Command and their chief predisposed a majority to accept that Harris was indeed overseeing a significant part of the war effort. In these circumstances it would have been expecting a lot of Portal to dismiss Harris simply because of his wayward reading of his instructions.

Personality factors also played a part in the relationship between Harris and Portal. The chief of the Air Staff was a rather austere and patrician figure, who, as a matter of instinct, strove to avoid embarrassing and painful confrontations with those around him. Once the war was clearly being won, Portal was all the more inclined to grin and bear Harris as long as he didn't go to really quite extraordinary lengths in defying policy. This seems to be the only ready explanation for the capitulation that Portal offered to Harris at the end of 1944, when the head of Bomber Command was clearly ignoring the spirit, if not the letter, of the instructions given to him concerning targets to be attacked in Germany.

Portal's somewhat ambivalent attitude toward Harris was also a reflection in part of his ambivalent attitude toward area as opposed to precision bombing. At times, he was vigorous in supporting attacks on what Harris called panacea targets, but on other occasions he seemed supportive of a full-bore assault on German cities. In the first days of the war, he threw his weight behind a concentrated assault on the Nazi oil infrastructure, but shortly after he seemed to go all out in his support for the theory of the area offensive. The official history records that Portal, as head of Bomber Command in early fall 1940, "believed that the time had come to launch a direct attack on the German people themselves. He believed that this course had been justified by previous German actions, and that it would be justified as a strategy in the outcome."[70] A year later, as chief of the Air Staff (a post he had assumed the previous October), Portal was a major proponent of the "4,000 bomber plan," which was offered as a scheme by which to defeat Germany singlehandedly by air power.

As the war progressed, however, he did increasingly come to favor precision bombing, e.g., synthetic oil facilities, the German transportation network, and so forth. Moreover, he suggested that bombing was hardly likely to gain victory over Germany by itself. At Casablanca he stressed that it was necessary "to exert the maximum pressure on Germany by land operations; air bombardment alone was not sufficient."[71] Nevertheless, even in the last year of the struggle, Portal occasionally reverted to his earlier predilection for area bombing. It was he, for example, who was the main driving force behind the planning of Thunderclap, and even during his disputation with Harris in the fall of 1944 he suggested that it might be desirable very soon "to apply the whole of the strategic bomber efforts to the direct attack on German morale."[72] The point is that because Portal was somewhat unresolved in his own mind about the merits of area versus precision bombing, it was all the more difficult for him to confront Harris about his commitment to the area offensive. Part of Portal always was drawn to the notion of a truly devastating assault on German urban centers.

If Portal's relations with Harris were somewhat complex, the same cannot be said for Sir Archibald Sinclair's association with the chief of Bomber Command. Sinclair had been the prewar leader of the Liberal Party, and had served as Churchill's second-in-command in the Sixth Royal Scots Fusiliers in 1916 (which Churchill led for a brief period after being dismissed from the government). Sinclair almost never could bring himself to confront Churchill personally, even when it would have been most useful to do so, and even then only after "considerable stiffening" from Portal. He was effectively excluded from broad questions of strategy and detailed matters relating to aircraft production, and in the process he became a rather marginal figure.

The evidence, in fact, rather convincingly suggests that Sinclair was a man who was considerably out of his depth, who was overawed by the single-mindedness of Arthur Harris, and who saw it as his function to deflect whatever criticisms might be advanced—both within and outside his Ministry—concerning the suitability of Bomber Command's strategy. Symptomatic of Sinclair's pliability was his position early in the war that we "could not gain a decision against Germany by bombing of the civil population. We achieve nothing by promiscuous bombing." After the War Cabinet had opted for the unrestrained area offensive, however, he became a fervent supporter of what he had earlier rejected.[73] One of Churchill's aides described Sinclair as being a "high-minded and patriotic" man but an individual who "could seldom, when the time eventually came, stand up to the stronger personalities with whom it was his fate to contend." Lord Beaverbrook, in his typically caustic manner, described the Air Ministry as being quite rotten and he added that Sinclair was "a thoroughly bad Minister who was hoodwinked by his subordinates."[74] Beaverbrook had few qualms about the area bombing offensive, but he certainly would have counted Harris among the subordinates who hoodwinked Sinclair on a regular basis.

In raising moral questions about the area offensive, what are we left with then after this discussion of the relationship between Harris and his superiors? If an indictment is justified, Harris may (as we have already argued) be rightly included among the accused, even if he can claim extenuating circumstances. His unwillingness to consider any reasonable alternative to the area offensive, indeed his virtual obsession with continuing urban attacks until the very last days of the war, is hard to defend or explain away. It is not enough simply to say that Harris's "character" was such that he could not have acted in any other way. His personality flaws, while they might command sympathy in another context, contributed to a degree of unnecessary and inexcusable human suffering such that he must bear his share of guilt for British bombing policy.

Even so, it is hard to escape the conclusion that the ultimate moral culpability for the inhumanity of the area offensive must lie at the feet of those who had the power, not just in theory but in actuality, to force a change of policy. Harris did the work of his masters in the way they wanted it done, at least in the earlier phases of the war, and the fact that they allowed him to retain command even after he entered into a period of defiance of orders from above could reasonably be interpreted as at least indirect complicity in his methods. To be sure Churchill had overarching political considerations in retaining Harris, Portal was a victim of his own mixed attitudes toward bombing strategy, and Sinclair was ill-suited as a general matter to exercise control over strong personalities. Yet none of this gainsays the fact that Harris was ultimately only a tool, ordered to—or allowed to—conduct a quite indiscriminate air offensive against Germany that was in violation not only of the traditional norms of war but, even more, of the traditional norms of civilized society that Britain laid proud claim to represent. Harris's sin was one of commission, but the others was ultimately one of omission, and it is difficult to think that the former was more reprehensible than the latter.

3

The Servants of the Realm

"Be men first and subjects afterwards."
—Henry David Thoreau

We have analyzed personalities and institutions who had direct power of command in the British area offensive against Germany. In an enterprise of this sort, however, there are many others whose biographies—and participation—present issues for consideration. The focus here is on two groups of individuals who were outside the inner circle of decision-making but whose roles in the area bombing offensive were nevertheless of great importance. One of them was involved in calculations about how to drop the bombs most efficiently; the other was involved in dropping the bombs.

THE BOFFINS

At first glance, the credentials of Professor Freeman Dyson would seem to make him a fairly typical representative of the fabled military-industrial complex. Born and raised in England, he came to Cornell University in 1947 as a Commonwealth Fellow. He subsequently decided to settle permanently in the United States, and in 1953 he took a position as professor of physics at the Institute for Advanced Study in Princeton. In the years since, he has consulted at various times for the Defense Department, and has worked as a member of Jason, which, as Dyson describes it, is a "group of scientists who work on technical problems for the Department of Defense and other agencies of the American government." For our purposes, there is one other item in Dyson's resumé that is of particular interest: during World War II he worked for the British Royal Air Force in the area of operations research. He was a scientific analyst for Bomber Command and thus had extensive knowledge of the strategy behind British air strikes against Germany.

Given his professional background, Dyson's description of his contribution to the British war effort is rather striking: "I felt sickened by what I knew. Many times I decided I had a moral obligation to run out into the streets and tell the British people what stupidities were being done in their name. But I never had the courage to do it. I sat in my office until the end, carefully calculating how to murder most economically another hundred thousand people."[1]

His *mea culpa* extends even further than this. He recalls reading reports after the war about the men who had worked in the Adolf Eichmann organization, and admits that he had a certain sympathy for these individuals. "Probably many of them loathed the SS as much as I loathed Bomber Command," Dyson reflected, "but they, too, had not had the courage to speak out." When it came down to it, the main difference between his work and that of Eichmann's operatives "was that they were sent to jail or hanged as war criminals, while I went free."[2]

There are two objections that may be raised to this sort of language. The first concerns retrospective admissions of moral culpability. One might well challenge the relevance, even the moral consistency, of Dyson's offering an apology for his actions some 40 years after the event. An even harsher verdict might be that the author is citing a moral anguish now that he did not really feel, at least in the same degree, in the original circumstance. There is also the matter of equating Bomber Command and the Eichmann organization. The former, it may well be argued, was created precisely to *combat* the evil that Eichmann represented; indeed, the former was made *necessary* by the latter.

These are not small objections, but it is not the purpose here to offer a detailed moral or political critique of Dyson's writings (such as *Weapons and Hope,* which in fact impresses as a book of considerable power and integrity). Instead, his comments are offered by way of introduction to an assessment of the British scientific community's role in the strategy of area bombing. Certainly as far as aerial combat was concerned, the British struggle against Germany could in some real sense be called the "war of the boffins," the latter a generic term used to describe civilian specialists advising the Royal Air Force on technical matters. Scientific talent was systematically recruited from the universities, industry, and various branches of government to contribute to the development of Bomber Command and its tactics, and scientists became important players in various types of operational decisions. They were involved in calculations on the lethality of various types of bombs, the properties of different metals for aircraft, communications, and navigational devices, and alternative targeting strategies.

Aside from specific technical contributions (the most famous being the development of radar, which was actually achieved before the war broke out), perhaps the most salient role of the scientists was in the new field of "operations research." As a discipline, operations research purported to use methodology employed by various of the sciences to construct a rational overall plan for the development and deployment of military resources. *Science in War,* an influential tract issued by 25 prominent British scientists in 1940, described operations research this way: "The waging of warfare represents a series of human operations carried out for more or less definite ends. Seeing whether these operations actually yield the results expected from them should be matter of direct scientific analysis."[3] The whole idea of operations research was to make systematic in military decision-making what had previously been based largely on received wisdom or personal judgment. As the war progressed, each of the branches of the RAF (Bomber Command, Fighter Command, Coastal Command) developed their own operational research units.

The issue that Dyson's plaintive lament raises is simply this: how common was his anguish among other of his fellow scientists, particularly those who were engaged in some form of operations research, which was the scientific endeavor that had the most direct connection to the area bombing of Germany? More generally, what stance did the British scientific community take toward the moral questions raised by the area bombing offensive of Germany? There is an interesting analogy to their situation in the case of the Manhattan Project, the code name for the development of the atomic bomb.

In 1940 a young American scientist, Dr. Volney Wilson, was asked to prepare a report on whether a chain reaction could be produced using ordinary uranium. Wilson worked intensively for two months and finally submitted a positive report on the matter. At the same time, he delivered himself of the following comments: "I believe it can be done, and if so it will be of great importance. But please take me off this job. It is going to be too terribly destructive. I don't want to have anything to do with it."[4]

Following the successful testing of the bomb at Alamagordo, New Mexico, on July 16, 1945, various American scientists who had worked on the Manhattan Project banded together to urge their government to wait before using the bomb on a Japanese city. Their idea was to explode one of the devices off the coast of Japan in a demonstration that would (hopefully) persuade the Japanese authorities to surrender once they had seen the bomb's enormous destructive power. The evidence is ambiguous as to whether President Truman ever actually had contact with, or was even aware of, this group. As it turned out, their efforts were in vain, and Hiroshima was to receive the first atomic bomb dropped in anger. A major factor in the abortive attempt by the scientific community to forestall immediate military use of atomic energy was, in any case, moral in nature: those involved felt that the weapon was so terrible in its effects, and carried such an ominous portent for future generations and future wars, that it behooved all involved to hesitate before the abyss. Robert Oppenheimer, the "father" of the atomic bomb and scientific director of the Manhattan Project, perhaps caught the essence of these feelings when he commented shortly after the explosion at Hiroshima that "the physicists have known sin."

Such sentiments carried over after the war, and with equally unavailing result, with respect to plans for developing the hydrogen bomb. Enrico Fermi and I. I. Rabi, as members of the General Advisory Committee charged with developing recommendations on further American nuclear weapons policy, argued that the creation of the hydrogen bomb "cannot be justified on any ethical ground which gives a human being a certain individuality and dignity even if he happens to be a resident of an enemy country." Such a bomb, they suggested, "is necessarily an evil thing considered in any light."[5]

At first glance, it would appear that roughly similar attitudes may have developed in the relationship between (and among) certain scientists and Bomber Command. There was the occasion in early spring 1942, for example, when Churchill's Chief Scientific Adviser, Lord Cherwell (Professor F. A. Lindemann), submitted his famous paper to the Prime Minister on the "dehousing" of German workers. Cherwell offered precise calculations as to the number of bombers, the weight of bombs, and the number of sorties necessary to dehouse a critical mass of the German workers and thus break the spirit of the German population and their support of the war effort.

His calculations, however, did not go unchallenged. Particularly forceful in his objections was Sir Henry Tizard. Tizard was perhaps the most distinguished scientist of the day in the professional civil service; before the war he had been chairman of the Committee for the Study of Aerial Defence, which had proved crucial in the development of radar. Tizard wrote to Cherwell that "I am afraid that I think that the way you put the facts . . . is extremely misleading and may lead to entirely wrong decisions being reached, with a consequent disastrous effect on the war."[6] Tizard questioned Cherwell's cost-gains equation, suggesting that it was out of order by a factor of five (other scientists, such as P. J. Blackett, then director of Operational Research at the Admiralty, mentioned an error on the order of six). Essentially, Tizard doubted that enough bombers would be available to dehouse the Germans in sufficient numbers, and he questioned the accuracies that could be achieved by the bombers that were available. As it turned out, both Tizard and Blackett were off in their own calculations: Cherwell's minute was in error by a factor of ten.

In many ways Lord Cherwell's personality mirrored that of Sir Arthur Harris himself. Modesty, self-doubt, a sense of humor, and a willingness to consider the views of others, especially subordinates, were all traits that he found foreign and even incomprehensible. As one description had it, "he had time for a few physicists and a few peers, but regarded most of the human race as furry little animals."[7] Tizard, by contrast, was regarded by virtually everyone as gentlemanly, witty, and self-effacing to a fault. This may partly account for the impression that has lingered over the years that the clash between the two man was essentially one between the former's brutal insensitivity to death and destruction and the latter's humanistic concerns about undue death and destruction. In reality, their argument seems to have been more about the basic allocation of men and materiel than the ethical implications of area bombing. Tizard even wrote to Cherwell that "I should like to make it clear that I don't disagree fundamentally with the bombing policy."[8] Where he did disagree with Cherwell was on the question of whether, in terms of the overall war effort, it made sense to give Bomber Command such a high percentage of the available resources. Tizard was convinced that a commitment to other areas, e.g., the campaign against the U-Boats and tactical support of the ground forces, would pay greater dividends.[9]

Tizard, in fact, emerges as being as tough-minded in his own way as was Cherwell. One of the chief students of the bomber offensive stresses that at this time "although some scientists were revolted or distressed by the moral implications of area bombing—as obviously were many reflective men and women privy to the issues—Tizard and company were not."[10] This analysis seems borne out by a comment that the English scientist-novelist C. P. Snow made about the Cherwell-Tizard controversy. He admits that even though he personally and the people he knew best were frequently uneasy about strategic bombing, partly on military and partly on humane grounds, "when it came to the point it was not Lindemann's ruthlessness that worried us most, it was his calculations."[11] In any case, Tizard's and Blackett's objections to Cherwell's arguments were brushed aside by the government. Not only were they dismissed but, as Snow further recalls, this "minority view was not only defeated, but squashed. The atmosphere was more hysterical than is usual in

English official life; it had the faint but just perceptible smell of a witch hunt. Tizard was actually called a defeatist."[12] In the aftermath of his humiliation he was retired to an honorific post at Oxford and had no further influence on the British war effort.

Aside from the Tizard-Cherwell controversy, there was one other well-known imbroglio on bombing policy during the war that, at first glance, would seem to reflect a morally sensitive scientific community's objecting to the crudity of the area offensive. The central figure in this instance was Sir Solly Zuckerman. Zuckerman was trained as a doctor; before the war, however, he had gravitated into the study of primates and in particular the sexual and social life of apes and monkeys, from which two books resulted. Because of his background in experimental work, he was called on in the early days of the war to undertake tests of the physical effects of blast and high-velocity fragments on living creatures (he used goats as particularly useful human approximations in these researches).

Zuckerman was subsequently assigned to a broader study of the effect of German bombing raids on Great Britain and in particular the physical and morale impact of German attacks on Birmingham and Hull, the results of which were used (or abused) by Lord Cherwell for his own purposes. Eventually Zuckerman found himself in North Africa as scientific adviser to RAF Marshal Arthur Tedder, in which capacity he remained, even while assuming other responsibilities, for the rest of the war. It was when he joined Tedder's staff that his contribution to bombing strategy emerged in a pronounced way.

Based on his analysis of the effect of Allied bombing in the North African campaign, Zuckerman developed some strongly held ideas as to how to maximize the effectiveness of airpower, particularly in support of the land campaign. In essence he became a strong supporter of precision bombing and one of those panacea merchants that Arthur Harris so constantly bewailed. An early test of his theories came with Allied air attacks on the island of Pantelleria, for which he was assigned considerable responsibility. Pantelleria was a small but heavily defended island that had to be occupied before the Allied forces could proceed with the invasion of Sicily. The bombing of Pantelleria was, as Zuckerman recalls, "planned down to the smallest detail, and I remember waiting for the reconnaissance photographs after each raid so that we would find out whether each bomb had or had not gone down exactly where we planned that it should go." The defenders of Pantelleria surrendered without a fight following this air assault, and Zuckerman's reputation rose accordingly.

It was further enhanced when he participated in plans for air strikes that would cut enemy communications down the length of Italy in support of the invasion of Sicily. The results again proved gratifying, with the enemy being unable to establish a functioning railhead to receive reinforcements of troops and supplies during the Sicily operation. Later, as Allied forces began to move up the Italian peninsula itself, the same concentration on rail targets continued to produce the same results. Zuckerman carefully checked the bombing plans against the projected outcomes, using both personal observations and the Italian railway records. As one assessment has it, "it was soon clear that by a scientific choice of targets, and a careful estimate of how confusion might be spread through a railway network like a chain reaction, it was possible to sterilize any railway system in Europe."[13]

Zuckerman's ultimate triumph as a scientific adviser to the RAF, however, took place during the planning for the D-Day operation. The man for whom he worked, Air Marshal Tedder, was appointed deputy to General Eisenhower, the supreme commander of the Allied invasion force. Tedder was effectively given overall command of Allied air forces in support of the invasion, and thus Zuckerman's position was considerably enhanced. Basically, he urged a continuation of the strategy that seemed to have been so effective on Pantelleria and especially in Italy—in this case, a generalized assault on the German transportation system in France and the Low Countries prior to D-Day.[14]

Not surprisingly, Arthur Harris was dismissive of this scheme. He wrote to Portal in January 1944 that "it is clear that the best and indeed the only efficient support which Bomber Command can give to *Overlord* is the intensification of attacks on suitable industrial centres in Germany." If his aircrew were diverted from such targets, Harris concluded, and forced to concentrate on panaceas such as the German railway network, "this might give the specious appearance of 'supporting' the Army [but] in reality it would be the greatest disservice we could do them. It would lead directly to disaster."[15] In the event, Harris's plea for a continuation of the area offensive was turned aside by Allied planners. There was little confidence that area bombing could prove decisive in the few months remaining before D-Day, and what came to be called the Transportation Plan thus received an imprimatur as the basic Allied air strategy leading up to the invasion.

Hearts and Minds

In view of Solly Zuckerman's role in the adoption of the Transportation Plan, and the rejection (for the time being) of continued area attacks on German cities, he might seem to be a reassuring figure to those searching for a general moral uneasiness among the boffins concerning the policy of area bombing. His constant stress on precision air strikes would seem at the least to suggest a certain queasiness about the indiscriminate slaughter of civilians that was at the heart of the area offensive. Zuckerman's putative role as a moral critic of area bombing might seem to be established as well by some of his later writings, in particular a small volume which he published in 1983, in which he dismissed any notion that a limited nuclear war might be winnable or even conceivable. He paid tribute to E. P. Thompson, at the time the leader of the movement for unilateral nuclear disarmament in Britain, saying that "there can be no answer" to Thompson's fundamental moral argument. "I am fully sensitive to the moral objections of weapons of mass destruction."[16]

This seems a pretty straightforward indictment of the notion of targeting civilians as an ingredient of national strategy. A closer examination, however, reveals a somewhat different picture about Zuckerman's stance on airpower. For one thing, his subsequent objection to the idea of a rational nuclear war-fighting strategy was based as much on technical considerations as on fine points of moral philosophy. He stressed the difference, not just in degree but in kind, between the effect of nuclear weapons and that of conventional bombing: the key distinction was that, for all practical purposes, there was no limit to the destructive power of nuclear bombs. More to the point, he suggested that all the destruction that Britain suffered in World War II from conventional bombing would pale before that caused by the explosion of a single megaton nuclear device over a single British city.[17] This is all sensible enough, but it is apparent that the argument rests not on the inherent rights of civilians in wartime but on the level of destruction that both sides would suffer in even a minimal nuclear exchange, which rendered nugatory any military rationale for such a conflict.

It is also important to recognize that Zuckerman's theories about precision versus area bombing in World War II evidently had very little to do with uneasiness about excessive non-combatant suffering. He comments rather impatiently that "no more than a handful of prominent British citizens pontificated [sic] about the immorality of reprisal attacks on German cities." Ironically, in fact, one of the objections to Zuckerman's Transportation Plan was that it would involve a large number of civilian casualties among the friendly populations of France and the Low Countries (since the relevant targets were generally located within urban areas). We will return to this issue in a different context later on, but suffice it to say here that Zuckerman seemingly saw little reason for questioning the Transportation Plan on the grounds of its possible effect on civilians. Once again, it was calculations of pure military efficiency that drove his thinking. There is little evidence that had he been convinced on instrumental grounds that the area offensive was militarily more effective, he would have shrunk from supporting such a strategy.

Zuckerman's essentially utilitarian approach to matters of bombing strategy in World War II is amply illustrated by his review of a notable book on questions of morality and bombing that appeared in 1985.[18] He declares, as a general matter, that "declarations of morality in international affairs almost inevitably become overshadowed by the realities. . . . moral principles about the possible killing of civilians were [never] a consideration that consciously affected the choice of targets in the implementation of some particular bombing plan." He takes pains to suggest that the USAAF's concentration on precision bombing in World War II had more to do with the Americans air force's desire to carve out an independent role for itself than with "the American air generals wrestling with their souls about the morality of their actions." Zuckerman also notes with some asperity that the United States engaged in area bombing against Japan with a fervor matching that demonstrated by British Bomber Command against Germany.

In sum, it is clear that Zuckerman, now as then, feels no need to offer moral *mea culpas* for his role as scientist in British bombing strategy in World War II. In an earlier book on the relationship between the scientific community and military operations, he states flatly that "we cannot invest pure scientific knowledge with any inherent moral direction. That is imparted by the way science is used." He makes much of the fact that the seat of effective power is elsewhere and that it is there that moral considerations in policy-making (to the extent that they may be relevant) ought to be considered.[19] In adopting such a view, Zuckerman apparently reflected the prevailing mood of the British scientific community during World War II. Freeman Dyson, in fact, emerges as a relatively rare creature among the boffins. For the vast majority, the challenge of operational research was simply another scientific problem that engaged their intellectual curiosity. Indeed the war seems in many instances to have been something of a tonic to their scientific creativity. Zuckerman comments (without seeming irony) that "a state of war can stimulate the scientist to great feats of the imagination and to great practical achievement," especially since in wartime scientists enjoy "resources on a scale they had never dreamed of in peace."[20]

It is only right to recognize that the stance of British scientists was reinforced by a belief that they were part of a truly just war and were contributing to the vanquishing of an undoubted evil. As one of the main historians of the role of British science in the war has stated, there was an unusual consensus concerning the military conflict with Germany, "largely, no doubt, on account of the political and ideological beliefs of the enemy." The Nazi regime was essentially anti-scientific in its orientation and, even worse, used racial criteria in judging scientific talent (e.g., the obsession with developing a purely "Nazi physics" that would be uncontaminated by non-Aryan thinking). "Whatever the colour of a British scientist's beliefs in 1939 he was therefore united with his colleagues against the common enemy in a way that might not have been so certain had the enemy been a different one."[21]

Among the principal British scientists of World War II, Professor P. S. M. Blackett may perhaps be taken as a final example of the prevailing ethos within the scientific community. Blackett was widely regarded as the father of operations research on the British side in World War II. He served as an operations research specialist to RAF Coastal Command and later to the Admiralty, where his most renowned accomplishment was the development of the convey system to defeat German submarines. After the war, he acquired additional fame for his research in nuclear physics. Blackett was hardly unfamiliar with the world of military realities. As he once commented, "During nearly twenty years of my lifetime of sixty years, I [was] either training for war, fighting wars, or studying and thinking about them."[22]

It was Blackett, of course, who protested vigorously at Lord Cherwell's attempt to justify the area offensive by his calculations on the effect of dehousing German workers. Moreover, Blackett suggested that the bombing offensive appealed in a perverted way to what he called the "Jupiter complex" in Great Britain (as well in the United States), in which the Allies saw themselves as righteous gods, raining retributive thunderbolts on their wicked enemies.[23] He denounced what he called a policy based on "gusts of emotion" that promised great things yet provided little if any standard by which realistic measurement of results could be obtained. Finally, Blackett was quite critical of the decision to use the atomic bomb against Japan. In a book written shortly after the war he even went so far as to suggest that the bomb was used primarily for political and not military reasons, particularly in order to impress the Soviet Union with the overwhelming power of the Western Allies. He suggested in this regard that "many American scientists undoubtedly felt morally distressed at finding the results of their brilliant scientific work used in a way which seemed to many of them [and, by inference, to Blackett] to lack adequate moral or military justification."[24]

Blackett was considered by his colleagues to be something of a radical in his politics and this may account in part for his attitude toward the use of the atomic bomb. Even so he does emerge as one of the few major scientists who, in the heat of the conflict, did manage to ponder some of the implications of what was being done in the name of the struggle against the

Axis. Yet it is well once again not to make too much of his moral doubts about the area offensive. His attitude toward Hiroshima and Nagasaki was, after all, shared by a good many others who nevertheless felt that Allied bombing policy had been fundamentally legitimate. The issue here was complicated by the fact that Japan may have been on the verge of surrender even before the dropping of the bomb. Moreover, Blackett's stance on the area offensive was heavily influenced by his conviction that British airpower could be much more effectively deployed against the German U-Boat menace (particularly in the critical years 1942-1943). Blackett by this time was scientific adviser to the Admiralty and not unnaturally tended to adopt their view of the appropriate allocation of British resources. Blackett's conscience may have been troubled by some of the more extreme manifestations of the area offensive, but on balance his criticism of this effort was largely utilitarian. His moral disagreement (to the extent that it existed) with others in the scientific community was at the margins, not at the center.

In assessing the relationship, moral and pragmatic, between the boffins and the application of British air power in World War II, there is a certain irony that deserves at least brief mention. The moral critic may be tempted to dwell on the abdication of ethical responsibility on the part of the scientists with respect to the area offensive. But a constant refrain in studies of the boffins' influence on air strategy is the difficulty they had, at least initially, in getting the airmen to take them seriously. As one writer puts it, "they had to persuade men who were responsible for ordering, and for doing, dangerous and difficult tasks, that these tasks would be less dangerous and less difficult if the implications of objective figures were considered and acted upon."[25] An early example of this tension came in the summer and fall of 1941, when scientists actually tried to measure the accuracy of the bombing that had heretofore been undertaken. Cameras were installed in the bombers so that photographs could be taken at the time of the bombs' release in order to establish exactly what was being hit. As R. V. Jones—an important figure in the boffin community and a scientific officer on the staff of the Air Ministry—recalls, "this aroused much resentment among the aircrew, who thought that the Air Staff must doubt whether they had actually gone in to attack their targets. Ultimately, they were convinced that no one had doubted their courage."[26]

There was also another, rather bizarre example of an underlying tension between the cool calculations of the scientists and the folk wisdom of the aircrew. The idea had developed among the pilots that by turning on their IFF (Identification Friend or Foe), a radar pulse designed to separate friendly from hostile aircraft, they could incapacitate German searchlights who had caught a plane in their light. R. V. Jones recalled that doing so was actually counterproductive and possibly dangerous and that the practice should be most emphatically discouraged. At a major conference of Bomber Command staff attended also by various pilots, Jones laid out the scientific evidence arguing against this use of IFF. To his amazement, the pilots continued to insist that it was an effective tactic. Later the operational research section of Bomber Command was formally charged with determining if using IFF in this way had a beneficial impact. The conclusion was that it had no effect one way or another. Bomber Command argued, however, that it was good to have the pilots believing in it, since otherwise they might abort their missions if caught in the glare of the German searchlights. As Jones says, this "was a thoroughly immoral argument."[27]

Eventually, the aircrew and the leadership of Bomber Command (sometimes grudgingly) accepted that the boffins did have something to offer in terms of making their missions both more efficient and more safe, even if the underlying prejudice against the supposed ivory-tower abstractions of the scientists continued to linger. In an unusual tribute to those outside his immediate circle of staff, Arthur Harris conceded that Bomber Command's operational research section became a "body of brilliant young civilian scientists and technicians . . . who did work of inestimable value in subjecting all aspects of our operations to an impartial scrutiny."[28]

This assessment doesn't help much, of course, in answering the question of what the boffins' moral role should have been in the development of Bomber Command's area offensive against Germany. The British historian A. J. P. Taylor was unsparing in his criticism of area bombing and, perhaps not incidentally, also had acerbic views on the role of modern science in questions of war and peace. He dismissed the scientists' mentality that accepts that "any argument will do" so long as they "can go on with their terribly sweet problems" (a phrase attributed to J. Robert Oppenheimer). Taylor argued that "the scientists think they are God. They want to remake the universe; and we pay the price for their mad ambition. . . . Shall we knock the power out of their hands before it is too late?"[29]

It is unclear how in the contemporary age one would go about depriving the scientific community of their powers. There is also a quibble that can be made about scientists' being consumed with a "mad ambition." Perhaps a fairer judgment on the boffins, curiously enough, might take at least something from that which we rendered on Sir Arthur Harris himself. British scientists, after all, were in the final analysis only servants of the state. One might have hoped that they would have spoken out more forcefully against the moral implications of the area offensive, particularly since they were in some position to judge the problematical military effects of such a massive departure from the war convention. In this sense, they could have harnessed their technical perceptions to a broader moral vision. Even as Arthur Harris was ultimately only carrying out the dictates of his political masters, however, the scientists were engaged in working on problems that those in a supposed position to know seemed to think were critical. Moreover, the fact that one is a specialist in radar impulses does not necessarily mean that one is also unusually sensitive to issues of moral judgment. Perhaps the British scientific community should have spoken out more forcefully against the abuses of the area offensive, but then so should have a number of others. Their responsibility may have been no less, but it may also have been no greater.

THE AIRCREW

It is said that old men start wars that young men must fight. This may seem like a fairly jejune proposition, yet it is also a truism that the morale of young men in combat is an important factor in the capacity of a state even to wage war, let alone to wage it successfully. Some wonderment has been expressed at the ability of the German *Wehrmacht* to retain its cohesion virtually to the last days of World War II, even when ultimate defeat was a foregone conclusion. The evidence on this score suggests that a major reason for such cohesion was that the average German soldier continued until final defeat to feel a sense of loyalty to his immediate unit as well as some general commitment to the necessity, and even the rightness, of continuing to fight.[30]

If it is surprising that the German army held together reasonably well, it appears almost miraculous that Bomber Command was able, with only a few exceptions, to sustain the morale of its own aircrew until the German surrender. This achievement is all the more remarkable when we draw up actuarial tables for those joining Bomber Command during the war. Aircrew were normally required to fly 30 missions before they were offered other duties. There were some who, after a period of stand-down, volunteered for an additional 20 missions. For much of the war, to attempt 30 sorties over Germany, or even the occupied territories, was virtually to sign one's own death warrant. The British radar specialist R. V. Jones summarized the situation as follows:

> One could hardly contemplate what our bomber crews were up against. They frequently had to fly about 800 miles through the German defences, at a speed

less than 200 miles an hour, and at any time they were liable to unexpected attack.
The chances of surviving a tour of thirty operations in Bomber Command in
1943 were about one in six, but morale never faltered.[31]

The overall odds on a person's joining Bomber Command and surviving the
war totally unscathed was about one in five. Once assigned to an aircraft, the
average individual had a service life of about 40 days.

The picture that presents itself is of thousands of young men crowded
together on dank air bases in East Anglia, waiting for assignments that
almost inevitably would spell either death, injury, or a long period as a
prisoner of war. In "Lincolnshire Bomber Station," a pilot named Henry
Treece penned some lines that seemed to catch the whole atmosphere of
the proceedings:

> Across the road the homesick Romans made
> The ground-mist thickens to a milky shroud;
> Through flat, damp fields call sheep, mourning their dead
> In cracked and timeless voices, unutterably sad,
> Suffering for all the world, in Lincolnshire.
>
> And I wonder how the Romans liked it here;
> Flat fields, no sun, the muddy misty dawn,
> And always, above all, the mad rain dripping down,
> Rusting sword and helmet, wetting the feet
> And soaking to the bone, down to the very heart.[32]

How to explain the psychological strengths that sustained what otherwise
might seem an irrational commitment? How could R. V. Jones say (evidently
quite accurately) that "morale never faltered"? Enlistment in Bomber Command, after all, was entirely voluntary—for most it would have been much
safer to go to sea or join the Eighth Army. Part of the explanation lies in the
esprit de corps fostered by Arthur Harris, which convinced his personnel that
Bomber Command was the elite service of the war. As one former Flight
Sergeant said of Harris, "We had all the confidence in the world in his
strategy. We felt that we and we alone in Bomber Command were winning
the war."[33] It was also true that for much of the war, for those eager to have
a direct role in fighting the Germans, Bomber Command seemed to be the
one service that was engaged in continual day-to-day combat with the Nazi
regime. Once one joined Bomber Command, moreover, there was considerable pressure to stick it out and, above all, not to let one's fellow aircrew

down. Those who did waver were disciplined under the rubric LMF, or "Lacking Moral Fibre," and were officially styled as "Waverers." To be dismissed or reassigned to other duties under a LMF indictment, to be a Waverer, was considered a moral blot on one's record (symbolized by the removal of the individual's flying brevet), and the possibility of such a fate provided at least negative reinforcement to do one's duty.

If we accept that the aircrew of Bomber Command were sustained by the feeling that the bombers were playing a decisive role in bringing down the Nazis, there was nevertheless one potentially troublesome cloud on the horizon that could perhaps have affected their morale. Very few combat soldiers like to think that their actions violate all the common rules of humanity in the practice of war. There is an interesting comment in Neil Sheehan's biography of John Paul Vann, the quintessential American career soldier in Vietnam, that provides a reference point here. Vann was appalled by the indiscriminate shelling and bombing of "suspected" Viet Cong hamlets. He adhered to the

> ideal of the soldier as the champion of the weak. A soldier who valued his honor
> and understood the purpose of his profession did not deliberately kill or wound
> ordinary people. . . . Vann had come to Vietnam to wage war on other men, not
> on their mothers and fathers or on their wives and children. That these people
> . . . undoubtedly did sympathize with the Viet Cong and helped them did not
> strip them of their noncombatant status and make them fair game in his mind.[34]

How did the aircrew of Bomber Command deal with the fact that they were in effect reversing a basic principle of civilized warfare, that is to say, the distinction between combatant and non-combatant? In plainer English, how did they react to having to drop bombs night after night on German civilians, even if the targets were technically "military" in nature?

Conflict and Conscience

In examining the evidence on this matter, a rather complex and in some ways surprising picture seems to emerge. There was, for the most part, seemingly little revenge motive in persuading aircrew to continue their work. When we recall that the Nazis had earlier attacked British cities, that they were widely recognized to have committed all sorts of crimes, and that many in Britain (including at times the Prime Minister himself) seemed to draw no distinction between the Nazi regime and the German people as a whole, it might have

been expected that Bomber Command personnel would revel in the opportunity to exact retribution for earlier German sins.

In reality, most aircrew seemed to be relatively less bellicose in their attitude
toward the Germans than many on the home front. A leading expert on British
airpower and staunch defender of Bomber Command observed that the fliers
were indeed "far less bloodthirsty than some whose activities [were] less
intimately connected with the tragic realities of modern war."[35] This phenomenon may have been widespread among all Allied fighting men. An American
veteran of the war recalls that as a foot soldier in Europe it was his impression
that hatred for the "devil-enemy" increased the more one was *removed* from the
combat zone. Civilians back home could be far more intransigent in their attitude
toward the enemy than those doing the actual fighting. He recalled that "many
a combat soldier in World War II was appalled to receive letters from his girl
friend or wife, safe at home, demanding to know how many of the enemy he had
personally accounted for and often requesting the death of several more as a
personal favor for her!"[36]

The reality seems to be that for most in Bomber Command the business of
carrying bombs to Germany was essentially just that: a temporary occupation
that one did more or less well depending on talents and energy levels. There was
comparatively little gloating that the German people were finally being taught a
lesson, or that they deserved the nightly calamities being visited on them.
Moreover, there seems to have been some general impatience with the glowing
accounts appearing in the British press about the invariable success of the
bombing raids. At the very least, there was very little echo of the romanticism
of Rupert Brooke and other British servicemen in World War I concerning the
nobility of the cause. Indeed the largest impression one has of the attitude of
Bomber Command aircrew toward their role was a pervasive fatalism and even
melancholy. An RAF fighter pilot recalled how Bomber Command aircrew
conducted themselves just prior to a raid on Berlin.

> [There were] a hundred or more young men, who walked silently and unsmiling
> to their allotted aircraft. Accustomed as I had already become to the gaiety and
> laughter of fighter pilots, I was distressed by the tense bearing and drawn faces
> of the bomber crews. At that time, late in November, 1943, some eighty per
> cent were failing to complete unscathed their tours of thirty operations. Of
> course they had plenty, but there was nothing but lip-biting gloom registered
> on those faces.[37]

In their time off-duty the aircrew seemed to take pleasure in removing
themselves as much as possible from the reality of their normal existence.

In doing so, they revealed that they were, after all, basically only a group of very young men thrust into a macabre situation. After parties away from the base, for example, they typically brought back such schoolboy trophies as toilet seats and street signs. Their essential innocence was also reflected in various aircrew rituals, such as the dropping of empty beer bottles from aircraft during raids over Germany (they made a noise that upset the "bystanders" beneath). Some crews urinated communally on their plane's tail wheel before taking off, as a talisman against danger; others did so on returning, as a thanksgiving for having survived.[38]

To suggest that the aircrew were essentially resigned to their roles as technicians of violence may provide a mixture of satisfaction and dismay to moral critics of British area bombing. On the one hand, it exculpates the fliers from the grosser charge that they actively "enjoyed" what they were doing or took positive satisfaction in the deaths of thousands of German civilians. On the other hand, the critics might want to feel that the aircrew themselves had moral doubts about their actions, which would only add support to an ethical indictment of the basic strategy itself. One of the prevailing myths about the American use of the atom bomb against Hiroshima, for example, is that one of the crew of the *Enola Gay* was so morally shattered by what he had done that it had a permanent and ruinous effect on his subsequent life. Even though the evidence for this assertion later proved to be quite dubious, it has often been cited in condemnations of the bombing of Hiroshima.[39]

The reality, fortunately or unfortunately, was that most fliers in Bomber Command were simply indifferent to the moral debate. Even the most sensitive aircrew generally found that they "felt no guilt or dismay at dropping bombs, simply because [their] fear entirely submerged any more noble or humane motive."[40] One survivor of the bombing of Dresden recently wondered why there weren't any humane bomber crews who simply dropped their bombs off target in order to avoid the moral atrocity of attacking Dresden. The reason most aircrew would have given was that such an action might have at least slightly delayed the war's end and thus extended their own period of personal danger.[41]

At times Bomber Command pilots even offered a mocking assessment of the supposed moral issues raised by the area offensive. Thus two officers from 617 Squadron wrote a sardonic letter to *The Times* following the famous raid on the Mohne dam in the Ruhr Valley in May 1943. The letter denounced the dams raid because a pair of "ring-necked whooper swans" nested regularly on the lake created by the Mohne.

> They are almost the rarest of Europe's great birds. Has anything been heard of the fate of the Mohne pair, probably the last in Europe? And, in view of the

rarity of these beautiful birds, why was the bombing of their home permitted? Furthermore, assuming that this operation was necessary, could it not have been deferred until the cygnets (if any) were full grown?[42]

The Times declined to publish this supposed defense of avian rights.

Consider as well this passage from a former RAF pilot who did not serve in Bomber Command but who presumably revealed some of the basic attitudes of all the fliers.

> There were occasional treats [in France] when, usually contrary to orders, we would sweep down on German trucks, petrol bowsers or staff cars and riddle them with shot and shell. It was like an enjoyable day's rabbit shooting; nobody gave much thought to the human suffering we caused, for we had been at war for nearly five years and our sensitivities were dulled, at any rate in battle. It would have been hard to survive if they had not been. When it was all over we shed quicker than might have been expected the hard skin of callousness with which, quite naturally it seemed, most of us had so long covered our emotions.[43]

Samuel Johnson once commented that the prospect of being hanged in the morning concentrated the mind wonderfully. In the case of Bomber Command, the daunting challenge of surviving in the skies over Germany did seem to lead to a shuffling off of other considerations.

It is a fine question whether any blame should attach to the aircrew for the fact that they generally had few moral doubts about their wartime operations. A first principle of the Nuremberg trials was that superior orders are not in themselves a defense for an individual soldier committing acts in violation of the laws of war and humanity, although the existence of such orders could be considered a mitigating factor in assigning punishment. Even so loathsome a figure as German propaganda minister Joseph Goebbels rather bizarrely insisted on this principle (although somewhat less so with airmen in the Luftwaffe): "The pilots cannot say that they as soldiers acted upon orders. It is not provided in any military law that a soldier in the case of a despicable crime is exempt from punishment because he blames his superior, especially if the orders of the latter are in evident contradiction to all human morality and every international usage of warfare."[44] Perhaps Bomber Command aircrew should have questioned more stringently the legality and ethics of what they were doing, but the argument is a rather problematical one when we consider that the area bombing of Germany was in accordance with specific directives from the highest political authority and was constantly defended as being crucial to the war effort. If we add to this the pressures to maintain group cohesion, that is, not to let the (flying) team down in extremely adverse conditions, it would have been expecting a lot for individual crew to engage in philosophical disputation on the morality of their actions.

Perhaps our focus here should be not so much on the (unsurprising) failure of Bomber Command personnel to question area bombing on moral grounds, but rather on another issue: the numbing effect that modern military technology has on those assigned to employ it. A report by the Air Ministry in June 1942, based on letters from aircrew opened by the censors, stressed "the effect of airmen's remoteness from their attacks on human beings." Clausewitz identified the basic dilemma a long time before the Lancasters were sent over Germany. He referred to the depersonalization of violence, which exists when soldiers can't directly observe the consequences of their actions and thus develop an increasing callousness. "Weapons with which the enemy can be attacked while he is at a distance allow the feelings, the 'instinct for fighting properly' so-called, to remain almost at rest, and this so much the more according as the range of their effects is greater."[45] Presumably the act of dropping bombs from 20,000 feet would fall into this category.

It is also important in this context to recognize that aircrew were generally shielded from the idea that their mission was simply to devastate German cities. Indeed, the subterfuge consistently used in explaining the area offensive to the average British citizen was also applied in the briefing of the pilots. As one authority on Bomber Command has written, "Crews were given all the information available about the target's importance [but] given it in terms which organizations disenchanted with Bomber Command like the Foreign Office, the Ministry of Economic Warfare and (increasingly) the Anglican hierarchy could accept. They were rarely given much which could stand up to stringent examination on the basis of known facts."[46] The truth of this observation is attested to by the comments of a pilot some years after the war. He recalled that his one clear memory of being briefed to bomb whole areas was at Essen in July 1943. "At that point we were not aware that we were bombing civilians as such, because we had always been given an aiming-point like the docks, or a rubber factory or railway yards. But on this occasion the briefing said that we were to bomb the workers' houses or residential quarters and this came as something of a personal shock."[47] The point is that whatever moral doubts aircrew may have felt were assuaged by assurances that their aiming points were critical German military installations.

In reinforcing Clausewitz's assertion about depersonalized violence, it is instructive to consider an example of a situation in which a pilot was not able to depersonalize what he was doing. The Master Bomber (basically the target indicator) for the RAF's second attack on Dresden was a very experienced pilot with more than three tours under his belt. In November 1944, about three months before the Dresden raid, he had been asked to serve as Master Bomber for an attack on Freiburg im Bresgau. He declined, since he had studied at the university there and had many friends in the area around the Freiburg Cathedral, which was the aiming point selected for this particular assault. However, he had never been to Dresden, and even though he regretted the destruction of such a fine city, he went ahead with this assignment, since he could offer no compelling personal reason for not carrying it out.[48]

As this incident suggests, it would be a mistake to leave the impression that the moral issue never impacted on the consciousness of the fliers in Bomber Command. Perhaps their engagement with the matter was a lot less than critics of the area offensive would have hoped for, but what is striking from a somewhat different perspective is the degree to which the ethical question did emerge from time to time. The evidence on this score is scattered but nevertheless suggestive. A former navigator recalls, for example, that after a briefing on an apparently non-military target, someone in the back of the room called out, "women and children first again" (a comment which was studiously ignored). Air-gunner Geoff Parnell remembered his feelings during the great raid on Hamburg in July 1943: "There were people down there being fried to death in melted asphalt in the roads, they were being burnt up and we were shuffling incendiary bombs into this holocaust. I felt terribly sorry for the people in that fire I was helping to stoke up."[49] There is also this recollection from a long-serving Pathfinder navigator who touched both on his own qualms and on the difficulties of giving them practical expression:

> Area, or town bombing, upset many of the aircrews, myself particularly. I always hated the thought of indiscriminate bombing and always thought of women, children, hospitals and suchlike. But to whom could you express such doubts? Raids on our cities helped to still the small voice of conscience but it worries me still to this day.
>
> Had the Germans won the war, should we or ought we to have been tried as war criminals? If we believed it morally wrong, should we have spoken out to our squadron commanders and refused to participate? What would have been the result? Court martial!
>
> It would have needed much more courage to have spoken out on this matter than the mere fact of continuing to fly on operations. So no one voiced his reservations but the thoughts live with me to this day.[50]

In May 1943, some members of 76 Squadron, based in Yorkshire, expressed their unhappiness with attacking Wuppertal simply because, as their intelligence officer told them, they would be able in doing so to catch thousands of refugees crowded into the area after an earlier Bomber Command assault on the Ruhr. As German air defenses drastically declined in late 1944, an increasing number of British airmen were sufficiently relieved of their fear for survival to develop a pity for the fate of those below. For some of the aircrew of Bomber Command, as for many others, the attack on Dresden seems, for example, to have represented at long last a step too far. One reflection of the disapproval was symbolic in nature: certain of the squadrons assigned to attack Dresden voted to forgo a customary ritual—the dropping of bits of concrete and other junk intended as an insult to the Germans. There is also the comment from one of the men involved in the Dresden raid that "for the first time in the war I truly felt sorry for the people below."[51]

It is interesting to note that even though they may have felt no qualms themselves, certain major figures in authority during the war worried that the aircrew might become infected by moral criticism of their activities, and thus they attempted to shield them from such talk as much as possible. Arthur Harris, for one, constantly fretted that the relatively unfettered British press might undermine the morale of his personnel by giving space to the ethical musings of area bombing opponents. We have previously referred to his objecting to Archibald Sinclair and others dissimulating as to the real character of the area offensive; such a stance, he thought, might lead his aircrew to conclude that they were being asked to do things that the Air Ministry was ashamed to admit. A member of Parliament who also happened to be a flight-lieutenant in the RAF spoke for many when he deplored all the statements calling into doubt the purpose of the bomber offensive. "It is tough to ask these chaps to undergo great dangers and perils, which they do cheerfully and bravely, unless they are convinced ... that it is worth doing."[52]

The concern that existed about the sowing of ethical doubts among the aircrew was well-illustrated by an incident that took place at High Wycombe and involved the socialist Minister of Aircraft Production, Sir Stafford Cripps. Cripps was an ascetic and a devout Christian who took it upon himself to remind the pilots of their duty to God as well as to country. In a lecture shortly before the attack on Dresden, he took as his text "God is my co-pilot," and suggested that officers should send men on a bombing mission only if, with a clear conscience, they were convinced that such a mission was justified not only on military grounds but on moral grounds as well. In case his point was missed, he reminded the fliers that "even when you are engaged in acts of wickedness, God is always looking over your shoulder." These observations were received with some hostility, particularly since some in Bomber Command believed that Cripps's ministry was deliberately starving them of aircraft for pseudo-moralistic reasons.[53] During the question period one or two officers commented that if his advice was followed the result would be an undermining of discipline and would hinder the war effort. The meeting was called to an abrupt halt by the chairman. Churchill soon learned about this curious session and expressed his displeasure. He was described as "incensed with Stafford Cripps for making a speech about brotherly feelings for the Germans." In the typical Churchillian fashion, he said that he "might agree with such sentiments when victory is won, but not with a great battle raging and the Huns shooting captured soldiers in cold blood."[54]

The sensitivity that existed on this matter could be seen in the angry comment offered by one of the chief defenders of Bomber Command to the effect that "no chivalrous airman wants to slaughter grandmothers or babies."[55] If there was this degree of concern about the receptivity of aircrew to the moral question, one can only conclude that either the problem was greatly exaggerated or that alternatively—and more interestingly—there was perhaps a greater degree of moral uneasiness among the fliers than might be apparent from the surface evidence.

The Legacy of Guilt

There is a final point to be made concerning the men of Bomber Command. Even if it is assumed that most aircrew were relatively free of moral doubts while they were undertaking their missions against Germany, they can have hardly been impervious to the widespread moral questioning that was levied against their activities after the war. Particularly bitter must have been the comments of fellow airmen who now denounced their comrades' former behavior. One man, for example, with 26 years' commissioned service in the Royal Air Force, noted that "I was a fighter pilot, never a bomber pilot, and I thank God for that. I do not believe I could ever have obeyed orders as a bomber pilot; it would have given me no sense of achievement to drop bombs on German cities."[56]

The veterans of Bomber Command were, in any case, confronted after 1945 with a level of moral condemnation of area bombing that had been generally absent during the struggle itself. As we have already recounted, they received no Campaign Medal, and the general attitude of many—both in the government and outside—seemed to be that it would be best to forget their activities as quickly as possible. This *ex post facto* implied (and often outright) censure can hardly have failed to have at least some effect on many of those who had served in the bombers. The damage to self-esteem that could take place is movingly conveyed in this passage from Max Hastings's history of Bomber Command.

> One night after I had visited a much-decorated pilot in the north of England in the course of writing this book, he drove me to the station. Suddenly turning to me in the car, he asked: 'Has anybody else mentioned having nightmares about it?' He said that in the past ten years he had been troubled by increasingly vivid and terrible dreams about his experiences over Germany.
>
> A teacher by profession, he had thought nothing of the war for years afterwards. Then a younger generation of his colleagues began to ask with repetitive, inquisitive distaste: 'How could you have done it? How could you have flown over Germany night after night to bomb women and children?' He began to brood more and more deeply about his past. He changed his job and started to teach mentally-handicapped children, which he sees as a kind of restitution. Yet still, more than thirty years after, his memories of the war haunt him.[57]

The reality seems to be that some in Bomber Command ultimately became casualties of the war just as much as their comrades who suffered more conventional injuries in missions over Germany.

4

The Subjects of the Realm

"It is not always the same thing to
be a good man and a good citizen."

—Aristotle

In the summer of 1944, a certain Mr. John Brophy, a writer then serving in the Home Guard, wrote a remonstrative letter to his good friend Captain Basil Liddell Hart, the distinguished British military historian. Brophy was particularly aroused by Liddell Hart's argument that British wartime conduct was hardly morally superior to that of the Germans. While admitting that certain wicked things had been (and were being) done in the interests of victory, Brophy heatedly denied any comparison between German and British standards of behavior: "Taken as a whole the British [record] is morally clean, and the German filthy. The concentration camps alone are enough to indict the Nazis. I stick to the general proportion, and I see the British with all their faults as the most civilized and innocent nation in the world."[1]

A rather similar sentiment was expressed by a regional information officer (RIO) of the British Ministry of Information in April 1941. The RIOs were local officials charged with distributing and supporting the government's approved line on British military policy. In this instance, the RIO strongly objected to instructions from the ministry on how to represent the actions of Bomber Command to his constituents. He was told to stress that the government, in developing its bombing strategy, didn't want to make the "mistake" of diverting its efforts from key military targets to attacks on "secondary targets" (i.e., cities). The point to be emphasized was that simply killing civilians was not militarily efficient. The RIO demanded to know if this was really the only reason that could (or should) be given for not smashing German cities. "Why must Government always shirk the moral issue? Have we not the courage to say that to take reprisals is wrong in itself, unethical, unchristian and unworthy of the British people?"[2]

There are some who might quibble at the notion that Britain has always been the most civilized and innocent nation in the world. Nevertheless, one of the images of British society that has prevailed—and not only among Britons themselves—is that, historically, standards of civility have been unusually high and there has been a comparatively strong devotion to norms of humane conduct. Assuming that these perceptions have at least some basis in fact, it is a matter of considerable interest to evaluate the general reaction of the British citizen to the area bombing offensive against German cities conducted in his or her name during World War II.

In what follows there will be a focus on groups and individuals from various walks of British life. They can be considered together in the sense that none were directly involved in the strategy or operations of Bomber Command. Some held official posts outside the inner circle of decision-makers involved in directing the war effort, i.e., backbenchers in Parliament. Others were prominent in the religious community or in various literary or social realms. Attention is also given here to British society as a whole, since the views of the average citizen concerning the strategy of British arms were ultimately of considerable importance in a political system that remained basically responsive to popular will.

A few preliminary observations are in order. There is an obvious tendency in all societies—both authoritarian and democratic—to give the benefit of the doubt to official authority during great crises such as a major war. It may have been asking too much to expect that the typical British citizen would question the analysis, and even more the morality, behind what the government was doing in the air offensive against Germany. Some private doubts may exist, but there is considerable inclination to accept that what one's leaders say is necessary and right, indeed *is* necessary and right. The alternative—accepting that one's government is either incompetent or immoral—is distinctly unappealing. The fact that so many Germans continued to support Hitler's war effort until the very end is only one piece of evidence attesting to the wide latitude that governments normally enjoy in wartime.

There was also the character of the Nazi threat itself. Even among those who might have had doubts about the violation of traditional rules governing combatants and non-combatants, the specter of Nazi brutality and its denial of basic human dignity loomed large. In April 1945, an air force historian visited the recently liberated death camp at Buchenwald. After observing this charnel house, his comment was that "here is the antidote for qualms about strategic bombing."[3] To be sure, the evidence available earlier about the extent of Nazi atrocities was not as clear-cut, but enough was known to make it understandable that a general unfeeling toughness might develop toward the suffering of Germans who had tolerated or even abetted such abuses in the first place.

It has to be recognized as well that a great many in Britain, in fact a majority of the population, seem to have had little real sense of what the area bombing of Germany actually involved. Official government spokesmen, of course, went out of their way to deny that Bomber Command was attacking German civilians. The steady claim was that British aircrews were targeting strictly military objectives. As late as 1944, a public opinion poll revealed that 75 percent of those questioned assumed that Bomber Command was being directed solely at military targets. Only one in ten was aware that bombs were falling on other sites as well (e.g., the center of German cities.)[4] Perhaps more people should have been able to infer the actual strategy, but as one analysis on the subject has it, people preferred to feel rather than know about strategic bombing. In any event it remains that ignorance about the specifics of the air war was seemingly widespread among the British people virtually to the end of the war.

A distinction does have to be made here between what specialists in public opinion generally call the mass public and the attentive public.[5] The latter are those who, as a matter of interest or practice, pay fairly close attention to the details of politics and current affairs. In most democratic societies they are estimated to comprise around a quarter of the population. For members of the British "attentive public," there was information available to those seeking it that suggested that Bomber Command was targeting German cities themselves.[6] Given this fact, one might conclude that there was often an unspoken conspiracy between government spokesmen and many in their intended audience: we pretend that we are attacking only military targets and you pretend to believe us.

Press accounts of the bombing of Dresden did have the effect of dropping the scales from all but the most unfocused eyes. In one of the more bizarre episodes of the air campaign, an Associated Press correspondent received a briefing from an RAF spokesmen who spoke of the necessity of disrupting the flow of relief supplies from the German government to civilians (and of destroying cities in which refugees were congregating). The correspondent then filed a dispatch in which he said that "Allied air commanders have made the long-awaited decision to adopt deliberate terror bombing of the great German population centers as a ruthless expedient to hasten Hitler's doom."[7] This article was inexplicably cleared by the military censor at Allied head-quarters, and caused considerable embarrassment to both American and

British spokesmen on the air campaign. As the official historians of Bomber Command put it, the dispatch "undoubtedly contributed to the widespread misunderstanding of the conduct of the British Air Staff and of the Commander-in-Chief, Bomber Command, which has prevailed ever since."[8] The "misunderstanding," of course, related to the fact that attacks on German civilian targets had been a prime objective of British air policy for three years and that Dresden represented not the beginning but the culmination of such a policy. The British government quickly took steps to forbade publication of the AP dispatch in Britain, but its contents had already been widely circulated.

Given what we have said above about the factors shaping British opinion in the war years, one might have expected something close to uniformity in support of the bombing offensive against Germany, at least prior to the raid on Dresden. In actuality, there was a surprising degree of diversity in the British people's reaction to the bombing, both among the mass public, who had little evident idea of what the area offensive entailed, and among the attentive public, whose knowledge was (sometimes) more in tune with reality. There was a steady drumbeat of criticism of Bomber Command from the few and an even wider expression of uneasiness from a good many others. A survey undertaken by the British Institute of Public Opinion in April 1941, for example, found that 53 percent of those questioned approved (in theory) of bombing civilian targets in Germany, 38 percent did not, and 9 percent were undecided. A later poll revealed that Londoners, when asked their opinion of bombing raids on Germany, replied in the following proportions: about six in ten gave "unqualified verbal approval," two out of ten had qualms about the bomber offensive, and one-tenth felt the raids were too terrible to be condoned.[9]

In sorting out public reaction to British air policy in World War II, it is possible to divide opinion into three general categories, even if there was some overlap among them on certain issues.

THE CROMWELLIANS

In May 1942, Mr. Geoffrey Shakespeare, Liberal MP for Norwich, wrote a letter to Sir Archibald Sinclair setting out his views on the bombing of Germany. "I am all for the bombing of working class areas of German cities," he informed Sinclair. "I am Cromwellian—I believe in 'slaying in the name of the Lord,' because I do not believe you will ever bring home to the civil population of Germany the horrors of war until they have been tested in this way."[10]

The people referred to here as the Cromwellians robustly supported, and virtually without qualification, the area bombing of Germany on the grounds that it was ultimately designed to have a military effect even if the achieving of same was somewhat roundabout. This meant that the qualms of others about attacks on civilians were dismissed with a rather impatient shrug. Since the heart of Germany's social, political, and industrial infrastructure lay in its cities, so much the worse for German cities. A common argument advanced in this context was that if German civilians were to be spared because of humanitarian concerns about sanctuary for non-combatants, this would perforce bring Bomber Command to a grinding halt. It was not that the mass bombing of urban centers was desirable in itself. Precision strikes against oil, transportation, aircraft factories, and so on were obviously preferable in military terms *if they were feasible*. But since such strikes were for much of the war outside the capabilities of Bomber Command, the obliteration of cities was not only the logical but also the legal and moral alternative indicated.

Yet there was often a darker note to the Cromwellian case, quite aside from these utilitarian calculations. At times the rhetoric seemed to imply that not only was area bombing militarily justified in itself but perhaps it was especially justified given the "character" of the German people. There is no way to get around this theme except to say that, at the very least, it carried the suggestion of racism. Even Churchill himself, celebrated by many for his compassion and generosity toward a defeated enemy, was not immune to this temptation. In April 1941 he offered the sociological observation that "there are less than seventy million malignant Huns— some of whom are curable and others killable."[11] The crucial premise here seemed to be that there was essentially no difference between the German people and the Nazi regime itself. Since the latter was universally regarded as a pariah by civilized opinion, it was only a short step to the argument that German society itself was also an outcast among mankind. Given this attitude, there was no need to shed tears about any calamity that might befall it. Indeed, there was a lot to be said for the argument that such a society deserved to experience some calamity.

Perhaps the leading British voice arguing that the German people were somehow tainted by original sin was that of Sir Robert Vansittart, who was a veteran of the Foreign Office and one of the principal men arguing for a firm policy against Hitler in the late 1930s. Vansittart was still chief diplomatic adviser to the British Government in the autumn of 1940 when he was allowed (or encouraged) to make a rather striking series of broadcasts on the Overseas Service of the BBC, which subsequently appeared as a pamphlet

entitled *The Black Record*. Sir Robert suggested that throughout history the
Germans had been the "butcher-birds" of Europe, the invariable cause of the
trials and tribulations of civilized humanity. Envy, self-pity, and cruelty were
identified as the fundamental traits of the German people. Even though
Vansittart conceded there were a few good Germans, he claimed that for the
most part Hitler "gives to the great majority of Germans exactly what they
have hitherto liked and wanted."[12] What came to be called "Vansittartism"
was embodied in an organization called the Win the Peace movement, and
even though Vansittart had no direct role in the operations of Bomber
Command, there is little question but that his basic thesis provided at least
spurious intellectual support for those who viewed the area bombing offensive in important ways as simply a just punishment for past and present
German misconduct.

It has to be recognized that the Cromwellian impulse wasn't just confined
to bloody-minded members of the Tory elite in Britain during the war.
Support for this notion sometimes came from rather surprising sources. For
instance, the President of the Trades Union Congress told the annual conference in late 1942 that "until the German people, not alone their gangster
rulers, have meted out to them what they have meted out to millions of their
fellow creatures . . . the German people will again, if not prevented, make
another attempt to enslave Europe." Even Clement Atlee, the eminently
civilized leader of the Labour Party, opined that "a great moral and mental
revolution" would be needed before the Germans could be trusted again. "It
was idle," he said, "to think that the process of converting the Germans from
the barbarities into which they had sunk to civilization was not going to take
a long time."[13]

In gaining a further insight into the mindset of the Cromwellians, we
might take a look at a small book published in 1944 entitled *Bombing
Vindicated*. It was offered by Mr. J. M. Spaight (CB, CBE), former
Principal Assistant Secretary at the Air Ministry, and a well-known writer
on matters of airpower. This book may well be regarded as the principal
(indeed the only) full-length defense of the area offensive to be offered
during the war itself by a private author. The arguments presented in
Bombing Vindicated are a curious melange, consisting in part of a vigorous
trumpeting of the military effectiveness of the area offensive alongside
rather defensive denials that there was any real moral issue at stake in the
tactics of Bomber Command.

The title of his first chapter reflects Spaight's fundamental thesis: "The
Bomber Saves Civilization." Spaight goes out of his way to assure his readers
that he is not an unfeeling man and that he is as sensible as the next person

concerning the suffering of woman and children. He admits that the notion that the bomber had saved civilization may strike some as a perversion of the truth, and he concedes that British opponents of area bombing are sincere patriots and had the courage of their convictions even if they were wildly misinformed. He constantly frets that he may be misunderstood when he extols the virtues of the bombing offensive, saying that "I seem . . . to have been exalting military expediency and discounting the humane motive."[14]

Despite this bow in the direction of moral rectitude, Spaight's references to the supposed ethical issues raised by the area offensive are essentially *pro forma*, using language that was commonplace in virtually everything written or said by the Cromwellians. The real thrust of his analysis is to dismiss the idea that there was actually any issue to be debated concerning the area offensive. This attitude is reflected in his comment that "unfortunately the German propagandists were able to count upon a certain amount of support in their campaign [against area bombing] from within this country of free speech." He stressed that Hitler's supposed conversion to humanitarianism (his protests against British terror bombing) was no more than an attempt to blunt the extraordinary effectiveness of Bomber Command's campaign over Germany. This argument for bombing on utilitarian grounds also contained a warning to his audience that British civilians would themselves pay the price of any "forbearance shown by our airmen," which implied that a curtailment of the area offensive would prolong the war and cause further suffering for the British people. In any event, Spaight concluded, the "loss of civilian life which bombing causes is almost trivial in comparison with that due to blockade."[15]

This was an old theme that was a favorite of Sir Arthur Harris. The gist of it was that the naval blockade of Germany in World War I was far worse in its impact on the civilian population than British bombing in the current war. If any were left unconvinced by his dismissal of moral problems in the area offensive, Spaight added that what the Germans were doing to others was more terrible than anything the British were doing, which supposedly exculpated Great Britain from any putative violation of humanitarian principles in the conduct of the war.

What is especially striking about *Bombing Vindicated* is how the author— who, given his professional background, presumably had accurate information on Bomber Command's strategy—consistently denies that his country was actually targeting the urban population in Germany. In a chapter entitled "The Bombing of Civilians," Spaight simply rejects the notion that there was any plan for the bombing of civilians. Indeed he accepts that "indiscriminate bombing is certainly not justified," yet suggests that this is not a matter that need engage the concern of his readers since such was not being pursued. Certainly there was some unintended death and destruction visited on German cities, but military industries and workers, as well as famous cultural sites, were unfortunately generally located in the middle of urban centers. Spaight especially denies that German morale was anything other than a quite incidental object of British bombing.

None of these claims, of course, were in any way reflective of the fact that morale indeed was mentioned prominently in various directives given to Bomber Command during the war, that Arthur Harris's own statements described his aircrew as simply aiming their bombs at the middle of German cities, or that German military industry was generally located not in the center but on the outskirts of the cities. Spaight's dissimulation on this score was, to be sure, reflective of the public relations stance taken by official governmental spokesmen, for example, Archibald Sinclair, concerning Bomber Command's tactics. Perhaps the fact that Spaight felt it necessary to engage in such a deception, even while extolling the great accomplishments of Bomber Command, is one of the most important points to emerge out of his book.

THE MODERATES

As they have been defined and described here, the Cromwellians almost certainly never constituted more than a distinct minority of opinion in Britain with respect to the activities of Bomber Command. For the great majority of the British public, the attitude adopted toward the area offensive might properly be described as a general (if at times uneasy) acceptance of a military necessity combined with considerable admiration for the courage of Bomber Command aircrew, not to mention considerable pride in the fact that Britain was taking the war to the Germans in a demonstrable way even though she may have been suffering military reversals on other fronts. A report sent to the Air Ministry analyzing a sample of civilian letters opened by the censor in the wake of the 1,000-bomber raid on Cologne summarized what seems to have been the prevailing position: "There are those who are pleased, and those who regret that so much suffering should have to be inflicted. There are those who fear reprisals. Many of the letters contain two or more of these elements. Predominant is satisfaction, but many women express regret."[16]

I refer to this majority as the "moderates" not because they were hesitant in their commitment to victory over the Nazis but because they generally seemed unresponsive to the argument that the German people as such needed and deserved the terrible punishment of the area offensive. Indeed, the moderates at times demonstrated at least some empathy for the suffering of the German civilian population under bombing; this was especially so for those who had themselves experienced air attacks in an earlier period. Calls for reprisals against Germany in response to the Luftwaffe's attacks against Britain, for example, tended to be concentrated in areas that had been least affected by German bombing. A Gallup Poll published early in May 1941 showed that the most determined demands for revenge came from Cumberland, Westmorland, and the North Riding of Yorkshire, which were rural areas barely touched by bombs, whereas in Central London there were far fewer individuals who simply wanted to punish the Germans for their sins.[17] The British Institute of Public Opinion took a similar poll a month earlier and found that "sentiment in favour of reprisals is almost in inverse ratio to the amount of bombing experienced."[18]

Typical of those who viewed the area offensive (at least partly) more in sorrow than in anger, even while accepting its basic legitimacy, was a certain Brigadier Cecil Aspinall-Oglander. In a letter to *The Times* on May 1, 1942, he criticized the sometimes gloating attitude that he perceived in publicity about the bombing of Germany:

> Britain and her Allies and well-wishers must all be devoutly thankful that the RAF is at last able to repay Germany in her own coin and to inflict upon her cities the same devastation that she has inflicted on ours. But it must offend the sensibilities of a large mass of the British population that our official broadcasts, when reporting these acts of just retribution, should exult at and gloat over the suffering which our raids necessitate. . . . Let us at least preserve the decencies of English taste. An Englishman does not exult when a criminal is condemned to the scaffold, nor gloat over his sufferings at the time of his execution.[19]

In describing and assessing what might be called middle-of-the-road British opinion on the area bombing offensive, some particularly interesting material is to be found in the stance taken by members of the British religious community toward the bombing. One representative effort by religious leaders to deal with the issues raised by the war was the establishment in August 1940 of a movement known as the "Sword of the Spirit." Its most prominent figure was Cardinal Hinsley, the liberal-minded Roman Catholic Archbishop of Westminster. The avowed aim was to unite all people of goodwill—not just Catholics—in a crusade of prayer and action against the atheistic, totalitarian challenge of the Hitler regime. The ultimate goal was the restoration of a system of justice and peace in the world.[20]

For present purposes, however, it was the position adopted by the hierarchy of the Church of England that is of greatest interest. The latter was, after all, the established faith in Great Britain and more generally was seen at the time as a bulwark of the Establishment, "the Tory party at prayer" as one phrase had it. Under these circumstances, it might have been expected that the Anglican clergy would pretty much accept the government's definition of military necessity and support the bombing offensive without undue demurrer as a means to defeat the enemy. Such support was perhaps even more to be expected given the Church's record in World War I, where its generally enthusiastic—some would say jingoistic—offering of religious sanction for the struggle against Berlin was a matter of record.

In the event, the attitude of Church authority toward the war effort in 1939-1945 was a good deal more ambiguous and contradictory than might have been expected. Certainly there was general support for the notion that this was after all a just war and that the Nazis represented a fundamental threat to basic Christian values that could only be defeated by force of arms. Yet this stance must be set alongside a fairly lively debate evident amongst various Anglican luminaries as to what means were legitimate in the prosecution of this particular just war. At the very least, Church of England clergy tended to avoid the fairly unsubtle linking of God's will with English interests that characterized their behavior in World War I.

One reason for so doing may have been their perception that the Church's credibility had been undermined—particularly among the young and the better-educated—by the unabashedly propagandistic stance taken by clergy in the earlier struggle. Perhaps as one consequence of this alienation, organized religion was at relatively low ebb on the outbreak of World War II. On Easter Sunday, 1940, for example, only 6 adults in 100 took communion in Anglican churches. A subsequent survey indicated that six of ten in Britain never went to any church at all, and a third of those under 40 described themselves as non-believers. The nonconformist churches (Methodist, Baptist, Congregationalist) had their own fall-offs in membership, with a decline of about 50 percent from 30 years earlier.[21]

To the extent that there was a debate among religious leaders about the means (although not the ends) of the war effort, the primary focus clearly seemed to be on strategic bombing, and in particular the area bombing of German cities. It needs emphasizing that only a handful of the clergy objected outright to area bombing. George Bell, Bishop of Chichester, was the most prominent and his case will be considered in detail later on. The Bishop of Birmingham, the Moderator of the Church of Scotland, and the Methodist leader Donald Soper were others who expressed their concerns about the very concept of the area offensive, as did Cosmo Gordon Lang, Archbishop of Canterbury from 1928 to January 1942. The small Quaker community in Great Britain added their voice to these protests, particularly in the form of the Bombing Restriction Committee organized by T. Corder Catchpool.

Even if most clergy felt unable to go so far as to flatly condemn area bombing, however, it remains that a number of them were troubled by the implications of a strategy that seemed to eliminate all traditional distinctions in just war theory between combatant and non-combatant as well as proportionality in the means of warfare. An early indication of this concern came in 1940, when a group of pacifist leaders asked the Archbishops of Canterbury and York at what point the Church would rather see the war lost rather than won with methods that were totally inconsistent with Christianity. Their reply was that when the bombing of "open towns" was undertaken, not as a reprisal but as a regular national policy, such a divide would have been reached.

Perhaps the most bizarre interaction between British bombing policy and the British clergy came during the tenure of the Reverend John Collins as the official Chaplain for Bomber Command. After the war Collins became a prominent figure in the Campaign for Nuclear Disarmament (CND), which was opposed to any nuclear weapons for Britain, and his general attitude toward Bomber Command can be seen in his description of High Wycombe:

> Bomber Command Headquarters was perhaps the most soul-destroying, the most depressing of the . . . places in which I had to serve. For there, in contrast with the natural beauty of the surroundings, the evil . . . policy of the carpet bombing of German cities was planned.[22]

When Arthur Harris laid on a lecture for his aircrew entitled "The Ethics of Bombing"—in response to an earlier talk by the devout Christian and socialist Sir Stafford Cripps, who had seemed to question the morality of what was being done—Collins stood up to say that perhaps he had misunderstood the title of the talk, which should have been "The Bombing of Ethics." Needless to say, Harris was unamused by this and other interventions from his Chaplain, and Collins was threatened with court martial on four different occasions during the war for his unorthodox behavior (he was perhaps saved from such a fate by the curious circumstance that he was related to Arthur Harris by marriage).

The Reverend Collins later argued that the Anglican hierarchy had a fatal tendency to side with military authority in whatever disputes arose over the independent conduct of clergymen assigned to them. In making such a comment, he perhaps had in mind the august personage of William Temple, who had succeeded Lang as Archbishop of Canterbury early in 1942. Temple's attitude toward British wartime policy stands as a particularly interesting example of the position that leading churchmen adopted concerning military matters during World War II. His elevation to the highest office in the Church was greeted with almost universal enthusiasm. He presented a notably benign appearance, possessed a sparkling humor, was well-rounded (in both the physical and intellectual sense), and exuded goodwill and tolerance toward one and all. As one description has it, he was the "quintessence of compromise . . . firmly in the centre of British politics." Churchill himself was initially rather doubtful about his appointment, since Temple had formerly been a member of the Labour Party and was identified with quite progressive social views, expressed in books such as *Christianity and Social Order,* but in time he too came to appreciate the qualities of the new Archbishop of Canterbury.[23]

As the champion of compromise, and perhaps even more as the presumed spiritual leader of the British people, Temple trod a very delicate path during the war whenever questions of military policy arose. He echoed with approval the old saying that "it is the duty of Lambeth [the Church] to remind Westminster that Westminster is responsible to God; but this does not mean that Westminster is responsible to Lambeth." Translated into concrete terms, this attitude seemed to suggest that the Church had no right to criticize the government over area bombing, even though there might be some standards of restraint to which the government should be sensitive.

Temple's attitude on military matters could at times be exceedingly opaque. With respect to the British naval blockade of Germany, for example, he said that "it seems to me that in the phase the war has now reached [June 1942], to object to the blockade on the ground presumably of the suffering that it will cause is stark materialism."[24] The "materialism" referred to presumably reflected the German civilians' desire to continue to eat and be clothed. As far as area bombing itself was concerned, however, Temple was fairly forthright. He declined flatly to be enrolled in the ranks of those protesting the strategy as contrary to Christian norms and British values. In July 1943 he was asked by the dissident Bishop of Chichester to request a statement in the House of Lords on the aims of British bombing. Temple refused, saying "I am not at all disposed to be the mouthpiece of the concern which I know exists, because I do not share it."

Even while rejecting the Bishop of Chichester's appeal, Temple did recognize that there was serious concern over area bombing, and on various occasions he paid tribute to the sincerity of the protesters and to their right to raise questions. Even while strongly anti-pacifist himself, he spoke admiringly of Quakers and others who followed their beliefs. He called as well for understanding treatment of the small conscientious objector community in Britain. Moreover, Temple declined to emulate his World War I predecessor in issuing "prayers for victory." His attitude was that there were many sincere German Christians as well, and that to pray for victory over them was inappropriate.

Ultimately Temple can be seen as a man genuinely struggling with diverse considerations. He was a firm supporter of the British war effort, and eschewed any temptation to dictate to the government on strategy. At the same time, he recognized the essential tragedy of what was happening and agonized over the human cost of the struggle, both to friend and foe. As he described his position, "To kill is right, if at all, relatively and not absolutely; that is, it can only be right in special circumstances." The need to defeat Naziism was for him that special circumstance, but that did not mean he exulted in the struggle, as some others did. He rather mournfully summarized his thinking: "We are involved in an entanglement due to the sin of mankind, including our own, in which the best thing we can do is still a bad thing. None the less, it is right to do it because it is the best possible. And so we have got to do it and be penitent while we do it."[25]

Adopting this sort of stance, of course, left Temple open to criticism and from quite opposing points of view. On the one hand there were those who felt he was being unduly precious and perhaps even self-righteous in agonizing over the dilemmas of violence in service to a just cause. His colleague Dr. Cyril Garbett, the Archbishop of York, for example, dismissed Temple's unwillingness to pray for victory unless the qualifier "if it be Thy will" was appended. As Garbett wrote in his diary, "I disagree entirely. Unless we thought it was God's will that we should war against the Nazis, we ought to have opposed the war: if it is His will, then we must pray for victory." Garbett himself was asked in 1943 to join in the protest against area bombing, but not surprisingly he rejected such appeals. "Often in life," he said, "there is no clear choice between absolute right and wrong; frequently the choice has to be made of the lesser of two evils, and it is a lesser evil to bomb a war-loving Germany than to sacrifice the lives of our fellow-countrymen who long for peace, and to delay delivering millions now held in slavery."[26] Even though Garbett distanced himself from the easy certainties of the Cromwellians, there is no question but that he was impatient with those who seemed prone to agonizing over the morality of the means adopted in a righteous cause.

Temple's attempt to find a middle course in the debate over British bombing policy was also subject to criticism from quite a different quarter. Those opposed to the area offensive found his rather circuitous reasoning something of an abdication of moral leadership in a crisis. Their chagrin was reinforced when the Church, after the war, seemed to accept belatedly that city bombing was after all quite unacceptable. In a report by a Church commission appointed by the Archbishop of York and the Archbishop of Canterbury (now Dr. Fisher, who had succeeded Temple in 1944 after the latter's death), the following judgment was rendered: "The commission is agreed that 'obliteration' bombing of whole cities . . . must be condemned. It is inconsistent with the limited end of a just war; it violates the principles of discrimination which we have established; and it is not necessary for the security of the attacking aircraft. In fact it constitutes an act of wholesale destruction that cannot be justified." One of the leading opponents of the area offensive commented sourly at the time that the isolated protests of the tiny Bombing Restriction Committee would have been enormously helped if the members of the commission had taken this stance during the war. Of the sixteen eminent churchmen involved, however, only the Archdeacon of Stoke had spoken up while the bombing was going on.[27]

Perhaps one could have expected William Temple and others in the church to be more forthcoming in their opposition to area bombing, yet it is well to remember the pressures under which they were operating. It bears repeating that if truth is the first casualty of war, the willingness, even the ability, to oppose one's government on a major issue of wartime policy is perhaps the second. One authority on the role of the church in wartime summarizes the factors that seemed to dictate a cautious attitude by clergy:

[Their] reticence is usually explained in terms of 'prudence' as manifested in a desire to avoid making a 'rash judgment' based on only partial access to the facts; a desire to avoid subjecting the Church and its individual members to the persecution that would almost certainly follow such a denunciation; and, finally, a desire to avoid placing the individual in an impossible conflict of conscience which would probably be resolved in favor of the nation's demands anyway.[28]

All these are strong and understandable factors bearing on the role of the church in a war situation. To be sure, their full acceptance carries the risk of making the church essentially irrelevant during a time when its moral guidance is most needed, and may even render nugatory the church's traditional devotion to just war doctrine. Putting it this way, however, may somewhat misstate the issue. The fact is that Temple and others felt that the air offensive was indeed a morally legitimate method of defeating a universally-recognized peril. One can criticize their insensitivity to questions of proportionality but hardly their *bona fides* in attempting to decide on the lesser evil. That they managed to avoid the sort of unalloyed Vansittartism that affected some in British society was also no mean accomplishment, given the general antipathy toward the Nazi regime felt by all. Yet there were some at the time who argued that simply avoiding the extremes of anti-German racial prejudice was not enough. They were convinced that area bombing *was* inherently an illegitimate act of war and an affront to the conscience. They openly attempted to convince their fellow citizens that a crime was being conducted in their name.

THE DISSENTERS

It might fairly be said that there has rarely, if ever, been a more convincing set of reasons for the citizens of a democratic society to give the benefit of the doubt to their government's conduct of a war effort than was the case with the British in World War II. The issues behind the fighting seemed about as practically and morally compelling as any that are likely to appear in war. That Hitler was embarked on a program of essentially unlimited aggression was plain to all but the most obscurantist opinion. That the regime that he directed was an affront to all decent human values seemed beyond question. Under these circumstances one did not have to be morally oblivious to feel that any and all methods that were available to bring him down should—and ethically could—be employed. The pressure to take such a position was all the greater when one considers that the prospects of a German victory in the war were seen by many not just as an abstract possibility but as a real and immediate one, at least in the beginning and middle years of the struggle.

Despite all this, however, there was public dissent against the British government's handling of the war effort, and in particular moral protest at the policy of area bombing of Germany. The dissenters included several members of Parliament, at least one very prominent religious figure, two famous military historians, the playwright George Bernard Shaw, and the classicist Gilbert Murray as well as a number of others in the literary and artistic community. The existence of such opinion even in the midst of what could reasonably be regarded as a true just war seems remarkable in retrospect. It is also a testament to the capacity of some in a democratic society to draw distinctions and make discriminations even as they supported the overall effort to rid Europe and the world of a genuine evil.

Aside from the inherent courage of individuals willing to speak out against what they saw as a repugnant strategy, it does have to be recognized that the climate for dissent in Britain during World War II was in some ways noticeably more tolerant than during the first great war. One significant reflection of this fact was the attitude toward conscientious objectors. In World War I, three out of ten were sent to prison for their beliefs. In the period 1939-1945 only 3 out of a 100 were treated so. Almost 60,000 people registered as conscientious objectors (four times the number in World War I), and of this number only one-fifth were rejected as insincere and thus liable to the draft. Prime Minister Neville Chamberlain had set the tone even before war had broken out. In introducing the Act of 1939, which brought back conscription, he said that "where scruples are conscientiously held we desire that they should be respected and that there should be no persecution of those who hold them."[29] Several years later, the Home Secretary, Herbert Morrison, was queried in the House of Commons as to whether it might not be time to suppress the Bombing Restriction Committee, among whose members were a number of conscientious objectors and pacifists. Morrison responded that "if people sincerely hold the view that bombing should be abolished or restricted, I cannot see that it is terrible to say so." Morrison did go on to assure the House that they should not be unduly concerned since there was "no danger that the bombing will leave off, anyway."[30]

Contributing to this generally permissive atmosphere for public protest against the doings of Bomber Command was the fact that the British society as a whole appeared unreceptive to the grosser types of anti-German propaganda fostered during the first war. We have already discussed how Vansittartism, for example, never caught on with the majority of people, with its implication that the German civilian "deserved" everything that was delivered to him. As Mass Observation (a leading opinion survey) observed, "Few people think the crimes of war should be visited on the ordinary citizens of Germany."

One factor that likely contributed to this relatively restrained public opinion was the memory of greatly exaggerated stories of German atrocities circulated by British propaganda in World War I. This caused people to view with some skepticism any statements about the inherently evil characteristics of the enemy (ironically, such stories had far more basis in fact in the second war than in the first). The British government displayed some concern about the lack of a suitably anti-German attitude among the British people. In the so-called Anger Campaign, which took place early in the war, the government attempted to arouse feelings of outrage concerning the aggressive qualities of the German people. The point, in any case, is that the general moderation in public opinion was an important factor in at least mitigating, although certainly not eliminating, anger against those who were openly calling for greater respect for the welfare of the ordinary citizens of Germany.

The British press had played an important part in circulating German atrocity stories in the first war and was generally noted for its unabashed jingoism. At least some segments of the press, however, themselves displayed a newfound moderation in World War II. To be sure, the majority gave more or less unqualified support to the bombing of Germany. The *Sunday Dispatch* was typical with its comment that "it is right that the German population should 'smell death at close quarters.' Now they are getting the stench of it." Still another outsized headline screamed "NO PITY! NO MERCY!" and the writer went on to argue that "if we are to succeed we must not harbour cant and humbug. Voices are already heard, crying that mercy must temper justice, that vengeance belongs alone to God. . . . All these sentimental appeals are bunkum and hypocrisy . . . whether they come from a familiar prelate or some unsuspecting quisling." Especially virulent in their support of the area offensive were the Beaverbrook newspapers, for which a typical headline was, "Why all this bosh about being gentle with the Germans after we have beaten them when ALL GERMANS ARE GUILTY!"[31]

Even when this type of flamboyant language was avoided, a consistent pattern in the popular press's treatment of the air war was the use of sporting metaphors and rather flip characterizations that were as offensive to critics of Bomber Command as the more overt chauvinism often seen on the front pages. An early example was this headline following one of the major engagements in the Battle of Britain: "Theirs, 78, Ours, 17," which implied that the killing overhead was not very different from a cricket match. Another headline in July 1943 read, "Hamburg has been Hamburgered" (a variation of "Coventried" to describe the devastation of Coventry). One officer in the RAF reacted to what he called this coarsening of rhetoric by saying that "the tragic evolution of war was commented on in the language of a gang fight in a school playground."[32]

At the same time, there were occasional, more temperate voices in the press who, even while giving support to the war effort, raised some troubling questions about air strategy. Such popular papers as the *Daily Mail* and the *Sunday Times* both published editorials opposing indiscriminate area bombing as being inconsistent with British values. The *Sunday Dispatch* opened its pages to the well-known figure of C. E. M. Joad of the BBC for an article attacking the inhumanity of bombing German civilians. *The Economist,* a highly regarded journal dealing with international affairs, also questioned some of the particulars of Bomber Command's activities. To be sure, such commentary was in the distinct minority, but it did exist and offered at least some comfort to the equally small minority among the public who were openly critical of the area offensive.

It is important to recognize that the dissenters against Bomber Command's tactics were hardly united on their premises or their proposals. Some came from an avowedly pacifist background, which in some sense greatly uncomplicated their approach to the question. These individuals were against all war, however waged, and area bombing was seen as only a particularly repugnant example of the larger evil. Others, however, favored military resistance to the Nazis but stopped short of sanction for air attacks on German cities. Then there were those who seemed to underpin their moral outrage with a pragmatic judgment: they asserted that area bombing was not militarily efficient and consequently it was not morally justifiable. In many ways the debate between these latter two groups was the most interesting. The former suggested that even if the bombing was producing real military results, it still was intolerable because of its violation of traditional humane standards in warfare (the distinction between combatant and non-combatant). The latter seemed to say that if they could be shown bombing was efficient, they might tolerate it, but since such evidence was not at hand they necessarily had to oppose it.

There was a final difference in the behavior of the dissenters that merits attention here. Some attempted to work essentially through "back-channels," that is, via private communications to those in authority. Typical was the Marquess of Salisbury, and not surprisingly those who took this route tended to have prominent Establishment positions that gave them some inherent credibility with the decision-makers. Others, such as the writer Vera Brittain, took a more public route and again for somewhat understandable reasons: Brittain had no cachet with Churchill's inner circle, and moreover she had an instinctive faith in the morality and good sense of the average British citizen. In these circumstances, it was natural that she should use her published writings and public speeches to press her views. There were still others who employed both public and private avenues, such as Bishop George Bell. Because of his ecclesiastical position, not to mention his seat in the House of Lords, he had ample opportunity to preach on the immorality of area bombing. At the same time, again because of his relatively exalted status, he attempted to sway the views of other notables in more discreet ways.

One may debate whether, as a general matter, it is most effective to go public or private in dissenting against government policy, and each of the individuals to be examined no doubt had his or her own theory as to the right way to proceed. At the same time, it is unmistakable that their strategy depended at least in part on their opportunities—those on the outside attempted to speak to the broader society, those on the inside endeavored to use their contacts to influence policy. The only ultimate test of strategy here remains the relative effectiveness of the different methods pursued. As it turned out, none of the protesters against the area bombing of Germany found a way to have a major, or even a minor, impact on policy. This does not mean, however, that the efforts and the anguish of several of the most prominent dissenters do not merit closer examination. An awareness that there are individuals who have the courage to oppose the (often passing) wisdom of the many is rewarding in itself.

The Military Historians

Perhaps the most surprising source of dissent against the area offensive came from the British strategic analyst Captain Sir Basil Liddell Hart, who was extremely influential in the interwar years and was sometimes described as a shadow CIGS (chief of the Imperial General Staff) It was he who, in the 1920s, had been one of the most prominent voices arguing for an emphasis on the strategic air offensive. At the time Liddell Hart had also expatiated on the comparative humanity of fighting a war through strategic bombing. His theory was that such bombing was likely to produce victory far more quickly than the land operations of World War I and thus on balance would save lives. He argued that this might be especially so if the bombers employed gas rather than high explosives. "Gas may well prove the salvation of civilization from the otherwise inevitable collapse in the case of another world war."[33] In his memoirs Liddell Hart recalls how impressed Sir Hugh Trenchard, chief of the Air Staff, was with his analysis, and how Trenchard ordered a number of copies of *Paris, or the Future of War* for his senior officers and for the new RAF Staff College.[34]

Trenchard presumably would have been somewhat less pleased with Liddell Hart's reaction to Bomber Command's attacks on Rostock, Cologne, and other German cities in 1942. In a Reflection that he wrote at the time, Liddell Hart delivered himself of the following sentiments:

> It will be ironical if the defenders of civilization depend for victory upon the most barbaric, and unskilled, way of winning a war that the modern world has seen. . . . We are now counting for victory on success in the way of degrading it to a new low level—as represented by indiscriminate (night) bombing and indiscriminate starvation. . . . If our pounding of German cities, by massed night-bombing, proves the decisive factor, it should be a sobering thought that but for Hitler's folly in attacking Russia (and consequently using up his bomber

force there, as well as diverting his resources mainly into other weapons) we and the Germans would now be 'Cologning' each other's cities with the advantage on Germany's side, in this mad competition in mutual devastation.[35]

How to account for this rather remarkable conversion from enthusiastic supporter of strategic bombing to captious critic?[36] In any such transformation there is bound to remain an element of puzzle, and for the cynic, grounds for skepticism or even derision. It is curious in this regard that in his memoirs Liddell Hart is virtually silent in explaining why his views did change so greatly. He devotes a few offhand remarks to relatively minor technical matters involving strategic airpower in World War II but says nothing at all about his condemnation of the area offensive as immoral, or, for that matter, as militarily ineffectual. Since his memoirs appeared some 20 years after the end of the war, perhaps he thought it best to let his seemingly contradictory position on the air offensive simply remain a moot point.

In hunting about for an explanation of Liddell Hart's dramatically altered view on airpower, it seems evident that even before World War II he had come to have serious doubts about the strategic bombing force's technical ability to actually locate and hit defined targets, at least with a weight of bombs sufficient to affect morale and arms production in any decisive way. Moreover, he seemed to feel that Germany, not Britain, would have the advantage in any mutual competition in strategic air strikes, and that modern air defenses would in any case likely prove far more effective than could have been anticipated in the 1920s. In a reflection of his changed strategic analysis, Liddell Hart in the late 1930s strongly urged that Britain concentrate on building up its fighter defenses against possible German air attacks rather than devote major attention to Bomber Command.[37]

It also seems unmistakable, however, that part of the basis for Liddell Hart's condemnation of the area offensive in World War II had to do with specifically moral concerns. He seemed to be genuinely appalled by the continual "Cologning" of German cities and, paradoxically, his ethical outrage could perhaps be seen as consistent with his earlier support of the air offensive. That position after all had been heavily influenced by his revulsion at the mindless trench slaughter of World War I (he himself served for some months at the front and participated in the Battle of the Somme) and more generally by his virtual obsession with finding a means of conflict that would avoid the slide from limited to total war. To be sure, Liddell Hart had seemed to condone area attacks in his earlier writings, but only on the basis that these might prove militarily decisive and in a short period of time. Given his later conclusions that Bomber Command's operations were not having much of an effect on the German war effort, their moral justification became increasingly problematic.

The purist might wish that Liddell Hart had condemned area bombing simply because it involved the death of innocents. In fact, his moral stance derived, at least in part, out of questions of military utility. Yet it hardly seems fair not to allot him at least a measure of credit for arriving at—and accepting—the moral conclusion to which his strategic logic led him. There were a good many others who agreed with his strategic analysis but were unable or unwilling to draw the appropriate moral inference; their attitude was that the area offensive, while limited in utility, must be having at least some effect on the German war effort and thus was worth continuing.

There are two other aspects to Liddell Hart's views on the area offensive that, for some, might call into question his being awarded the moral high ground. In the first place he felt an unremitting personal hostility toward Winston Churchill. Before the war he had gone so far as to question whether Churchill's power for evil wasn't potentially greater than his power for good: "his almost unique egocentricity, his dramatic sense, his lack of scruple, and his lack of judgement, make a combination that might be destined to lead this country to disaster." This antipathy may well have caused him to criticize the efforts of Bomber Command at least partly because the airmen were the favored creatures of the Prime Minister for much of the war. In his papers, Liddell Hart noted a conversation with General Sir Frederick Pile, Britain's air defense chief, in which Pile allegedly said that "Winston is pinning all his faith to the bombing offensive now. The devastation it causes suits his temperament, and he would be disappointed at a less destructive ending to the war."[38] This seems a remarkably bitter, and perhaps unfair, description of Churchill's attitude toward violence. In any case, Liddell Hart's distaste for the Prime Minister was returned in full measure. Churchill commented at one point that the military analyst seemed "more a candidate for a mental home than for more serious action."[39]

Perhaps what Churchill had in made when he offered this remark was Liddell Hart's attitude toward Hitler and the German threat generally. His position here was the other point that might give some pause in applauding his wartime denunciation of the area offensive. Basically Liddell Hart felt that Hitler was no more than a classic exemplar of the European power politician intent on expanding his geopolitical domain. Hitler, in this view, was essentially a rational leader who would accept limitations to his designs once superior power was manifest. As he wrote in the summer of 1943, the Allies had "succeeded in crippling the enemy's power of aggression, and making him anxious for peace on the terms we defined on entering the war, or on any terms, indeed, that did not involve his complete downfall."[40] Liddell Hart was particularly dismissive of Vansittartism, the notion that there was some peculiar defect in the German character that led them toward polices of domination and racism. Not incidentally, he tended to stress that at least in terms of military tactics the Germans generally were more observant of the war convention than their democratic opponents, that is, they concentrated on traditional military objectives in their operations (even if the Nazi political apparatus was in itself abhorrent). Finally, Liddell Hart assumed that the anti-Nazi opposition in Germany was a serious factor that, if given the proper encouragement, might prove decisive in changing German leadership and thus Berlin's war aims.

These assumptions taken together led him to suggest that a compromise peace with the German government was a distinct possibility once the high tide of German conquest had passed. Even a government led by Hitler might be persuaded of the virtues of a return to the *status quo*. Failing this, an alternative German regime could be dealt with on the basis of traditional European security arrangements. Such convictions naturally led Liddell Hart into opposition to a military strategy that had as a prime objective the progressive devastation of German society and institutions. On the one hand, he saw such a program as undermining the prospects for a compromise peace either with Hitler or a successor regime. Even more, he viewed the effective elimination of Germany as a factor in the European power balance as something that would invite Soviet domination of the Continent once the war was ended.

The latter analysis, at least in hindsight, seems fairly perceptive. Perhaps the same cannot be said perhaps for some of his other arguments: the evidence that Hitler was a "traditional" European statesman was particularly problematical. The point for present purposes is that, given his views on the character of German strategy, Liddell Hart was predisposed to regard the area offensive as actually counterproductive to Allied interests. This was especially so since British policy seemed to be directed not so much at a discrete foreign threat—in the mode of earlier challenges such as that presented by Louis XIV or Napoleon—as at the very capacity of the German people to wield a role in European politics. The policy of unconditional surrender was a particular *bête noire* to Liddell Hart in this sense.

It should be noted in passing that Liddell Hart was not the only military historian in Britain to express his outrage at the area offensive. Major General J. F. C. Fuller was in many ways Liddell Hart's equal in prestige as an analyst of military affairs. Both had written widely on the offensive potential of mobile armored warfare, and their ideas had made a considerable impact in various quarters, especially in Germany itself. Fuller was, if anything, more outspoken than Liddell Hart in his comments on Bomber Command's activities. In August 1943 he drafted an article for the London *Evening Standard* in which he opined that "the worst devastations of the Goths, Vandals, Huns, Seljuks, and Mongols pale into insignificance when compared to the material and moral damage now wrought" by British bombing of Germany.[41] The newspaper's editor wrote back saying that he lacked the nerve to publish Fuller's article. Fuller was similar to Liddell Hart in that he was appalled not only by the sheer destruction being visited on German cities but also by the inherent strategic flaw in the area offensive. The declaration on unconditional surrender, in his view, made the notion of ending the war through shattering German morale a *non sequitur*: how could one terrorize the Germans into demanding peace if there were no peace terms to be negotiated?

Fuller and Liddell Hart also shared something else, and that was an almost total ostracism by the government during the war. Despite the fact that they could rightly be viewed as two of Britain's most perceptive military (if not necessarily political) analysts, their talents were evidently not seen as needed in any capacity by those in authority. Liddell Hart thought that perhaps his banishment from an official role might be changing in March 1944, when he was summoned for a session before the War Cabinet. Instead, he was subjected to a withering cross-examination as to how he had obtained advance notice that the coming invasion of Europe would take place in Normandy. He had considerable difficulty in convincing his interlocutors that a memorandum of his two months earlier had merely reflected his reasoned assessment given Allied troop deployments in southern England.[42]

Perhaps the stringent critique that both Liddell Hart and Fuller offered of one of the prime strategic commitments of the government makes this exclusion from its affairs unsurprising. In Liddell Hart's case his violent personal antipathy toward Churchill was obviously a factor as well, not to mention the thinly veiled contempt he had shown for many of Britain's major military figures. Moreover, some of his earlier thinking on British security had been badly contradicted by events. He had argued in the 1930s for an essentially defensive strategy, in which relatively few resources would be given to the army on the expectation that France could alone resist a German land campaign in the West. The rapid Germany victory in the spring of 1940 at least temporarily undermined his reputation for military sagacity. Finally, Liddell Hart's seemingly rather benign view of Hitler, reflected in his comment that the German dictator "had been remarkably reluctant to get into war" as well as his doubts about the actual existence of concentration camps, made him appear (in the minds of many) quite unsound, to use the classic British phrase dismissive of the eccentric.[43] As for Fuller, his reputation was clouded by his strong anti-Semitism as well as his supposed sympathy for fascism (a charge levied in particular connection with his admiration for Mussolini in the 1930's).

Nevertheless, the isolation in which these two existed at the time was vivid testimony to the truth of C. P. Snow's comment (quoted earlier) that "the atmosphere [of support for the area offensive] was more hysterical than is usual in English official life." Neither man, after all, could be accused of ignorance of the real world of military affairs, each of them having served on active duty and having an admittedly vast knowledge of the details of military technology. They were not pacifists and were quite prepared to offer thoroughly unsentimental analyses about how British and Allied military power could bring the Germans to heel. If such men were consigned to the wilderness for their views on British bombing, how much more likely was it that other critics—without any military background— would also be dismissed as irrelevancies? Members of the religious community in Britain, for example, and in particular George Bell, with whom Liddell Hart had a close association during the war because of their mutual abhorrence of the area offensive.

The Bishop

George Bell was 56 when the war broke out, and he was considered to be one of the genuine luminaries in the Church of England. Soft-spoken and with refined tastes, Bell was a patron of the arts and a man of unusually broad interests. At the same time, he seemed to many to be always a man in search of a special cause. Before the war, he had devoted particular attention to the plight of German refugees. In the early months after war was declared he turned to succoring interned enemy aliens, visiting their camps, and complaining to the authorities about the deplorable conditions there. Somewhat later he chaired the Famine Relief Committee, whose aim was to provide dried milk and vitamins as well as other foodstuffs for mothers, children, and invalids in Belgium and Greece, even though this meant having to get the supplies through the British blockade of the continent. Initially, the government resisted the appeals of the committee on the grounds that it was the Germans' responsibility to feed the people of the occupied territories. They did eventually allow 8,000 tons of wheat to be sent to Greece under the auspices of the International Red Cross.[44]

In May 1942, George Bell traveled to Sweden to meet the German Lutheran Minister Dietrich Bonhoeffer, who told him of an opposition group in Germany planning the overthrow of Hitler. Bell eagerly relayed this information to the government on his return to Britain, but their response was one of indifference. The meeting with Bonhoeffer nevertheless reinforced Bell's deep aversion to Vansittartism on both moral and practical grounds. One of his consistent themes was that Germany and National Socialism were not the same thing, and in *The Church and Humanity* he attempted to identify the common human bond that in his view linked the British and German people: "There are very many in Germany . . . who long for deliverance from a godless Nazi rule, and for the coming of Christian Order in which they and we can take our part. Is no trumpet call to come from England, to awaken them from despair?"[45] Not surprisingly, Bell felt that the unconditional surrender formula was hardly such a trumpet call, and at least in the earlier period of the war he favored some sort of negotiated settlement with Germany. In a speech to the House of Lords, he summarized the case against a Carthaginian peace being imposed on the Germans.

> To line up the Nazi assassins in the same row with the people of Germany whom they have outraged is to make for more barbarism, possibly to postpone peace, and to make certain an incredible worsening of the conditions of all Europe when at last peace comes. . . . The remedy is to tell those inside Germany who are anti-Fascist that we want their help, that we will help them in getting rid of the common enemy, and that we intend that a Germany delivered from Hitlerism shall have fair play and a proper place in the family of Europe.[46]

Bishop Bell's preeminent cause during the war gradually came to be the issue of British bombing policy, and in particular what he suspected (or knew, drawing on neutral sources he questioned during his trip to Sweden) was the strategy of indiscriminate attacks on German cities and civilians. As far as Bell was concerned, the bombing of civilians was a "degradation of the spirit for all who take part in it." He expressed particular repugnance at the doctrine of destroying enemy morale and called on his fellow clergy to set themselves firmly against the "propaganda of lies and hatred" that in his opinion contributed to the area offensive. His firm belief was that the church's function was "at all costs to remain the Church. . . . It is not the nation. It is not the state's spiritual auxiliary with exactly the same ends as the state."[47]

As the war progressed, Bell waged an increasingly lonely campaign to convince the government—and, more broadly, the British people—that area bombing was an insult to their better instincts and in fact to their basic values. In making this argument, he became a growing embarrassment to his fellow churchmen and to the church hierarchy itself. The one notable (and rather surprising) exception was the former Archbishop of Canterbury, Cosmo Lang, who echoed Bell's concerns about the inherent inhumanity of the area offensive and was particularly sharp in demanding that the government publicly confront its apparent hypocrisy concerning bombing policy. In a typical statement to the House of Lords, Lang delivered himself of the following remarks:

> We were always told that [Government] policy was to limit attacks to definite military objectives or their immediate neighbourhood, and not directly and purposely to involve the destruction of the lives and homes of people. I do not think it can be said that that policy has been adhered to in these apparently deliberate attempts to destroy whole cities, and I venture to think there is some force—I think we must all admit it—in the plea that either the hitherto declared policy is to be changed or this new policy is to be definitely adopted.[48]

Such expressions of support for Bell's position were rare indeed, however. More typical of his experience was the letter he wrote in July 1943 to the current Archbishop of Canterbury, William Temple, asking him to request in the House of Lords a clear statement from the government concerning the tactics of Bomber Command. Temple's curt dismissal of this suggestion set the tone for Bell's treatment at the hands of other leading church figures. Even within his own diocese, Bell felt growing disapproval for what he was saying about the brave fliers of the RAF. In September 1943, he wrote in the *Chichester Diocesan Gazette* that "when a Minister of the Government speaks in exulting terms of a ruthless and destructive bombing of the German people . . . the subjection of fifty German cities to the same terror as Hamburg (or Coventry) has suffered . . . then we have real cause to grieve for a lowering of moral tone, and also to fear greatly for the future."[49] Organizers of a Battle of Britain Commemoration, held in Bell's own cathedral in September 1943, were so outraged by his pronouncements that the Dean had to gently persuade him not to appear at the convocation.

In February 1944, Bell decided to do what Temple had refused, and directly raise the issue of area bombing himself in the House of Lords. Lord Woolton sat next to him on the bench of bishops and pleaded with Bell not to go ahead: "George, there isn't a soul in this House who doesn't wish you wouldn't make the speech you are going to make."[50] The Bishop of Chichester was undeterred. In his remarks directed at the government, he expressed dismay that they didn't seem to realize that the progressive devastation of cities was threatening the very roots of civilization.

> I desire to challenge the Government on the policy which directs the bombing of enemy towns on the present scale, especially with reference to civilians who are non-combatants, and non-military and non-industrial objectives.
>
> I fully realize that in attacks on centres of war industry and transport the killing of civilians when it is the result of bona fide military activity is inevitable. But there must be a fair balance between the means employed and the purpose achieved. To obliterate a whole town because certain portions contain military and industrial establishments is to reject the balance.
>
> The Allies stand for something greater than power. The chief name inscribed on our banner is 'Law.' It is of supreme importance that we, who, with our Allies, are the Liberators of Europe should so use power that it is always under the control of law. It is because the bombing of enemy towns—this area bombing—raises this issue of bombing unlimited and exclusive that such immense importance is bound to attach to the policy and action of His Majesty's Government.[51]

These remarks were received in silence, save for two peers who expressed support, and were then followed by a statement from Lord Cranbourne for the government, promising that far from ending city attacks, Bomber Command would increase its efforts in future.

George Bell was very far from being a pacifist, and in fact he strongly supported the overall war effort because of his abhorrence of Naziism. He was also hardly a total political *naif*: on a number of occasions, in response to the pleading of colleagues he respected, he agreed not to raise his favorite subject at particularly inopportune times. Given these facts, it is striking how much antagonism his criticism of area bombing did arouse in various quarters. Bell was not some wild-eyed radical on the fringes of society, baying away at the perniciousness of the Establishment. In fact, Bell *was* the Establishment, and he generally attempted to operate within its unstated code. If his relatively moderate and restrained form of protest was met with so much anger, how much more difficult it must have been for those who were against area bombing because they were against war itself or who did not have the advantage of wearing bishop's robes.

Ironically, Bell's very moderation was in some ways his Achilles heel as well. When true pacifists criticized the bombing, their remarks could be dismissed by supporters of Bomber Command with benevolent condescension: there was a willingness to accept the sincerity of their beliefs and even a certain sneaking admiration for the probity of their idealism. To be sure, they were quite naive about the real nature of the world, and the ways in which war necessarily had to be conducted, but all the same they deserved at least some credit for their consistency. Bell, on the other hand, often couched his criticism of area bombing at least partly on grounds of military efficiency. Since he felt the devastation of German cities was not efficient in winning the war, he was all the more aroused by the moral repugnancy of such a policy. His opponents were in this sense given a very large opening for riposte, which they eagerly seized. Bell was essentially accused of hypocrisy—the charge was that he wasn't really against killing large numbers of Germans but simply wanted to do it in a particular way. Moreover, who was he to set himself up as a military expert? Wiser (military) heads than he were convinced that the bombing was indeed crippling the German war effort. Should he be respected as a saver of strategy just because he was also an accomplished saver of souls?

All of this George Bell had to contend with, yet in retrospect he stands out as perhaps the most incisive voice protesting area bombing. In fact, one suspects that one of the reason his arguments aroused so much anger was that his critics were uncomfortably aware that he was offering a fairly sophisticated and measured critique of the bombing strategy, one that could not be set aside so easily as that coming from innocents such as the pacifists. Bell accepted the so-called real world and indeed operated in it. His essential argument, however, was that pursuit of a just cause did not legitimate any methods, that good ends did justify bad means. This was hardly a radical position to take, except perhaps in the fevered atmosphere of wartime. Bell deserves considerable praise for being determined to stick to it.

One of the reasons for the patriotic outrage at Bell's stance during the war was the fact that the true character of the area offensive was systematically concealed from the British public. When the reality of British bombing policy (not to mention its doubtful military utility) was revealed in considerable detail after the war, Bell's moral opposition assumed much greater credibility. Liddell Hart spoke to this point in the obituary that he penned on the occasion of Bell's death in 1979. "The wisdom and foresight of George Bell's wartime speeches in the House of Lords . . . have now come to be widely recognized—and especially by military historians of the war. Hardly anyone would now question the truth of his repeated warnings about the folly of the Allies' unconditional surrender formula. . . . George Bell, standing for the principles of his creed, came to achieve a far clearer grasp of grand strategy than did the statesmen."[52]

His stance had its price, not just in strained relations with many colleagues and with his parishioners, but in terms of his own professional advancement, especially after the war. Paradoxically, his fate was in some ways a mirror opposite of that of Sir Arthur Harris. The latter was snubbed at the end of the war because he was so closely identified *with* area bombing. Bell was snubbed because he was so closely identified with *opposition* to area bombing. Under normal circumstances, he would have been in line to succeed Temple as Archbishop of Canterbury, but in the event, he never achieved such exalted status (the post instead went to the Bishop of London, Geoffrey Fisher). The evidence is that his trouble-making during the war caused a sufficient number to regard him as unsound that his prospects were permanently stifled.

The lesson seemed to be that it was acceptable to have been involved in and supportive of area bombing during the war as long as one was not unduly boastful about it. It was also acceptable to have been rather critical of area bombing as long as one was suitably discreet and private about it. The point in each case was to be able to resume one's career after the war without having been identified strongly with one side or the other. Neither Bell nor Harris, for perhaps similar reasons, found it possible to cover their tracks in this way.

The Politicians

Dr. Alfred Salter was a Labour member of Parliament from the depressed constituency of West Bermondsey in the East End of London. He was widely respected as a force for the renewal and at least modest beautification of his otherwise rather grim district. He made no secret of his loyalties: his entire life was spent as a socialist, a pacifist, and a Quaker. His opposition to his government's bombing policy against Germany was rather less subtle and complicated than George Bell's. Salter simply felt that the taking of human life for whatever reason was an illegitimate act. Yet it would be facile to dismiss his protest against area bombing as merely the rote expression of pacifist beliefs. In reality, Salter may have been against war as a tool of policy, but it was Britain's strategy of indiscriminate attacks against the German civilian population that aroused his special ire. Moreover, the MP for West Bermondsey was, like Bell, hardly unaware of the pressures for compromise and the commonsensical necessity of sometimes adjusting one's views to the prevailing political realities. Salter dwelled not in the ivory tower but in the rough-and-tumble of his blue-collar constituency (unlike many British MP's then and since, he actually lived in the district that he represented in Parliament).

There was still another circumstance that made the consistency of Salter's condemnation of Bomber Command's tactics rather compelling. West Bermondsey was particularly hard hit by the German Blitz of London. Of approximately 19,500 properties in the district, only 730 escaped some damage from German bombs. Alfred Salter's own residence was leveled by the Luftwaffe. For him to protest against the area bombing of Germany thus seemed to be conduct almost unique in its dispassion and devotion to principle. As with Bell, such conduct also carried a price.

Salter was acutely aware of his relative isolation from the political mainstream almost from the beginning of the war. He calculated that only about six Labour MPs, led by the redoubtable George Lansbury, were actively opposed to the war at the outset. Perhaps another 20 to 30 MPs desired a truce with Germany following the collapse of Poland (22 of these signed a demand for a conference with Berlin to work out the terms of such a cease-fire). Salter figured that some 70 constituency Labour parties were in favor of a truce. All in all, not an impressive support network, especially when compared to the far greater body of those demanding a fight to the finish against German transgressions. What was particularly painful to Alfred Salter was his perception that his old allies in the West Bermondsey Labour Party essentially abandoned him once he made his opposition to the war clear. He reflected with some bitterness that his colleagues' earlier pacifist inclinations vanished once the government called for support in the military struggle against Germany. Symptomatic of the new mood, in Salter's view, was the decision of the Bermondsey Borough Council—once one of the most progressive in the country—to fire all conscientious objectors from its service, even elderly World War I veterans.[53]

It would be idle to pretend that Alfred Salter's efforts had any noticeable impact on British opinion. Like many protesters against area bombing, he was tolerated but hardly taken seriously by the majority. The MP for West Bermondsey spent his time in organizing groups such as the Peace Pledge Union, a pacifist organization lobbying for immediate peace with Germany, and the Peace Aims Group, which was centered in the House of Commons and sponsored talks throughout the country on the issues of the war. Yet his condemnation of the strategy of Bomber Command has a considerable power when examined in retrospect. Particularly notable was his final address to the House of Commons in 1941 (delivered before only a scattering of MPs). Arthur Harris had not even assumed command of British bombers at this point, although air strikes against German cities were becoming increasingly common. What gave his remarks a special poignancy was the fact that Salter was in extremely poor health at the time, suffering from thrombosis of the brain. He was to die not long after delivering himself of these words, which stand as a fairly compelling statement of the case against British surrender to the immoralities of total war.

> Open retaliation and revenge are now being advocated in the highest quarters. No apologies are now offered for the indiscriminate bombing of women and children. . . . In the early days of the war only strictly military targets were said to be the objectives of our Air Force. Now we have photographs showing whole streets of working-class houses being blown skyhigh by our bombs. . . . Every day the war continues it will become harder, not only materially but spiritually, to build a new and better world.[54]

The House listened in silence to this speech, without any of the normal heckling that might typically confront such remarks. There seemed to be some unspoken respect for the valor—and perhaps the insight—of a member who could address such issues regardless of possible political retribution. Salter's peroration was particularly moving and summarized all the anguish which he felt at the course of events. "Is there no pity in the whole world?" he asked. "Are all our hearts hardened and coarsened by events?"

There are two aspects of Salter's protest against area bombing that induce uneasiness perhaps even in the most sympathetic. It could legitimately be objected that as a pacifist Salter wasn't particularly concerned about area bombing *per se*. He was opposed to all violence, and bombing just happened to be a particularly dramatic example of the phenomenon that he abhorred as a general matter. One could admire his consistency in this sense but be uneasy about how his opposition to all matters military blurred the specifics of his (and others') case against area bombing. Salter's pacifism also led him into certain political stances that were at the least uncomfortable for his fellow opponents of British bombing policy. The reason he urged an immediate truce with Germany after the Nazi conquest of Poland was that he now saw no further issue to prolong hostilities, Poland having disappeared from the map of Europe. Salter also allowed as how he was prepared if necessary to accept a Nazi victory in the war, since pacifist principles were eventually bound to prevail. These were not sentiments that were calculated to ease the path of those wanting to sway British opinion toward a more restrained use of military technology in the struggle with Hitler.

Alfred Salter's biographer offers a final salute to his subject when he comments that "history should at least have evidence in the Parliamentary records that amidst the destruction and madness of the second world war one voice was raised in protest and appeal."[55] In the strict sense, this comment can be regarded as an exaggeration. There was certainly more than one voice that was raised at the time, and later, against the steady progression of assaults on humanity by all sides in the war. Some might also question Salter's unyielding devotion to his singleminded and perhaps rather naive view of the world. What seems beyond question, however, is that his message calling for an emphasis on what joined, rather than on what divided, the peoples of the world has a powerful resonance even today.

Alfred Salter, as it happens, was not the only member of Parliament who consistently spoke out against the area bombing offensive. Mr. Richard Stokes, the Labour MP for Ipswich, was also a thorn in the government's side, and his background represents an interesting contrast to that of Salter. He was hardly a traditional pacifist; indeed he consistently supported the necessity for tactical bombing in close support of military operations. The son of a barrister, educated at Cambridge, head of his own engineering firm, Stokes could claim a distinguished military record, having won the Military Cross and the Croix de Guerre as a gunner major in World War I. Yet he was hardly less fervent than Salter in denouncing the inhumanity of Bomber Command's strategy. On a particularly notable occasion in December 1943, he demanded to know of the Secretary of State for Air whether the government wasn't simply afraid to admit that it was now committed to the indiscriminate bombing of residential areas in Germany. Archibald Sinclair dismissed Stokes as being "incorrigible" on the subject, and the House then passed to a consideration of why airmen were forbidden to send their pajamas to service laundries.[56]

Richard Stokes's protestations seemed to have had little more impact on the House than those of Alfred Salter, but they remain as yet another eloquent example of the dissent that was offered by a small group of Parliamentarians. His essential proposition, as he put it, was that "women and little children are women and little children to me, wherever they live." This former military hero also expressed considerable anger at the role the aircrew of Bomber Command were forced to adopt, saying that "it fills me with absolute nausea to think of the filthy task that many of our young men are being invited to carry out." Not surprisingly, the destruction of Dresden aroused Stokes to further outrage, although in this instance his protests were received somewhat more carefully, since numerous press dispatches had spelled out for the British people what area bombing in the case of Dresden had really meant. When he rose to speak in the House of Commons on March 6, 1945, he delivered a particularly effective summation of the moral case against the area offensive.

One thing gave his arguments special strength: he supported his ethical position in part by referring to quite pragmatic considerations that were even then in the minds of Churchill and others. He noted that the Russians seemed to have avoided the policy of devastating whole cities and thus the obloquy that was likely to follow those who had pursued such a strategy once the war was over. More to the point, he asked the following:

> What are you going to find, with all the cities blasted to pieces, and with disease rampant? May not the disease, filth and poverty which will arise be almost impossible either to arrest or to overcome? I wonder very much whether it is realized at this stage. When I heard the Minister [Sir Archibald Sinclair] speak of the 'crescendo of destruction,' I thought: What a magnificent expression for a Cabinet Minister of Great Britain at this stage of the war.[57]

Even at this late date, the member for Ipswich was also exercised that the government seemingly continued to follow its policy of disguising the reality of the bombing policy from the British people. He observed that the famous Associated Press dispatch had been widely printed elsewhere but suppressed in Great Britain (Stokes took the liberty to read it out in full to members of the House). Symbolic of the truth of Stokes's complaint was the fact that the Secretary of State for Air ostentatiously left the House chambers before Stokes began his speech, thus removing himself from the possibility of uncomfortable queries. Some hours after Stokes had delivered his remarks, the government did offer a response from the Joint Under-Secretary of State for Air, curious in itself since Sinclair had now resumed his seat. His comments represented something of a capstone to three years of governmental deception on the reality of the area offensive.

> We are not wasting bombers or time on purely terror tactics. It does not do the Hon. Member justice to come here to this House and suggest that there are a lot of Air Marshals or pilots or anyone else sitting in a room trying to think how many German women and children they can kill.[58]

Obviously Alfred Salter and Richard Stokes, together with a few others sitting in Parliament, were voices in the wilderness, but they nevertheless raised those issues of conscience that were largely ignored by other politicians in the fever of wartime. In passing, it might be noted that Richard Stokes too suffered the effects of having spoken out against the area offensive, at least before it became fashionable to do so. As we have already detailed, the postwar Labour government of Clement Atlee hardly disguised its disdain for Arthur Harris and other champions of Bomber Command, but this did not seem to translate into a willingness to welcome into the fold those who had been "premature" in their moral objections to the area offensive. Stokes had been so rash as to suggest during the war itself that the British government would live to regret ever having permitted such raids and that they would stand for all time as a "blot on our escutcheon." His reward for these and similar remarks was to be excluded from ministerial office, to which he could normally have expected promotion. The Atlee government may have regretted the area offensive, but Stokes was an uncomfortable person to have around, since he had spoken up while the air offensive was in progress. Many of the most distinguished members of the postwar Labour government had served in the wartime Cabinet that had authorized the air offensive, and their objections to it at the time had been hard to discover.

The Writer

Vera Brittain's opposition to British air policy in World War II was in its own way as curious and unexpected as that of Captain Basil Liddell Hart (with whom she otherwise had almost nothing in common). There was little in her earlier upbringing that would have suggested she would one day become a virtual outcast from mainstream British society for the virulence of her objectives to area bombing. Born in 1893, she was raised in a prosperous family headed by a successful industrialist of impeccable middle-class values. She spent a good deal of her youth immersed in a typical Edwardian lifestyle, with an elaborate house, long lawns, tennis courts, and many servants. Upon finishing school at the age of 18, she followed for a time the typical course of an eligible young woman from a good family, engaging in a round of tea parties and tennis engagements while waiting for Mr. Right to come along. A suitable marriage was seen as the highest goal to which she might (or should) aspire.[59]

Eventually Vera Brittain did decide to continue her education, and she took a second-class degree in history from Oxford. In subsequent years she established a growing reputation as a poet and novelist, public speaker, and prolific journalist. In 1933 she published a memoir entitled *Testament of Youth,* which became an international sensation, selling 120,000 copies over the next several years and marking her as one of Britain's best-known writers of the period. She was married to George Catlin, a British professor at Cornell University in the United States, and a prominent Labour Party figure. She was, in sum, an acknowledged figure in British public life with various ties to prominent personalities in politics and the arts.

Yet despite her seemingly unbroken string of successes and conventional fulfillment, there had also been a darker strain to Vera Brittain's life that perhaps was a factor in her later career as a dissident. The great love of her youth, whom she was engaged to marry, was killed in action on the Western Front during World War I. Her brother Edward was also a fatality of the war. Her closest female friend, the novelist Winifred Holtby, died in her early forties. Her father suffered from life-long bouts of depression and finally killed himself in 1935. All of these events may well have provided a steel to her character that made her willing to endure the subsequent obloquy that was to be her lot in the period 1939-1945.

Such personal tragedies, of course, don't in themselves explain why she became such a fervent opponent of her government's policy in the war. Although not originally a pacifist, she increasingly became attracted to pacifist philosophy in the 1930s and was an early supporter of the Peace Pledge Union, founded in 1934 by the Church of England Clergyman Canon Dick Sheppard. Around 130,000 people eventually signed the Peace Pledge, which stated that "I remember war and never again will I support or sanction another and I will do all in my power to persuade others to do the same." Moreover, Brittain, while not conventionally religious, came increasingly to stress Christian themes of peace and forgiveness in her writings and public statements, and such a commitment no doubt shaped her attitudes in an important way.

Above all, however, it may have been Vera Brittain's own experiences in World War I that eventually led her to condemn all war—and in particular the seemingly mindless slaughter of civilians—as reprehensible. She served as a VAD (voluntary nurse) in France and was assigned to care not only for British casualties but for German as well. Her witnessing of the suffering of both friend and enemy seems to have had a profound impact. She describes one occasion when, alone in a hospital ward, she was

> gazing half-hypnotized at the dishevelled beds, the stretchers on the floor, the scattered boots and piles of muddy khaki, the brown blankets turned back from smashed limbs bound to splints by filthy blood-stained bandages. Beneath each stinking wad of sodden wool and gauze an obscene horror waited for me—and all the equipment I had for attacking it in this ex-medical ward was one pair of forceps standing in a potted-meat glass half-full of methylated spirit.[60]

Given this memory, it may not have been difficult for her to envisage what the hospital wards in any German city were like after a visit from Bomber Command. Indeed, she stated later that her pacifism had its roots in her experience nursing wounded German POWs in France in 1917, since she saw them not in the abstract as the enemy but as fellow human beings.

For whatever reason, Vera Brittain emerged as one of the most prominent voices protesting her government's conduct of the war effort, and, in particular, the policy of the area bombing of Germany. In assessing her position, it needs emphasizing that as a pacifist she was similar to Alfred Salter in that she condemned the use of violence in whatever form. For both Salter and Brittain, condemnation of the area offensive was only part and parcel of a more general rejection of the tools of war to settle political disputes. The same objections to her views as to those of Salter could thus be offered: since Brittain was against all war, what special importance should attach to her opposition to the strategy of Arthur Harris (would she not have been equally opposed to less draconian methods of prosecuting the war)? At the same time Vera Brittain was similar to Alfred Salter in one other respect, and that was her belief that area bombing was a particularly repugnant manifestation of the application of violence. In other words, all war may have been evil, but the bombing of civilians stood in an (evil) class by itself.

Moreover, Brittain at times showed a capacity for mixing moral and pragmatic arguments about military strategy. Thus she referred to the raid against the Peenemunde rocket installations—a rare precision attack by Bomber Command—as one that made sense from a military standpoint. She also argued that research done after the war showed the area offensive to be "not merely wicked but stupid," that is, it was militarily ineffective. She describes the war as having been won by the land armies and by "the relatively intelligent precision bombing of aircraft factories and railway junctions."[61] Vera Brittain was hardly an expert on military questions, but these statements demonstrate that she was able to accept at least some differentiation in the rationality—and thus acceptability—of different military measures.

There is also little doubt that she regarded Hitler and the Nazi regime as a serious threat to the values she held so dear. In a trip to Germany in 1936, she heard Hitler speak and dismissed him as being in effect a religious maniac. In one of the few cafes in Frankfurt where Jews were allowed to assemble, she perceived with abhorrence the "collective sense of humiliation among the patrons." At the same time, she felt that the outbreak of war could not simply be attributed to the inherent aggressiveness of the Germans. The inequities of the Versailles settlement as well as the commitment to power-politics by all the European leaders played an important part as well. Brittain was especially critical of Vansittartism and described as hysterical the notion that the Germans were the butcher-birds of history. She felt that such racial stereotyping made it far easier for the British government to adopt a policy of systematic destruction of German cities.

There were some problematical aspects of Vera Brittain's attitude toward the German threat. Even she admitted that her old friend Bertrand Russell had abandoned his pacifism of World War I because he saw Hitler as a unique threat that could only be defeated militarily. Brittain seemed unable to go this far, and, moreover, tended to downplay evidence of Nazi atrocities. Early in the war she discounted stories about concentration camps as propaganda by the British government to justify bombing policy. Even when evidence on the Holocaust became undeniable with the entry of Allied troops into Germany in 1945, Brittain felt that accounts of the concentration camps were perhaps being emphasized to assuage the guilt that many in Britain felt about the destruction of German cities. In an analysis that even her admirers might find troubling, she demanded to know "what essential moral difference divided the murder of prisoners in concentration camps from the incineration of refugees in Dresden?"[62]

Throughout the war Vera Brittain attempted to rouse the conscience of the British people to the moral issues raised by area bombing through her lectures, writings, and a host of other activities. A principal focus of her efforts was the Bombing Restriction Committee (BRC), which was formed in the spring of 1941 by the Quaker T. Corder Catchpool and whose declared purpose was "to urge the Government to stop violating their declared policy of bombing only military objectives and particularly to cease causing the death of many thousands of civilians in their homes." Typical of its efforts was a pamphlet produced in 1943 entitled *Stop Bombing Civilians*. Questions were raised in the House of Commons about the government's willingness to provide paper (scare in wartime) for such a publication, and one Conservative MP actually demanded that the members of BRC be interned for the duration of the war.

Given her talent with the pen, however, it was not surprising that Brittain gave most of her attention to composing books and articles that laid out the particulars of her indictment of government policy. An early effort in this regard was the "Letter to Peace-Lovers," begun in September 1939 and eventually achieving a circulation of slightly under 2,000 in England and abroad. The letter was supported both by subscribers and donations and included among its readers some members of the government, including a future Colonial Secretary. It continued throughout the war and even for two years after. Aside from the letter, Brittain produced several books during the war that marked her out as one of the most articulate—and, for many, most objectionable—critics of the British air offensive. For example, a small volume entitled *England's Hour,* which appeared in 1941, was greeted with unconcealed disdain on the part of most reviewers because of its plea for forgiveness and humanity. As Brittain recalled, "emotional, egotistical, sentimental and hysterical were only a few of the adjectives hurled at me like a prepared collection of verbal rotten eggs."

Perhaps her best-known wartime writing was *Humiliation With Honour,* published the following year. The book consisted of letters composed to her son John and was dedicated to the "victims of power." She attacked the current cult of toughness and contempt for "squeamishness" that seemed then to be prevalent among so many in Britain. In describing her own philosophy, she argued that

> it is better to suffer disadvantage in war than to descend to the lower levels of barbarity. . . . an important function of pacifism in war-time is the preservation of certain human and religious values which might otherwise be lost.[63]

It says something about the relative tolerance of British institutions that even so radical and unpopular a critique of governmental policy as this found a publisher at the time. Even so, Brittain admits that its appearance did not come without considerable difficulty. Her regular publishers both in the United States and in Britain declined to accept the manuscript because of their commitment to the war effort against Hitler. She agreed to spare them the embarrassment of insisting on publication as a favored author. Eventually the book appeared under an obscure imprint in Britain and was offered by the Fellowship of Reconciliation, a pacifist group, in the United States. It turned out to have a surprisingly large sale, with the first edition of 6,000 sold out before publication and subsequent editions leading to an overall distribution of about 10,000. In a curious aside, Brittain claimed that the book was even read in occupied Norway and "circulated in typescript throughout the resistance movement."[64] How the Norwegian resistance movement found comfort in her message of forgiveness toward the Germans was left unstated.

The appearance of *Seeds of Chaos* (a history of the area offensive), published in 1944 on behalf of the Bombing Restriction Committee, represented yet another plea by Brittain for a return to traditional norms of international law and to the principle that a nation should even accept disadvantage in wartime if the alternative was the destruction of basic humane values. This particular publication led to some unforeseen, and for Vera Brittain particularly unpleasant, consequences. Her analysis appeared in abbreviated form in a special edition of the American pacifist magazine *Fellowship,* restyled as "Massacre by Bombing." Twenty-eight leading American clergymen and other opinion leaders appended a foreword to Brittain's article, denouncing what they called the "carnival of death" currently being created by Allied bombing. A storm of controversy erupted in the United States as a consequence of her (and her fellow authors') criticism, reaching even into the White House and causing both the President's Press Secretary and the Under-Secretary of War specifically to denounce the musings of the writers in *Fellowship*. Brittain mournfully recorded that the effects of this episode followed her even after the war: "Such writings as I could still publish [in the United States] never emerged from the shadow which had darkened my name."[65]

If Vera Brittain felt a cloud over her name in the United States, it was minor compared to the reaction she experienced in her own country. It is difficult to read her recollections of the wartime years and not be moved by the powerful sense of isolation and almost universal condemnation that became her lot at that time. The fact that official authority remained relatively tolerant of her activities did not mean that they turned a totally blind eye to them. She recalled how she became "a suspect, haunted by police supervision, thwarted by prohibitions in an England no longer tranquil or friendly."[66] She received official word that it was unlikely she would be allowed to visit the United States for the duration of the war. She had an invitation to give a series of lectures in India, but permission was denied for that trip as well. There were even inquiries in Parliament as to whether she should not be detained under the Emergency Powers (Defence) Act, which allowed those under suspicion to be incarcerated indefinitely without benefit of appeal or even detailing of specific charges. More painful was the general social ostracism that she had to endure, even from those who were old friends and companions. "Distrust did not only come from official quarters; friends who had known G. [George Catlin] and me for years coldly avoided me at public gatherings, and a growing spate of abusive letters increased the pain of such rejections." A famous writer of thrillers once wrote her to ask why "she did not keep her mouth shut." Brittain responded by asking whether the fight against Hitler was being conducted in order to shut peoples' mouths.[67]

All this might have been endured more easily if she had seen some evidence that her protests were having an effect on governmental policy. The obvious reality that she (and others) were essentially irrelevant to the direction of events made such indignities even harder to bear. At one point, Brittain feared that she might undergo a total physical and nervous breakdown if she were subjected to yet another barrage of criticism. In order to deal with the effects of what she called her long struggle against hostility and suspicion, she went for extended treatment to a facility in Coleford that featured a combination of physical and mental therapy. Some years later she wrote in moving terms to the director of this institution: "I shall never forget what it meant to come into a community where I was regarded neither as a fool nor a traitor, and how well you understood that what I needed then was just rest and that complete unquestioning acceptance of all I was and tried to be."[68]

There is a curious but perhaps not totally surprising postscript to the story of Vera Brittain's *crise de conscience* concerning British bombing policy in World War II. At the very moment that a veil was being drawn over the exploits and persona of Arthur Harris, a mood of forgiveness and even grudging approbation began to be extended to Brittain. Once the war was over, a good many people seemed to want to consign Harris and all that he wrought to forgetful oblivion, whereas Vera Brittain, perhaps in direct counterpoint, now came to be viewed with greater favor. She herself remembered how the climate totally changed in the immediate aftermath of victory and she was now readmitted into the circles of "respectable" opinion. The fact that she was no longer a pariah was attested to by the great success of a book of war anecdotes she edited called *Account Rendered.* The previously unfashionable motif of this volume was the capacity, even the duty, of civilized people to extend acts of kindness to an enemy in wartime. To Brittain's astonishment, the first edition of *Account Rendered,* some 50,000 copies, sold out before publication.

What might be called the rehabilitation of Vera Brittain was also given an unexpected boost from a most unlikely quarter. It turned out that she and her husband were on the so-called Gestapo List, which was a roster of people in Britain subject to immediate arrest upon a successful German invasion. Of even greater satisfaction and help to her was the fact that their names appeared alphabetically on the same page as those of Churchill and Chamberlain. The famous list was published in leading British newspapers and was much reproduced, thus indelibly associating Vera Brittain and her husband (if only indirectly) with two British prime ministers. As she wryly commented, this circumstance "answered the war-time heresy-hunters more effectively than argument." For a time there was a framed photocopy of the list on their dining room wall, but eventually they consigned it to the domain of the bathroom.[69]

The irony was that it evidently took the judgment of the Gestapo to convince a number of Vera Brittain's countrymen that she was a loyal defender of democratic, that is, anti-Nazi values, even though she condemned area bombing as a method to protect those values. It is also evident that the uneasiness many in Britain displayed about area bombing after the war translated into a belated embrace of the courage of Vera Brittain in opposing what many others, it now appeared, had also opposed (although in their case rather silently). In her typical penchant for the arresting phrase, Brittain once referred to such silence as the "Fifth Horseman of the Apocalypse." Perhaps this was overly dramatic, yet it seems hard to deny that Vera Brittain, in pitying the masses of German civilians subject to area bombing, was truly a rebel with a cause, and an unimpeachable one at that. The famous British classicist Gilbert Murray, in his introduction to Euripedes's *Trojan Women,* once drew a connection between compassion and dissent. "Pity is a rebel passion," Murray said. "Its hand is against the strong, against the organized forces of society, against conventional sanctions and accepted gods." Vera Brittain could hardly have asked for a better epitaph—nor, for that matter, could the other dissenters who protested against their government's policy of laying waste to German cities.

PART III

JUDGMENTS

5

Standards and Principles

"Do not do an immoral thing for moral reasons."
—Thomas Hardy

In discussing the views of various individuals concerning the morality of the area offensive, my own sympathies have clearly been with the dissenters rather than with the supporters. Given the fact that British bombing policy in World War II remains a highly controversial matter, however, and that the debate over it has generally produced a good deal more heat than light, it doesn't advance things very much simply to suggest a personal preference in the matter. Any serious critique of the area offensive has to set out the moral argument in a good deal more systematic fashion than has heretofore been attempted. The following two chapters are an effort to do so.

One very important caveat does have to be offered at the outset. There is a surprisingly sparse literature wherein specific historical problems of security or foreign policy are examined using an ethical framework. Such case studies as do exist, moreover, have often been rendered somewhat unsatisfactory by the tendency of the writer not to recognize the full complexity of the situations in which decision-makers found themselves. The primary emphasis seems to be on establishing at the outset certain moral precepts as virtually self-evident, after which a (generally negative) verdict is passed on the degree to which the decision-makers lived up to these moral absolutes. Much of the effort is spent on hunting and pecking through the details of the situation in order to find substantiation for certain moral conclusions already firmly held.[1]

Such a procedure generally gives only a very partial and skewed version of the historical events being examined. Even more important, it fails to consider this reality in its own terms, that is to say, as an evolving collection of circumstances and decisions that had to be dealt with at a particular time and at a particular place by a particular group of individuals. In what follows, we will basically be working *outward* from the history of the area bombing offensive against Germany. This requires that we first establish a set of admittedly broad moral guidelines that can form at least a tentative basis for judgment. In arriving at such a judgment, however, it is crucial to acknowledge the full complexity of what faced the relevant individuals in Britain at the time and to describe these complications as straightforwardly as possible. In one of the more notable studies of the ethical dilemmas facing public officials, Donald Warwick expresses the challenge here rather nicely: "An ethical framework built on an idealized conception of what public officials will do will tilt toward sanctimony or collapse into irrelevance; one erected on inadequate moral principles will incline toward cynicism or topple into description."[2] In considering the British area offensive against Germany, I want to assess what *actual* (or realistic) moral choices were open to British officials and what can be said about the quality of the decisions eventually taken.

THE SHERMANESQUE FALLACY

There is probably no writer on military strategy who has been more quoted (and misquoted) than Karl von Clausewitz, the famous author of *On War* and universally regarded as a basic source for insights into the relationship between war and politics. There is no doubt that Clausewitz, who was a scholar but also a man of considerable practical military experience, has much to tell us about the peculiar institution of war. Yet he also offered a moral definition of the practice of war that has been the bane of thoughtful analysts of ethics in wartime ever since. Clausewitz wrote that "war is an act of force which theoretically can have no limits." As if this invitation to undifferentiated violence were not enough, he went on to deny that what he sometimes called "philanthropic" principles could ever be logically used to restrain the instrumentalities of war: "Attached to force are certain self-imposed imperceptible limitations hardly worth mentioning, known as international law and custom, but they scarcely weaken it. . . . To introduce the principle of moderation into the theory of war itself would always lead to logical absurdity."

Particularly important to this argument was the concept of preemption. In what Clausewitz called the principle of "reciprocal action," the tendency toward ever more ruthless types of military activity is justified, or at least to be expected, on the premise that the enemy will likely do the same if given the chance. In this inversion of the Golden Rule, the idea was to do unto others before they did unto you. Clausewitz's calculation simply was that "the ruthless user of force who shrinks from no amount of bloodshed must gain an advantage if his opponent does not do the same." From this perspective, Clausewitz concluded, those "kindhearted people" who tried to place limits on the tools of war could make a brutal enterprise even more chaotic, for "war is such a dangerous business that the mistakes which come from kindness [can be] the very worst."[3]

Among later military figures who evidently adopted these dicta as operating principles was General William Tecumseh Sherman. In defending his tactics in the American Civil War, which included the burning of Atlanta and the mass destruction visited on a wide swath of the South during his march to the sea, Sherman argued that "war is cruelty and you cannot refine it." In a later speech to the graduating cadets at West Point, he summarized his stance in the famous phrase, "War is Hell." What he meant here is of some importance to our subsequent analysis. Sherman was not defending war itself; on the contrary, he stressed that it was a most terrible institution. He suggested therefore that it was those who were responsible for the *initiation* of war that had to answer to the moral philosophers. Those who were charged with bringing the war to a successful conclusion could hardly be held accountable for the methods they subsequently used to meet such a goal. It was not the techniques of war that were at issue, then, but rather the very use of it as a tool of policy.[4]

It is interesting to see how widely shared Sherman's attitude was by various figures in the British Government and, more specifically, the RAF during World War II. Consider the following examples. Arthur Tedder, a generally admirable figure who questioned Bomber Command's strategy and favored precision bombing, suggested that "the history of war affords little hope that nations which are fighting for their lives and beliefs will be restricted in their conduct of the war by moral factors."[5] Air Marshall Sir Robert Saundby, second-in-command to Arthur Harris, also employed the precepts of Clausewitz and Sherman in analyzing Bomber Command's attack on Dresden:

> It is not so much this or the other means of making war that is immoral or inhumane. What is immoral is war itself. Once full-scale war has broken out it can never be humanized or civilized, and if one side attempted to do it it would be most likely to be defeated. So long as we resort to war to settle differences between nations, so long will we have to endure the horrors, barbarities and excesses that war brings with it. That, to me, is the lesson of Dresden.[6]

The suggestion that the "realist" in wartime has to concern himself simply with the taking of lives cannot be taken in any serious sense as a self-evident proposition, however. Actually, to make such an assertion is frequently only an attempt to avoid a perhaps uncomfortable recognition that doubtful steps are being taken (or have been taken) in the search for victory. If ethics indeed have no place in wartime decision-making—an argument that can be offered as simply descriptive or as prescriptive, that is, it *shouldn't* have a place—then one's conscience is in some sense liberated. The true reality, however, is that nations, or at least those nations aspiring to a reputation as upholders of certain values, have always placed restraints on themselves in the application of violence. Indeed, the notion of violence unconnected to ethical considerations is inherently unsustainable. The distinguished British military historian Michael Howard is as well-placed as anyone to speak to this point. He dismisses the notion that war is *prima facie* "uncontrollable," not least because war "involves at every level of government and society the imposition of authoritative control." This means that the formal resort to war can be distinguished in a fundamental sense from mere acts of brigandage, mob violence, or riots, and involves the core values and beliefs of the nation. Howard summarizes the basic proposition:

> The prime characteristic of the military is not that they use violence, not even that they use violence legitimized by virtue of their function as instruments of the state. It is that they use that violence with great deliberation. Such violence, purposeful, deliberate, and legitimized is normally known as force, and the use of force between states is what we mean by war. War consists of such deliberate, controlled, and purposeful acts of force combined and harmonized to attain what are ultimately political objectives. . . . To control and limit the conduct of war is thus not inherently impossible. Indeed without controls and limitations war cannot be conducted at all.[7]

The key challenge here is to define what are meant by "political objectives," the preservation or expansion of which are the fundamental goal of warfare. Such objectives may be defined in relatively concrete economic or geopolitical terms, but any reasonable definition must also include the moral values of the nation, its sense of self-worth, and sometimes even the welfare of the international community more generally. From this perspective, the manner in which a war is conducted bears an intimate relationship to those ends that the fighting is designed to serve, that is to say, its "political" objectives. Winston Churchill himself appeared (at least at times) to recognize the truth of this proposition. When pressed in the House of Commons in January 1945 about the doubtful aspects of the unconditional surrender formula being presented to Germany, he shouted that this did not mean the Allies meant to "exterminate or trample on the German people. . . . Not at all. We remain bound by our own customs and our own nature."[8] Presumably this was a suggestion that the "customs and nature" of the British people forbade them from undertaking certain measures that other less civilized societies might contemplate.

A bizarre episode at the Teheran Conference in November 1943 provides an example of Churchill's sensitivity on this point. Stalin suggested at one point that the most effective way to prevent a resurgence of German aggression after the war would be to shoot out of hand at least 50,000, perhaps even 100,000, of the surviving German officer corps, thus decapitating at one blow future German military leadership. This idea may have been presented simply as an expression of Stalin's mordant sense of humor, but Churchill took it all quite seriously. He replied heatedly that he could never agree to such a proposal, that carrying it out would represent a permanent stain on the honor of the British people. Roosevelt attempted to lighten the somewhat strained atmosphere at this point by suggesting as a compromise that "only" 49,000 German officers should be shot. Churchill waved off this sally with impatience, and demanded that attention now be given to the next item on the agenda.[9] It might be noted in passing that slaughtering virtually the whole of the German officer corps would have been a fairly effective way of undermining German military prowess, at least in the short run. Clearly, however, Churchill did not see it in these terms and in consequence reinforced the notion that it was not just the ends of war but the means of it as well that required suitable attention.

The assertion that historically there have been limits to the degree and type of violence in wartime undertaken by various of its participants does leave the question of what general standards of restraint may be identified and also from what source these derive. The first of these matters is considered below, but as to the origins of—or rationale for—restraint in wartime, three primary factors seem to contribute. There are the particular values and institutions of the warring state itself, which may or may not dictate moderation in certain measures of violence. There is the general code of the international community, expressed not only in conventions but in custom, dictating legitimate conduct in wartime (and here referred to as the war convention). Finally, there is a body of essentially prudential considerations that stresses that the manner of fighting a war should not undermine the prospects for a more just or more favorable peace for the victorious parties or perhaps even for the international community as a whole.

The last factor in restraining uncontrolled violence may perhaps be persuasive at times even to those generally most skeptical of the notion of limits in war. The existence and, even more, the restraining effect of the war convention is generally met with a good deal more derision by these individuals, as noted above. The first consideration, that a nation's own peculiar character may dictate limitations in the use of force, presents a more ambiguous problem. Certainly all of the major figures instrumental in Bomber Command's air campaign against Germany were unalloyed patriots and convinced of the special virtues of the British people, which the struggle against the enemy was designed to preserve. The challenge in this case was to square Britain's seeming violation of previous standards of warfare (at least as practiced by their country) with their conviction that Britain was something special. The standard, if uneasy, solution was to assert that *necessity* forced the nation temporarily to set aside its traditional standards of discrimination. This was not an explanation satisfactory to the moral critics of the area offensive and, one suspects, not a totally comfortable notion with many of its proponents as well.

The notion of national character as something that does (and should) limit the measures of war remains as perhaps the most interesting of the three sources of restraint described above. Its essence was conveyed by a certain Lord Moulton of Bank, a 19th-century British parliamentarian, writing in the twilight of his career. In an essay for *The Atlantic* published in July 1924, Moulton distinguished between "three great domains of human action." The first was governed by "positive law," standards established by the lawmakers and enforced by the coercive power of the state. A second arena of conduct involved the "domain of free choice," such as the choice of a marriage partner, in which the law had no voice and the individual enjoyed complete freedom. Finally, there was a domain in which adherence to standards could not be compelled but in which obligations were nevertheless recognized and accepted, "the obedience of a man to that which he cannot be forced to obey [but where he is] the enforcer of the law upon himself." In a compelling conclusion, Lord Moulton asserted that "the real greatness of a nation, its true civilization, is measured by the extent of . . . obedience to the unenforceable."[10]

A FRAMEWORK FOR ANALYSIS

As far as the subject of ethics in wartime is concerned, the difficulty, of course, is in translating Lord Moulton's dicta bearing on individual conduct into something that is relevant to nations. Even if we are able to do so, in saying that a civilized nation should accept obedience to the unenforceable as morally commanding, the question becomes obedience to what? What are the standards of conduct in wartime that should be accepted and recognized by well-meaning statesmen even in the absence of coercion to make them follow such standards, and what initial assessment can be made about the area bombing of Germany in these terms?

The Legal Question

At the outset we ought to give brief attention to a legal assertion sometimes presented in moral garb. It is a commonplace that legal standards may (and should) reflect generally accepted moral principles, yet there are instances where they seem to bear little relationship to such norms. In the case of the area bombing of Germany, some supporters of that strategy have attempted to sketch out its legal admissibility and therefore its implied moral justification as well. It is evident that even if the first can be established, this hardly dictates that it was morally appropriate in the bargain. As it happens, however, the legal defense of area bombing is in its own terms so problematical that it can hardly be used as a moral assertion concerning British air attacks on German cities.

In a previous chapter we argued that prior to 1939 there seemed to be a general legal consensus within the international community that unrestricted aerial attacks on urban areas were prohibited by the war convention. As the fury of the area offensive mounted—and in the years since—the notion was advanced by some that, in actuality, there was no specific legal prohibition against city bombing. The case rests almost entirely on an interpretation of the provisions of the Hague Convention of 1907. In that convention there was no mention made of air operations as such, but considerable attention was given to the laws of war as they affected ground and naval operations against enemy cities. In attempting to capture or invest defended locales it was permissible for army units to shell a city despite the risk this involved to the non-combatant population (who, it was assumed, could leave the area of danger if they so desired). Even in this instance, such shelling had to be in pursuance of a legitimate military objective, that is, the capture of the besieged city. As far as the treatment of undefended towns was concerned, ground forces (e.g., artillery) were absolutely forbidden from attacks on such places. The general principles enunciated did give naval units rather more latitude than the army. Thus ships were allowed to shell specific *military* objectives in undefended cities, even if this might cause collateral damage among civilians. The rationale was that naval forces frequently were not in a position to actually capture the city whereas ground forces were, and thus attacks by the latter on an undefended town were quite unnecessary. Not surprisingly, supporters of the area offensive argued that by analogy air operations should be governed by the naval rules of the Hague Convention.[11]

Even if we accept this association, the Hague Convention of 1907 hardly constitutes a legal defense of British bombing policy, and most especially in its final climactic phase. One of the possible ways in which it might be held to do so is to assert that German cities actually remained "defended" to the last days of the war. From the evidence that has already been produced, it is clear that this was true only in the most formal sense and that its truth depends on an almost infinitely flexible definition of "defended." The reality was that the Allies had virtually unchallenged command of German airspace by the summer of 1944; to the extent that population centers were defended, this defense increasingly became a *pro forma* exercise (there was not a single Luftwaffe sortie against the Allied planes that bombed Dresden in February 1945). Given the helplessness of German cities by this point, the only activity that the Hague Convention allowed (on the naval analogy) was precise attacks against German military objectives in the effected areas. In actuality, Bomber Command resumed an unadulterated area offensive in September 1944 and continued it until the following April.

Initial Propositions

If a legal defense of the area offensive, particularly in its last year, seems hard to sustain, we turn now to a more general consideration of first principles in morality and warfare in order to establish a broader framework for judgment. It is standard in discussions of ethics and violence to employ some variant of "just war" doctrine as originally developed by Saint Augustine of Hippo, later refined by Saint Thomas Aquinas, and subject to constant elucidation (or re-elucidation) ever since. Indeed just war theory seems almost inevitably to lie at the heart of analyses about legitimate types of conflict and thus of the war convention itself. The theory makes a clear distinction between *jus ad bellum* and *jus in bello,* that is, between the legitimacy of the state's resorting to war in the first place and the methods by which the war is conducted. The framework of *jus ad bellum* emphasizes that there must be right intent, generally defined as self-defense or the protection of weak and innocent third parties. Even in these cases, the war must be started by legitimate authority and be resorted to only as a last resort. Wars begun basically for purposes of revenge or reprisal are proscribed.[12]

It would seem that there can be few, if any, quibbles with Great Britain's war against Germany in terms of *jus ad bellum*. This was indeed a classic example of a war of self-defense, not only of Britain itself but of other weak and innocent third parties in all areas of Europe who succumbed to the Nazi yoke in the early years of the struggle. Moreover, Britain's declaration of war on Germany on September 3, 1939 was a perfect example of war's being resorted to only as a last resort. The whole history of British foreign policy in the mid- and late 1930s was a tapestry of repeated attempts by London to arrive at a peaceful settlement of outstanding disputes with Hitler. The Munich agreement stands out as the most famous (and perhaps notorious) effort in this direction. It was only when it became plain to one and all, and not just in Britain, that Hitler was embarked on an essentially unlimited campaign of conquest and subjugation that Neville Chamberlain (as the legitimate authority) took the extremely painful step of declaring a state of belligerency with Berlin.

The moral case against the area bombing offensive of Germany, then, has to do entirely with the question of *jus in bello*. It is important to reiterate that just war theory does make a clear distinction between the purposes and the conduct of war. Even though the former can be entirely legitimate, this does not negate the demands (and the restrictions) of the latter, and indeed violations of norms of *jus in bello* can render a war illegitimate even if fought with right intent. It does have to be admitted that this is by far the most difficult and obscure part of the just war system. *Jus in bello* deals with such a potentially vast range of specific problems and issues that it is difficult to imagine there will ever be a universal consensus on what is just or unjust in the application of wartime violence. For our purposes, however, this problem need not be unduly obtrusive. The moral critique of the area bombing offensive rests on a few basic principles of *jus in bello* that are the recipient of more or less universal agreement and thus can be identified with relative ease.

The most primordial of these is the notion of "proportionality." The essential proposition is that the military utility of a given action has to outweigh the evil side-effects of such an action, that is to say, it has to be proportional in balancing the steps taken to achieve victory against the calamities that war can produce. One relevant consideration, for example, may be the attaining of a more just and stable postwar environment for the international community. Measures that may gain victory but undermine or even destroy the prospects of the latter are thus rendered dubious, if not totally excluded.

The concept of proportionality does present a problem as far as the definition of military utility is concerned. How useful does a particular action have to be in order to justify at least some evil side-effects? Clearly, there are few military men who will assert baldly that an operation contributed little to victory, but even so they remain indifferent to the suffering it may have caused. On the contrary, the consistent argument is that even though certain unfortunate consequences may have resulted from the event, it was militarily appropriate because it made at least some tangible contribution in vanquishing the enemy. Even given its ambiguities, however, the notion of proportionality continues to provide one of the surest bases on which to judge the moral legitimacy of various measures in wartime, and never more than when it involves the distinction between combatants and non-combatants.

Among the traditional stipulations of the rule of proportionality, it is this one that is perhaps the most fundamental. The general assertion is that those wearing uniforms or in some other way directly engaged in fighting are fair game for killing or wounding. Those not so engaged are supposed to be given sanctuary, that is, as "innocents," they are not legitimate targets for violent action. Where such takes place, the burden of proof is on the violator to demonstrate that the action was essential to the achievement of a just cause. It is true of course that in the modern era the definition of combatant and non-combatant has been a troublesome one. In an era of total war, of the complete mobilization of the resources of the nation in support of the war effort, are there any true "non-combatants"? Moreover, one might ask why the fate of civilians should be regarded as particularly sacrosanct compared to the young men in uniform who are doing the actual fighting? Are their lives somehow less valuable than those sitting in comfort before their hearth? Shall we shrug off the deaths of thousands in battle while bewailing the deaths of a relative few at home? As it happens, Hitler had his own answer to this question. When presented with evidence about the appallingly high rate of loss among young commissioned German officers on the Eastern Front, he replied with some puzzlement: "But that's what they are there for!" In his typically brutal fashion, Hitler was perhaps indirectly touching on a truth that seems to affect most governments at war: the sacrifice of combatants is viewed as less objectionable than grievous damage to the fabric of society itself, the protection of which, after all, is the ultimate purpose of war.

In the era of total war, the definition of combatant might seem to be reasonably expanded to include not just those in uniform or on the battle fronts but also those directly engaged in providing specific support for the armies. Thus civilian workers in defense plants, civil service personnel at military headquarters, railway workers supervising the shipment of military supplies, individuals engaged in petroleum production for use of the armed forces might legitimately (if regrettably) be regarded as combatants in the expanded definition. Even today the distinction between combatants and non-combatants loses all meaning, however, if we extend the definition of "combatants" to include all civilians whose activities in any way might be of service to the war effort of the state. Farmers produce food that soldiers (and civilians) consume, teachers educate young people who may serve as officers, postmen deliver mail to families from those serving at the front—in each instance there is some tenuous connection between the activity and successful prosecution of the war. Yet the link is so amorphous that to insist on it is to render one of the fundamental principles of the war convention, of *jus in bello,* a nullity.

The targeting strategy of Bomber Command over Germany during World War II, it will be clear enough by now, ignored any reasonable distinction between combatant and non-combatant, however broadly defined the former. We need only recall Sir Charles Portal's minute to Bomber Command on February 14, 1942: "I suppose it is clear that the aiming points [for the bombers] are to be in the built-up areas, not, for instance, the dockyards or aircraft factories." The effects of this order could be seen in Berlin just after the end of the war. An observer noted that there were an estimated 50,000 orphans living in holes like animals around the city, "some of them one-eyed or one-legged veterans of seven or so, many so deranged by the bombing and the Russian attack that they screamed at the sight of any uniform, even a Salvation Army one."[13] We have described in general terms the effect that the Allied bombing offensive had on German civilian life. Descriptions such as this help to make concrete what runs the risk of becoming a numbing abstraction because of its sheer enormity. There is a cynical but perhaps apropos aphorism that for many people one human death is a tragedy, a million deaths is a statistic.

TWO PRELIMINARY DEFENSES

The issue raised by the Berlin orphans is straightforward enough. By what calculation can we justify their suffering? Assuming that small children are not a legitimate target of wartime operations, is there any way in which their deaths and injuries may be defended as within the war convention?

In analyzing the position taken by defenders of Bomber Command on this question, one is struck by a rather curious phenomenon. There seems to be an acceptance among many of these individuals that area bombing was a departure from the war convention as previously understood, but they then set out a series of mitigating factors that make this departure (regrettably) both understandable and even on balance legitimate. The argument seems to be that, in most cases, countries should observe the distinction between combatant and non-combatant, and hopefully the city bombing strategy of World War II will not have to be repeated. In this particular case, however, other claims took precedence over the dictates of the war convention as they applied to the protection of innocents. The general proposition underlaying all of these assertions is that the area offensive, however much it may have (apparently) violated certain aspects of the war convention, was nevertheless in *overall* compliance with the rule of proportionality in just war doctrine. That is to say, the suffering of German civilians was more than counterbalanced by the contribution British bombing made to victory in a just cause. A reasonable evaluation of this claim necessitates a detailed look at the actual military effects of the area offensive and thus is left to the following chapter. At this point we consider two other claims offered in defense of that strategy that have appeared from time to time in the debate over the morality of bombing German cities.

The Principle of Double Effect

Innocents (non-combatants) have always died in wars, although more in some than in others. It seems inevitable that they will continue to do so. Philosophers of war over the centuries have had to face this problem squarely and, if possible, develop standards by which the destruction of innocents may at least in some cases be accommodated within the war convention. Perhaps the most famous attempt in this direction is the so-called "principle of double effect."

First developed by Catholic theologians in the Middle Ages, the principle of double effect is, as Walzer puts it, "a way of reconciling the absolute prohibition against attacking non-combatants with the legitimate conduct of military activity." Reduced to its essentials, the principle allows the killing of innocents *provided* that the following obtains:

1) The military action is in itself a legitimate act of war.
2) The "direct effect" is morally appropriate, that is, involves legitimate military targets, e.g., military supplies, enemy soldiers.
3) The intention of the actor is good in that he aims only at the acceptable effect and the evil side-effect (killing of innocents) is not one of his ends, nor is it a means to his ends.

4) The good effect (advancement of military goals) is sufficiently important to compensate for the evil side-effects.[14]

In order to render the principle of double effect meaningful, it should be added (as Walzer himself does) that it is not enough simply not to intend the killing of innocents. There must be a conscious and continual effort to limit the sacrifice of non-combatants as much as possible.

It is surprising how often the principle of double effect finds its way into the discourse of politicians and military leaders, even if they don't phrase their arguments in such abstract philosophical terms. In its often rather vulgarized version, the principle of double effect is reduced to the idea that I can do pretty nearly anything I want in wartime as long as I am actually trying to achieve military victory and not simply engaging in vengeful slaughter. In this version, double effect takes on an almost Shermanesque character, and use of the doctrine in this way was (and is) very common among apologists for the area offensive.

Consider, for example, this statement from Arthur Harris:

> Attacks on cities, like any other act of war, are intolerable unless they are strategically justified. But they are strategically justified in so far as they tend to shorten the war and so preserve the lives of Allied soldiers. To my mind we have absolutely no right to give them up unless it is certain that they will not have this effect.[15]

Notice that in this analysis any military action that "tends" to have the effect of shortening the war is rendered legitimate for that very reason (the reference to preserving the lives of Allied soldiers raises a somewhat different issue that needs to be considered separately). Clearly, this removes any conceivable restraints on violence, since it is well nigh impossible, and particularly during the conflict itself, not to make an argument that at least some progress toward victory will accrue from a given military action. The theologian John Ford effectively disputes this essentially unlimited extension of double effect: "It is illegitimate to appeal to the principle of the double effect when the alleged justifying cause is speculative, future, and problematical, while the evil effect is enormous, certain, and immediate."[16]

More to the point, the principle of double effect hardly can be offered as a defense of the area offensive simply because the evil side-effect in this case (the random killing of non-combatants) was not an unintended or regrettable consequence of a legitimate military action but was instead one of the main points of the strategy. In terms of the definition of double effect offered above, destruction of German civilians was in fact a "means to an end," that is, victory over the Nazis. Lord Cherwell's original minute on the dehousing of German workers, which implied large-scale loss of civilian life and formed much of the basis for the subsequent area offensive, stands as a prime piece of evidence in this regard.

The Sliding Scale

A second argument offered in defense of the area offensive is what has been called the theory of the "sliding scale." Reduced to its essentials, this suggests that the more just the cause, the greater latitude one has in ignoring, or at least temporarily setting aside, the principles of the war convention. The eminent theoretician John Rawls puts the point somewhat indirectly: "Even in a just war, certain forms of violence are strictly inadmissible; and when a country's right is questionable and uncertain, the constraints on the means it can use are all the more severe. Acts permissible in a war of legitimate self-defense, when these are necessary, may be flatly excluded in a more doubtful situation."[17] What this would seem to suggest is that area bombing by Germany against Great Britain (undertaken during the Blitz of 1940-1941) can be easily dismissed as morally repugnant whereas the subsequent British area offensive against Germany is far more defensible, since it was in pursuit of a compelling just cause. Noble Frankland makes precisely this argument. In discussing the morality of the area offensive, he suggests that a decisive consideration was "the causes for which the war [was] being fought and the nature of the enemy, for the means adopted must be in scale with the ends sought."[18]

There is hardly likely to be any war that provides more comfort and support to the adherents of the sliding scale hypothesis than World War II. The Nazi regime was so repugnant in all its particulars, and represented such a threat to all basic and decent human values, that it would indeed be tempting to argue that any methods efficient in bringing down such a regime were morally supportable. Yet two critical objections remain. The unalloyed adoption of the sliding scale in this instance would have logically removed any compunctions about the most savage application of military violence to defeat the Nazis. Even the most fervent supporters of Allied air power in World War II would (and for the record did) stop short of such an unvarnished commitment to destruction. There was, for example, the repeated assurances by British spokesmen that their bombers were attacking "only" military targets and that they were attempting to avoid collateral civilian damage as much as possible. The hypocrisy in such statements has already been remarked on, but it was the fact that they were made at all which is the point here.

Moreover, the argument of the sliding scale ignores the fact that the war against the Nazi regime was after all a defense of certain basic values, among which was a decent respect for the individual. In the ultimate sense this was the political purpose of the war (in the Clausewitzian sense), that is to say, the defense of a whole way of life. It will be recalled that one of the prime requisites of a truly just war is that the peace and justice to be achieved must not be compromised by the measures used to gain military victory. One of the leading historians of the area offensive observes that a great many people (among whom he presumably numbered himself) "felt that by embarking on a systematic attack on cities . . . the Allies sacrificed something of their own moral case and that they contributed substantially to the terrible moral collapse that took place in the Second World War, most especially in the treatment of prisoners and civilians."[19] To this argument the sliding scale thesis can present few rebuttals. The melancholy truth seems to be that in combatting a great evil, the British (and the Americans) condoned other evils that significantly lessened the whole moral purpose of the struggle.

SUPREME EMERGENCY AND MILITARY NECESSITY

References to the principle of double effect and the sliding scale may be found among those defending the area offensive, but the impression gained is that those making such arguments are generally rather uncomfortable with extending them too far, for perhaps obvious reasons. The supporters of Bomber Command, on the other hand, are a good deal less defensive when they discuss two other moral claims for the legitimacy of British bombing policy.

The first of these asserts the notion of "supreme emergency." The argument is that, in such a situation, even humane and civilized states may be forced (temporarily) to set aside the war convention in the interests of survival—and moreover, they have a (temporary) right to do so. An important assumption is that the state is fighting in accordance with the dictates of *jus ad bellum,* that is to say, it is fighting for a just cause. How to define a supreme emergency? Two ingredients seem to be necessary: there must be a clear and imminent danger of defeat by the enemy, and the consequences of such a defeat must appear to be truly catastrophic. In practical terms, this would mean that losing the war would threaten the very essence of the nation, would involve one's society and values being subjugated to a completely repugnant rule, and would perhaps even put one's existence as a separate state at risk. Notice that both elements have to be present in order for there to be a supreme emergency: if the threat of defeat is imminent but the consequences of defeat are limited, or if the potential consequences are dire but there is no immediate danger of defeat, then no supreme emergency exists. If such a peril does exist, however, Machiavelli for one argued that with "the entire safety of our country . . . at stake, no considerations of what is just or unjust, merciful or cruel, praiseworthy or blameworthy must intervene."[20]

From the concept of supreme emergency we move to the corollary notion of "military necessity." This term is found very widely in all discussions of ethics and military conduct, as well as in various conventions setting out the laws of war. The problem has been to interpret the scope and meaning of military necessity and to determine how it may or may not sanction certain measures that would be unallowable in the absence of it. As a general matter, military necessity may be said to obtain when a certain action bears a legitimate connection to the search for victory and when its non-performance would actively undermine that effort. Even so, there are certain military activities that the war convention rules out regardless of their possible contribution to victory, e.g., the mass slaughter of prisoners. For present purposes, I want to attach the notion of military necessity very closely to supreme emergency and to consider both of these ideas in the context of the British decision in February 1942 to launch a campaign of indiscriminate bombing of German cities.

We can summarize the implicit and, to some extent, explicit rationale of this decision as follows: Britain was indeed facing a supreme emergency in its war with Germany, and directing Bomber Command to attack German cities was a military necessity in the sense that Britain had no other significant way at the time of prosecuting the war against the Nazis. Not to prosecute the war was to accept the continuance, and perhaps the actual effectuation, of the supreme emergency, which was intolerable. Therefore, this particular violation of the war convention, that is, indiscriminate killing of German combatants and non-combatants alike, was morally defensible.

In assessing this argument, we need to look closely at both elements of the equation—that is, did a supreme emergency confront Great Britain as of February 1942, and was the area offensive a military necessity in that Britain had no other options open to her, or at least any that promised to do significant damage to the Nazi ability to make war?

On the first point, there is no question but that Britain was faced with at least one element of supreme emergency in February 1942. A Nazi defeat of Great Britain, and more especially a Nazi occupation of the British islands, would have ushered in a long night of barbarism that would have threatened all the basic norms of the nation as they had been developed over the past several hundred years. We have plenty of evidence that Hitler planned to remake British society and institutions along lines congenial to the New Order in Europe. A first step in this process would have been the systematic slaughter of all the leadership elements in Great Britain. We have already referred to the so-called Gestapo List of those scheduled for execution (both Winston Churchill and Vera Brittain claiming pride of place on this roster), which had on it the names of almost 2,000 individuals. Beyond this, there were plans for the mass deportation of British workers to Germany to work in factories and on farms, a process already established in other parts of occupied Europe at the time. Indeed, an item from the proposed plan of Military Government for England stipulated that the entire "able-bodied male population between the ages of seventeen and forty-five will . . . be interned and dispatched to the Continent with the minimum of delay." There was to be a draconian requisition of foodstuffs and raw materials beyond that required for the bare subsistence of the population. Finally, as need hardly be mentioned, British Jews would have been subjected to the same fate as their co-religionists on the Continent.[21]

But was German victory over Great Britain ever imminent, or more to the point, was it imminent in February 1942, the start of the area offensive? It seems possible to adopt one of two positions on this matter, the first of which is fairly categorical and the other somewhat more reserved. There is a lot to be said for the argument that if a supreme emergency ever did face Great Britain—in the sense of impending defeat by the Germans—it peaked in the summer of 1940 and rapidly ebbed after that time. Even though Britain had managed to extricate over 300,000 men from the beaches of Dunkirk, virtually all of their equipment was left behind, and the estimate was that there remained only two fully-armed divisions in the country itself to resist a German assault. Churchill and his advisers began to consider plans for moving the government to Canada in such an event. After a brief delay, Hitler ordered that preparations for the invasion of Britain, codenamed Operation Sea Lion, proceed with all due speed. He established as a prerequisite for the attack, however, that the RAF be essentially eliminated as a threat to the German invasion forces.

In considering the last point, it can be argued that September 15, 1940, represented the end of the crisis facing Britain. This was the climactic day in the Battle of Britain, the campaign by the Luftwaffe to nullify British airpower. After Fighter Command had inflicted heavy losses on the attacking German aircraft, with comparatively modest damage to its own, Hitler ordered the Luftwaffe to concentrate on the bombing of British cities at night rather than targeting the assets of the RAF in daytime. Shortly after September 15, he further directed that all preparations for the invasion be suspended. His mind now became increasingly focused on the coming campaign against Russia.

In assessing the situation facing Britain in February 1942, then, one might suggest that since any realistic threat of invasion had vanished, so had the specter of supreme emergency. There is still more to the argument, however. The critic might note that even though Britain was at this point free from the peril of actual military occupation, it was questionable how long she could maintain herself in the face of German control of the Continent. Might not her isolated position eventually result in the erosion of her capacity to resist Nazi pressure? In meeting this objection, reference can be made to perhaps the most important week of the entire war, which occurred at the beginning of December 1941. On December 5, the Soviets launched a major counter-offensive in the environs of Moscow which threw back the *Wehrmacht* from the gates of the city and inflicted the first major defeat of the war on German ground forces. The success of this offensive insured that Hitler's dream of a quick conquest of Soviet Russia in 1941 would prove unavailing. Two days later, on December 7, Japan attacked the United States at Pearl Harbor, which brought the Americans into the war not only against Tokyo but, three days later, against the Germans as well. At the dawn of 1942, therefore, it appeared that Russia had survived, the vast might of the Americans was now engaged, and the entire strategic situation had been dramatically transformed. Under the circumstances, the only supreme emergency that loomed was the one the Germans would face sooner or later. Winston Churchill himself happily assessed the entirely changed position:

> So we had won after all! . . . In dire stress, we had won the war. England would live; Britain would live; the Commonwealth of Nations and the Empire would live. . . . Once again in our long Island history we should emerge, however mauled or mutilated, safe and victorious. We should not be wiped out. Our history would not come to an end. . . . Hitler's fate was sealed [and] there was no more doubt about the end.[22]

If any vestige of supreme emergency had passed by February 1942, then, this concept cannot be used to justify the initiation of the area offensive, a military strategy that evidently violated one of the principal themes of the war convention, the distinction between combatants and non-combatants. There is, however, a more reserved position that one can take that would suggest that the supreme emergency had not totally vanished as of this date. Even though victory over the Nazis was seemingly assured, there was always the fog of war to contend with, Clausewitz's famous phrase describing the unexpected in military operations. What if Hitler should develop marvelous new weapons that might snatch victory from the jaws of defeat? Fears about the German atomic weapons program were, after all, a major spur to the Manhattan Project, and the launching of the V-1 and V-2 campaign as late as 1944 aroused concern that these earlier uncertainties might be justified. Moreover, the Soviet position in the summer of 1942 continued to be tenuous. The *Wehrmacht* was at the time making vast gains in the southern region of the country, and it was not unreasonable to wonder about the staying power of the Soviet people under such an onslaught. Finally, defeat of Hitler would almost certainly necessitate an invasion of the Continent, an amphibious operation dwarfing any that had ever been attempted and was by no means assured of success. The obvious point is that if one takes this more measured view concerning the prospects of German victory after February 1942, the legitimacy of the area bombing offensive can perhaps be defended more easily.

It can, that is, if we make certain corollary judgments about military necessity. The issue is plain enough: was the bombing of German cities the only realistic military option available to Britain that held out the prospect of doing serious damage to the German war effort? What alternatives were at hand for the British Government in using airpower (or other military resources, for that matter) in the war against Germany? In short, was the area offensive a legitimate military necessity in any real sense of the term? It is evident that an answer to these questions must be governed in part by one's position concerning the existence of a supreme emergency. If the threat to Britain was fundamental at the beginning of 1942, then presumably greater latitude may be given for the adoption of any and all measures for the protection of the state, even if they were violative of the war convention. If the peril was less, then a different standard of judgment must apply.

There seems to be a rather convincing array of evidence that to the extent Britain was to undertake a strategic bombing offensive against Germany in the period after February 1942, there was for the foreseeable future little alternative but to concentrate on general city attacks. We have already detailed the factors that effectively forced the RAF out of daytime bombing over Germany by the beginning of that year. Given the technical constraints operating on Bomber

Command in nighttime operations, a large urban area seemed to suggest itself as the only feasible aiming point for the aircrew. The British Bombing Survey Unit summarized the argument after the war: "The navigational and bombing accuracy actually achieved by Bomber Command in night attacks makes it doubtful whether target systems other than towns could have been effectively bombed before the beginning of 1944."[23]

If this was the case, obviously the moral argument is strongly affected. Noble Frankland makes the not unreasonable assertion that to criticize the area offensive on moral grounds in the period 1942 to early 1944 is to offer an ethical query quite unrelated to the operational circumstances confronting the decision-makers.

> In the case of bombing, strategic criticism, even when operationally unfounded, often seems to be reinforced by moral indignation and moral indignation often seems to have more to do with the formation of views about strategic bombing than do the strategic pros and cons of it. This need not be objectionable but it becomes so when, to serve a moral argument, Bomber Command is given in retrospect a function which, operationally, it could not have performed.[24]

This is fine as far as it goes, but of course the issue was just a bit more complicated than that. Perhaps the only type of strategic bombing that Britain could do in the middle period of the war was area bombing, but was strategic bombing itself a military necessity? Frankland, for one, leaves little doubt as to his views on the matter. "The alternative to area bombing was either no strategic bombing or daylight bombing. In the circumstances of the time, the idea of abandoning strategic bombing was scarcely a practicable proposition."[25]

This seems pretty strongly stated. *Why* was the idea of abandoning strategic bombing (at least temporarily) such an impracticable proposition? Consider this comment from a fairly important source, the British Prime Minister. Churchill stated in July 1942 that

> In the days when we were fighting alone, we answered the question: "How are you going to win the war?" by saying: "We will shatter Germany by bombing." Since then the enormous injuries inflicted on the German Army and manpower by the Russians, and the accession of the manpower and munitions of the United States, have rendered other possibilities open.[26]

These other possibilities included diverting the aircrew of the RAF from attacking Germany to direct support of the ground campaign in North Africa and later in Sicily and Italy, as well as to the destruction of the German U-Boat threat in the North Atlantic. Moreover, considerable resources could have been shifted away from the building of heavy bombers to the expansion of the army and navy (a possibility that many, although few within the RAF, strongly supported). Even in terms of strategic bombing itself, there could have been a continued effort to develop improvements in navigation and aiming until a more effective (and certainly more morally attractive) strategy of precision bombing was available for adoption. In the event, such alternatives were basically set aside, and the area offensive went ahead unabated.

OBLIGATIONS

If the bombing of German cities can not be defended in terms of an unequivocal military necessity, the obvious question is why it proceeded nonetheless. At this point, it is necessary to give a little more attention to the very notion of military necessity. The concept is usually framed in terms of what measures are necessary to gain victory, presumably in a just cause. Yet for some this definition is too narrow. They would assert that necessity implies anything that will have the effect of limiting suffering to one's own forces and, a connected matter, will bring victory as rapidly as possible, not just eventually. Thus this comment from General Dwight Eisenhower in his memoirs: "Military plans, I believed, should be devised with the single aim of speeding victory."[27] The issue here is raised in stark terms by Britain's decision to go ahead with the area offensive in 1942 despite the fact that other possibilities, as Churchill put it, presented themselves. It might be argued that abandoning the strategic air offensive in 1942, or at least postponing it until relatively precise air strikes against Germany became possible, could have lengthened the war and thus created the prospect of greater casualties for the British armed forces. After all, the systematic destruction of German cities was bound to have at least some effect on Germany's capacity to make war. Why abandon such an effort for the sake of saving German lives only to put at risk the lives of the just, that is, Allied soldiers fighting the Nazis?

The question becomes whether there are any limits to what a country may do militarily in order to save the lives of its own soldiers. Is it permissible to apply fire and sword to the enemy indiscriminately if this will have the effect of saving even one combatant on one's own side? This is a difficult issue to resolve, for obviously almost any type of military action theoretically can lead to the saving of lives amongst one's soldiers. Arthur Harris, for one, had no doubt about how to resolve this (apparent) dilemma. In response to Churchill's famous minute calling the bombing of Dresden a "serious query" against Allied policy, he observed that "I do not personally regard the whole of the remaining cities of Germany as worth the bones of one British Grenadier."[28] Among many extraordinary statements offered during the war by the head of Bomber Command, this must surely rank among the most extraordinary. Was Harris really arguing that the killing of indeterminate thousands of additional German civilians was morally counterbalanced by the saving of one British soldier's life?

What is really at stake here is the whole notion of obligations or what Kant called "perfect" and "imperfect" duties.[29] Simply stated, the former involve obligations that are absolute and commanding on the individual or the group; the latter are obligations that, while compelling, are nevertheless subject to modification or even temporary non-performance in certain circumstances. In terms of our own focus, the relationship between ethics and war, I would suggest that there are three categories of duties that present themselves to governments. The first and truly perfect obligation is to one's own soldiers and to the civilian population as a whole. Governments have no real purpose other than securing the life and welfare of their subjects, and such a duty can never be foresworn, at least by governments who genuinely aspire to serve their people's interests.

The other two types of duties impinging on governments in wartime may be described as imperfect but they exist nonetheless, the assumption being that all individual human beings have certain rights that continue to obtain even in the midst of war. Above all this means the right to life unless there are compelling factors that temporarily demand that this right be set aside (e.g., in battle itself). In descending order of obligation, such duties have to do with the population of "friendly" or allied countries and then with the soldiers and civilians of the enemy. Some might argue that the level of obligation toward friends and allies should be counted as perfect as that displayed toward one's own citizens, but in practice it is difficult to imagine—or expect—that governments will approach their well-being in precisely the same terms as their own.

The Case of the French Civilians

It is striking, in any case, that the British government in World War II did appear to recognize at least the second realm of obligation. Evidence for this may be found in British attitudes toward air strikes in the so-called occupied countries. Given the ferocity of Bomber Command's assault on German cities, and the seeming willingness by London to accept unlimited German civilian casualties, it is instructive indeed to observe how—in a different context—the British government displayed considerable concern about the vulnerability of civilians to air attack. A prime example can be seen in the period prior to the invasion of Europe and involved a debate over strategy to which we have already referred.

At a critical meeting on March 25, 1944, all the major Allied military figures involved in the air war against Germany met in London to decide how the British and American air forces could best be utilized in support of the coming D-Day invasion. One of the decisions that ensued from this conference was the effective suspension of Bomber Command's area offensive over the Nazi heartland. The British bombing force, until further notice, would be assigned to direct tactical support of Operation Overlord, and in particular concentrated attacks on the railroad marshalling yards and repair facilities of northwestern Europe (the so-called Transportation Plan identified with Solly Zuckerman). This would make it extremely difficult for the Germans to move men and supplies to the invasion front.

For present purposes what is important about this debate was London's uneasiness about the Transportation Plan. Concerns were expressed about the actual military effectiveness of a concentration on the German rail system. The British also presented a moral query, however, that focused on the large number of Belgian—but especially French—civilian casualties that were likely to result from implementation of the Transportation Plan, especially given the fact that the marshalling yards were concentrated in urban areas. Prime Minister Churchill asked Lord Cherwell, of all people, to undertake some calculations about the likely losses, and on the basis of his estimates the War Cabinet asserted that some 40,000 civilians in the occupied territories might be killed along with another 120,000 wounded. On this basis London suggested that attacks on transport targets be authorized only when civilian casualties were not likely to exceed 100-150 persons.[30]

Churchill went so far as to appeal to President Roosevelt to intervene to limit what the former called the anticipated "French slaughters" and "the apparently ruthless use of the Air Forces, particularly of the Royal Air Force, on whom the brunt of this kind of work necessarily falls, and the reproaches that would be made upon the inaccuracy of night bombing."[31] The President refused, saying he had full confidence in Eisenhower's judgment. Even Arthur Harris objected to the Transportation Plan, at least partly on supposed moral grounds, referring himself to the loss of civilian life to be expected from the campaign. It should be mentioned here that as far back as October 1942, the Air Ministry stated in a directive to Bomber Command that the official rules governing air attacks in the occupied territories forbade intentional bombing of civilian populations and required aircrew to take reasonable care to avoid undue loss of civilian life. All attacks had to be on strictly military objectives. This directive went on to state that given the enemy's adoption of a policy of "unrestricted air warfare," such rules did not apply to the enemy homeland itself.[32]

It has to be recognized that aside from their putative ethical qualms, Churchill and his advisers were concerned about a very negative political backlash, not only in occupied France itself but from De Gaulle's Free French government-in-exile as well, if a large number of Frenchmen were killed in Allied bombing raids. As it happened, pre-invasion bombing in the occupied countries had a less draconian effect on the civilian population than Churchill and others had feared. One reason was that the aircrew were given specific instructions that every target had to be identified visually in order to reduce the risk to civilians. Approximately 12,000 civilians lost their lives.

This was a somber enough figure, but what stands out is the concern that London displayed in this instance about the suffering of innocent Allied civilians, and it was one that could be seen on other occasions during the war. Even before the debate over air support for the Normandy invasion, for example, Admiral Sir Dudley Pound, First Sea Lord, fretted about the danger to French civilians as a result of attacks on ports in the Bay of Biscay. He admitted that the question was how "we balance the loss of French lives against those of our own merchant seamen."[33] Consider, as well, the attack by Mosquito fighter-bombers on the Shell House in Copenhagen, which was Gestapo headquarters in the city. The raid was designed to destroy all of the Gestapo records on the Danish resistance and to kill as many Gestapo personnel as possible. A major worry in this operation, however, was the possibility of extensive Danish civilian casualties. A debate unfolded on whether such casualties would be counterbalanced by the value of crippling Gestapo operations, and the decision was to go ahead. As it turned out, one of the Mosquitos crashed into a convent near the target, and a second wave of aircraft, thinking this was the target, bombed the wreckage of the convent, causing considerable loss of life among the children. As Air Chief Marshal Sir Basil Embry commented, "naturally this unfortunate incident caused great sorrow and distress in the [Bomber Command] Group," even though, he claimed, the Danes accepted it stoically as a legitimate "blow for freedom."[34]

Duties to the Enemy

The whole debate concerning Allied bombing strategy in the occupied countries raises a fairly important question. From an ethical standpoint, is there any defensible difference between killing "friendly" civilians and enemy civilians? If the British government was so sensitive to civilian suffering in France and other places, should this concern not have been expressed with respect to German citizens as well? Churchill may have revealed his own conceptions on this score when he deplored the death of French civilians as being "among a friendly people who have committed no crimes against us, and not among the German foe, with all their record of cruelty and ruthlessness."[35]

Such an attitude, however (perhaps) understandable, can not gainsay the fact that even in the case of the enemy duties do exist for a warring government. It may be reasonable to assert that these are more imperfect than in the case of one's own soldiers and civilians or those of Allied nations. Yet they hardly disappear even in the carnage of war. Indeed a standard philosophical proposition governing proper moral reasoning is the requirement of "universalization," which in essence means that before making a decision one must take into appropriate consideration the interests and rights of *all* effected parties. This does not mean that certain of these may not be given greater weight than others, but it does demand a reasonable attempt at balancing conflicting claims of groups or individuals.[36]

The idea that even the enemy retains certain rights in wartime inevitably rests on the notion that there is no essential difference in the sanctity of life. In the strictest sense, this applies even in the realm of the soldier. Thus few would countenance the systematic slaughter of enemy soldiers attempting to surrender on the basis that some might be concealing weapons and intending to do harm to one's own men. The principle applies even more, however, in balancing the welfare of one's own combatants with those of the enemy civilian population who are not combatants. By what moral calculus can we say that the death and injury of enemy civilians is essentially irrelevant as long as there is at least some prospect that such suffering will save a single life among one's soldiers? The mere fact that a state of war exists does not remove the legitimate claims of enemy civilians for a reasonable chance to go on living. In order to protect such rights, it may be necessary for the soldier to accept a somewhat higher degree of risk (no one is demanding that they simply sacrifice themselves for the sake of enemy non-combatants).

There are some professional soldiers who have at times recognized this principle. In the early days of the Vietnam War, for example, it was common for the South Vietnamese army to call in artillery or an air strike on a village in response to a single sniper shot from the hamlet. American adviser John Paul Vann strongly objected to this practice. He did so partly on pragmatic grounds, which was that such actions alienated the peasants and swelled the ranks of the Viet Cong. But he also offered a moral argument. Vann said that infantry should simply be sent in to find and kill the sniper. "If they did that," Vann admitted, "they would lose a soldier to a sniper every once in a while, but death was the risk of an infantryman's trade."[37] This seems a hard standard to accept, particularly from the point of view of those effected (one's own soldiers), but to abandon it would seem to remove any limits on the scale and type of legitimate violence in wartime.

There is something more here as well, and it is suggested by Vann's objections to the shelling of Vietnamese hamlets. Even if one takes the position that the only reasonable standard of conduct in war is what will gain victory most "cheaply"—effectively defined as the fewest casualties to one's own forces—it is often very difficult to know what a "cheap" policy would actually be. The indiscriminate killing of Vietnamese civilians, for example, likely made that particular conflict much longer, and much more costly, than a more measured strategy would have done, even if individual soldiers' lives were spared on particular occasions by the shelling and bombing. Moreover, there is a great deal of evidence (to be considered shortly) that the British concentration on area rather than precision bombing actually prolonged rather than shortened World War II. Since it is often difficult to demonstrate that a particular action is necessary in order to protect one's soldiers—the perfect duty of governments—all the more reason for proceeding cautiously in the decision to set aside the other standard rules of obligation, even when they involve the enemy himself.[38]

6

The Test of Experience

"It is worse than a crime, it is a blunder."

—French aristocrat Boulaye de la Meurthe
(commenting on the execution by Napoleon of the Duc d'Enghien)

In any discussion of applied ethics, one can speak of guidelines to moral judgment as deriving out of either "intuitions" or "consequences." An intuitive value judgment regards a certain action as invariably wrong (or right) regardless of its effects, and reflects the pure dictates of conscience. Consequentialism holds that a proper ethical analysis must depend on an estimate of the good and bad results of given actions or policies. Obviously, both of these standards presents complications. Thus there may be serious contradictions between and among different intuitive values. At the same time focusing on the consequences of actions leaves open how we can properly evaluate relatively better or relatively worse outcomes.[1]

In offering a moral critique of the area offensive, it is tempting simply to adopt an intuitive argument that the killing of over 500,000 German civilians by bombing was inherently a reprehensible act, an affront to the conscience, and an evil hardly to be defended because of its supposed contribution to Allied victory. Such a stance indeed commands respect, but it seems to me that the overall moral case against the area offensive is considerably strengthened—and indeed has to be strengthened—by a close examination of the real effects of British bombing policy and what type of contribution to victory it actually made. Examining the consequences of the area offensive is particularly important in this instance, because what we had was in fact a clash between two intuitive values: the sanctity of life and the sanctity of freedom (which required the defeat of the Nazi menace).

When this sort of contradiction exists, attention to the practical effect of different policies looms rather large. The central issue here thus becomes whether Britain's apparent violation of the war convention—overt attacks on the German civilian population—can be at least partially justified by their strategic effect in bringing about the Nazi defeat.

EXPECTATIONS AND RESULTS

Any overall assessment of the costs and benefits of British area bombing of Germany, invoking the principle of proportionality, is necessarily a complex one. Nevertheless there are certain conclusions about Bomber Command's operations that may be offered with a fair degree of confidence, and—a crucial point—should have been clear to one and all no later than the summer of 1944.

The Mirage of Morale

The notion that German morale could be shattered by a strategy of devastating German cities proved to be an entirely false premise. "Morale" in this sense basically meant the willingness of the German people to work for and support their government's war effort. For a variety of reasons, the carnage visited on Germany by British bombers never came close to having a real effect in these terms. The British Bombing Survey Unit itself conceded the point: "The effects of town area attacks on the morale of the German people were . . . very much over-estimated by all other ministries and departments through the course of the war. . . . There is no evidence that they caused any serious break in the morale of the population as a whole."[2] The United States Strategic Bombing Survey (USSBS) offered more or less the same conclusion:

> Under ruthless Nazi control they [the German people] showed surprising resis-
> tance to the terror and hardships of repeated air attack, to the destruction of their
> homes and belongings, and to the conditions under which they were reduced to
> live. Their morale, their belief in ultimate victory . . . and their confidence in
> their leaders declined, but they continued to work efficiently as long as the
> physical means of production remained. The power of a police state over its
> people cannot be underestimated.[3]

This analysis tends to stress the coercive capacity of the Nazi security apparatus to prevent disaffection, but one can also focus on the tendency of a population to rally around its leaders in times of crisis (especially in wartime) and to commit one's resources and will to the nation at a time of its maximum peril. In retrospect, it is surprising that any in the British government should have seriously argued that the Germans would be less resolute under the impact of bombing that the British themselves had been during the period of the Blitz, even given the fact that the weight of destruction visited on Germany was far greater than that delivered against Britain.

To say that the attempt to undermine German morale by area bombing didn't work is actually only one part, and perhaps the least important part, of a critique of this ostensible goal of British air attacks. Far more telling is the almost total lack of any systematic consideration on the part of British decision-makers as to *how* the "undermining of morale" was actually supposed to undercut the German war effort. In view of the fact that an assault on morale was one of the consistent items in the rationale for the area offensive against Germany, this is really rather an astonishing omission. Indeed, the idea that morale could well be the Achilles heel of the German war effort can only be regarded as an article of faith rather than rigorous analysis on the part of those directing Bomber Command's activities. Typical of the rather casual assumptions underlying it was the belief that German industrial workers, the main target of the area offensive, were far more likely to crack than the stolid German middle class (a premise particularly convincing to the aristocratic Sir Charles Portal).

The USSBS pointed to one gap in the reasoning concerning German morale: in a police state such as Nazi Germany, where individuals were executed for offenses as mundane as listening to foreign radio broadcasts, how was a loss of morale to be translated into some sort of mass political activity that would force the hand of the government toward peace? As the war progressed there was no doubt a growing disillusionment among the German people about the prospects for victory, and the devastation of bombing may have contributed to this feeling. At the same time people had to get on with their lives, produce an income from their jobs, try to sustain their personal relations, and so forth. The point is that, for the Germans as well as for the British (and presumably everyone else as well), the expected reaction of human beings under this sort of stress is simply to attempt to survive and hope for an end to the pain. This type of fatalism is reinforced when the state has a capacity and a willingness to employ large-scale coercion to prevent open disaffection.

Ironically, the Nazi authorities themselves seemed to have felt that Bomber Command's morale thesis might actually have some validity, and as a result they closely monitored the spirit of the German people as the war progressed. A whole raft of reports assessing the public mood reached the desks of the SD (*Sicherheitsdienst*), the Ministry of Justice, regional government leaders, school and labor officials, and the Ministry of Propaganda. Such reports generally distinguished between *Stimmung,* or the outward expression of attitudes toward the regime, and *Haltung,* personal behavioral patterns in the face of the stress of the war and especially the bombing. The former was often described as somewhat problematical, but *Haltung* was generally good, meaning that people were simply determined to struggle on as best they could.[4]

To the extent that the undermining of German morale was a seriously-conceived goal for the area bombing offensive, moreover, one is hard put to explain why, at the very conference (Casablanca) where the Allies decided on the combined bombing offensive against Germany, they also settled on unconditional surrender as the formula for ending the war with the Nazis. All that Washington and London offered to the German people after Casablanca was the total dissolution of German governmental authority and the handing over of the fate of the German people to the arbitrary judgment of the victors. One can hardly conceive of a formula more likely to restrain defeatist impulses among demoralized Germans than this one.

Certainly German Propaganda Minister Joseph Goebbels couldn't, and, considering the source, his reactions to the Allies' insistence on unconditional surrender is a significant one. He had written in his diary in March 1942 that

> If I were on the enemy side, I should from the very first day have adopted the slogan of fighting against Nazism, but not against the German people. That is how Chamberlain began on the first day of the war, but, thank God, the English didn't pursue this line.[5]

After Casablanca, Goebbels expressed his further relief that "the English are making the same mistake . . . of not saying anything tangible about their war aims. I can only add, thank God; for if they were to put up a peace programme on the lines of Wilson's Fourteen Points they would undoubtedly create difficulties for us."[6] What difficulties might have been created for him and the other Nazi leaders by a different Allied approach to peace terms may be inferred from the effect the Casablanca declaration had in undermining the German opposition movement at the time. After the German disaster at Stalingrad, there were serious discussions among dissident elements in the General Staff as well in the civilian opposition about a coup against the Nazi regime and the establishment of a new

German government that would negotiate peace with the Allies. The Casablanca pronouncement, according to one authority, "gave the death blow to any hope that may have been entertained either by the 'Shadow Government' or by the oppositional elements in the General Staff, that their enemies would negotiate with a 'respectable' government."[7]

All in all, then, the morale thesis was basically a chimera that received a rather ritualistic obeisance from many supporters of Bomber Command but can hardly be considered as a morally legitimate objective of the area offensive since its military relevance was quite undeveloped and indeed impossible to demonstrate. Lord Cherwell's famous minute about the dehousing of German workers and the effect this would have on the German war effort stands as a prime piece of evidence in this regard. Cherwell focused almost entirely on some rather elementary mathematical calculations about what weight of bombs would lead to what number of dehoused workers. How dehousing would disrupt the German military effort was left almost totally implicit. Actually, Cherwell's argument would have had a lot more coherency if he had simply said that the object of the area offensive was to kill a great number of German civilians who would then be unavailable for arms production or service in the military.

One is driven to the conclusion that the arguments about German morale were in effect adopted *ex post facto* by the British government in order to provide a rationale for something the government planned to do anyway, and for perhaps quite different and unrelated reasons. Putting it this way helps to deal with the consistent argument offered after the war by supporters of Bomber Command that even if morale wasn't significantly affected by the area offensive, the decision-makers had no way of knowing this at the time since the implementation of a massive strategic air offensive—and its likely effects—were quite without precedent in the conduct of war. The fact is that the decision-makers never had any reasonable standard for measurement of the loss of German morale nor for its impact on the German war effort. Since they had no actual notion of what they were trying to achieve, we can't exculpate them simply by saying they were "mistaken" in their assessments. In reality, they never had any assessments, at least as the term is commonly understood to mean a careful weighing of costs and gains, causes and effects.

Bombs To Prevent Bombs

A second inescapable conclusion about the area bombing offensive against Germany is that it proved to have only a modest impact on German arms production. Consider for a moment the devastation of Hamburg in July 1943. There is no question but that the old Hanseatic city suffered grievously on those warm mid-summer nights. Yet the question is what effect this particular famous victory really had in terms of damaging the German war effort. Within three weeks, gas and electricity had been restored to most homes and factories, and by September the port of Hamburg was able to handle 160,000 tons of cargo, only 40,000 less than in July. U-boat construction in the city was not significantly affected, nor was the output of aircraft.[8] Subsequent analyses revealed that overall war production actually returned to near-normal in the Hamburg area within a few weeks after the attack, and an earlier labor shortage was largely relieved since a large number of service workers, shopkeepers, and office personnel now were perforce seeking other employment. Professor John Kenneth Galbraith recalled his findings as a member of the United States Strategic Bombing Survey: "In reducing, as nothing else could, the consumption of non-essentials and the employment of men in their supply, there is a distinct possibility that the attacks on Hamburg increased Germany's output of war material and thus her military effectiveness."[9]

This is not to say that the area offensive didn't have at least some effect on the German allocation of resources, particularly in diverting such resources from other operations. Sir Arthur Tedder estimates, for example, that anti-aircraft defenses absorbed almost 600,000 men by 1943 and about 900,000 by 1944. He suggests that anti-aircraft guns took around 30 percent of total German weapons production.[10] Even we accept these claims, however, the essential fact remains that during the first major phase of Bomber Command's assault on Germany, dating roughly from the spring of 1942 to the spring of 1944, German output of war materials, far from declining, actually increased steadily. For example, construction of aircraft of all types went from approximately 15,000 in 1942 to about 40,000 in 1944. Production of tanks increased sixfold. Overall output of weapons and ammunition peaked in the summer of 1944, reaching almost three times the level achieved at the beginning of 1942.[11] Production rates declined rapidly after August 1944, but, as will be discussed later, this was due not to the area offensive but to precision attacks against the German energy and transportation systems.

How to account for this quite unexpected outcome (unexpected, at least, from the perspective of Harris and other adherents of the area offensive)? Aside from the organizational talents of Armaments Minister Albert Speer, who undertook Herculean efforts in sustaining arms production even after the most devastating air attacks, there were two factors that deserve special mention. Air Marshal Arthur Tedder stresses that the policy of area bombing was based at least in part on the idea that the German economy was fully stretched and "that any general loss to German industry as a whole would have to be borne by the munitions industry." He also admits that this idea proved to be quite fallacious.[12] The notion of a German economy totally mobilized and regimented in support of the Nazi war effort was in fact largely a myth, at least until 1943. In reality, Hitler had always been concerned that a drastic decline in living standards might undermine German support for the war, and consequently he tolerated for a good while a really quite extraordinary diversion of German manufacturing capacity to civilian consumption. As late as October 1943, Speer himself acidly noted that in the preceding year German industry had produced some 120,000 typewriters, 200,000 domestic radios, 150,000 electric blankets, and 512,000 pairs of riding boots.[13] The point is that there was actually a great deal of slack in German war production until quite late in the struggle, and this meant that Hitler had considerable leeway in meeting any falloff of arms production resulting from the area bombing offensive. Indeed, almost until the end of the war, German factories manufactured more arms than there were German soldiers to employ them.

The second factor mitigating against the area offensive's having any pronounced effect on German military production was essentially technical. In order for Bomber Command to interrupt seriously the output of a particular item of significance, it was necessary for it to undertake repeated raids against a single target. This went against Arthur Harris's tendency to want to deal in turn with all the German cities on his "hit list," that is to say, the 60 major urban centers that he had originally designated for destruction by Bomber Command. In practice, Harris would order a major strike against one target and then move on to the next, which gave the Germans ample opportunity to restore manufacturing capacity in the areas already attacked.[14] There was also the fact that simply destroying a large number of buildings in the target area did not necessarily result in an equivalent falloff in arms production. As the USSBS put it, "The destruction of buildings . . . did not involve a proportionate destruction of vital machine tools and, as it turned out, the enemy was able to salvage such tools and to resume production at a far more rapid rate than had been anticipated."[15]

The USSBS reference to "anticipated" results from the bombing offensive against Germany raises a critical point: to what extent can we, *in retrospect,* challenge Bomber Command's strategy in the air war? In other words, it was anticipated that area bombing would have a substantial impact on German war production. In the event, the actual results were far less than expected, yet this does not in and of itself lay the decision-makers open to moral condemnation. They can stand accused in this regard only if (1) they had ample reason to know at the time the area offensive was unfolding that it was not really producing the results that had been postulated for it, and (2) they remained essentially immune to the evidence as it accumulated. To take a famous line from the Watergate investigations, we have to ask: what did British officials know and when did they know it?

The Web of Intelligence

It is self-evident that we typically have more knowledge about an important historical event after it has occurred than when it is actually taking place. Even so it is remarkable how Harris and his immediate circle in Bomber Command throughout the war continually issued optimistic assessments about the effectiveness of the area offensive that seemingly remained unaffected by the evidence that was at hand. During the Battle of Berlin, for example, Air Staff Intelligence at High Wycombe freely circulated quite extraordinary (and quite inaccurate) estimates of the havoc that was being wreaked on the German capital. At the end of 1943, it was asserted that a minimum of 320,000 Berliners had been dehoused, and that the actual figure was probably a good deal higher (perhaps on the order of 500,000 to 800,000). All this despite the fact that, as Harris himself admitted, the consistent cloud cover over Berlin prevented his aircrews from directly observing any of the effects of their bombing. Goebbels took a curious satisfaction in Bomber Command's illusions.

> The British are greatly overestimating the damage done to Berlin. Naturally it is terrible, but there is no question of 25 per cent of the capital no longer existing. The English naturally want to furnish their public with a propaganda morsel. I have every reason to want them to believe this and therefore forbid any denial. The sooner London is convinced that there is nothing left of Berlin, the sooner they will stop their air offensive against the Reich capital.[16]

This willing suspension of disbelief (that the area offensive might actually be doing little harm to the German war effort) has to be considered in terms of what information on the effects of British bombing was actually available. It so happens that a great deal of new data on the performance and sources of British intelligence during World War II has become available in recent years. The most famous revelation came in 1974, when Wing Commander F. W. Winterbotham, the former head of the air section of SIS (Secret Intelligence Service, or British foreign intelligence), published the first account of "Ultra." He revealed perhaps the best-kept secret of World War II, which was that the Allies had cracked certain key German codes and had been privy to German communications on vital military, political, and economic matters throughout the war.[17] General Dwight Eisenhower described Ultra as having made a decisive contribution to Allied victory, and it turned out that Churchill himself was an avid consumer of Ultra intercepts. Perhaps the leading historian of British intelligence states flatly that "no British statesman in modern times has had a more passionate faith in the value of secret intelligence than Winston Churchill." So intense was Churchill's interest in the subject that he often demanded to see raw intelligence reports before they had been analyzed by the professionals.[18]

Aside from Ultra, Britain also had several other important sources of information on the situation in Germany. Among these were Japanese diplomatic communications from Berlin to Tokyo (which could also be read), reports from German prisoners of war, accounts from neutral-country business and diplomatic personnel in Germany, and SIS agents in place. Also of some value were decryptions of German police signals as well as assessments by the Political Warfare Executive (PWE) of German newspaper and radio reports and propaganda. Finally, there was considerable information available from photographic intelligence. The Central Interpretation Unit at Medmenham, close to Bomber Command and USAAF headquarters, was a key contributor in this regard. Taking all these together, it now seems that London had a fairly wide range of data on the actual situation in Germany, even if precise estimates on given issues were sometimes hard to produce.

As the war progressed, the British had at their disposal a whole series of indicators bearing specifically on the effects of the area offensive. Some of their information suggested strongly that certain things were *not* happening as a result of the bombing; other data seemed to demonstrate that certain things *were* taking place despite the bombing. The most important example of the former had to do with German morale, whereas in the area of German arms production a quite different picture emerged.

One of the prime sources of information on the morale question was Japanese diplomatic decryptions, and these admittedly painted a somewhat ambiguous picture. On the one hand, they referred to moments of general panic, such as after the Hamburg raid, and they also depicted an increasing apathy among the German populace as the fortunes of war turned against Berlin. On the other hand, none of the data available to London suggested that a general revolt of the German people against their masters was foreseeable. In January 1944, for example, a message from the Japanese Ambassador in Berlin to Tokyo stressed that "internal collapse will certainly not be brought about by means of air raids; the vicissitudes of the war situation as a whole will constitute spiritually, as well as otherwise, the most important factor."[19] It is notable that Arthur Harris objected to the growing use of the term "apathy" by the intelligence analysts to describe the average German's reaction to heavy bombing, since this seemed rather passive in connotation and unlikely to produce any measurable effect on the Nazi regime

Perhaps equally displeasing to him were other intelligence assessments that the effect of the unconditional surrender formula, together with the repressive capabilities of Gestapo and SS detachments, were important in keeping German popular restiveness within limits. The Chiefs of Staff Joint Intelligence Committee (JIC), charged with coordinating information on conditions in Germany, summarized the situation as it seemed to be in early June 1944: "There is no evidence to suggest that the Allied bombing may shortly foment any effective opposition to the regime, or that the stamina and discipline of the German people have deteriorated to such an extent that a collapse may be considered likely within the next month or so." Almost three months later, the JIC issued an even stronger disclaimer to the effect that area bombing "was most unlikely to foment such opposition or produce such chaos as might lead to a collapse of the home front."[20]

It has to be accepted that there were, at times, divergent reports coming out of Germany concerning the effects of bombing on particular locales and population groups. The point is that there was never any solid body of evidence available, from open or secret intelligence sources, to suggest that the area offensive could undermine German morale to the extent of producing a tangible effect on the German war effort. As far as the material effect of Bomber Command's efforts was concerned, however, particularly the impact on German arms production, there was considerably more definite information at hand.

On the basis of the data available to it, the Air Ministry in November 1943 foresaw a steady increase in German fighter production despite Harris's area campaign of the previous months against the Ruhr and other targets. The predicted increase was of almost 300 aircraft, from a total of about 1,400 in July 1943 to 1,700 by April 1944 (these proved to be something of an underestimate). When the Casablanca Directive had first been issued, it was hoped that the total German fighter force would be no more than 650 by the spring of 1944 as a result of the Allied air campaign. Harris was seemingly unmoved by these figures, however, and moved resolutely ahead to the Battle of Berlin, yet another application of the theory of the area offensive. He did so despite the objections of the director of Bomber Operations, Sid Bufton. Bufton argued that the decision to focus on Berlin—in preference to targets having a bearing on Germany's fighter strength—was as great a mistake as that made by the Germans in the summer of 1940, when during the Battle of Britain they turned their attention away from Fighter Command's infrastructure to attack London and other British cities.[21]

We have already detailed how overall German arms production actually reached its peak in the summer of 1944 despite (or because of) Bomber Command's commitment to the area offensive. Again, Allied planners had ample information testifying to this fact, including a decryption of a report by the Japanese Ambassador in Berlin describing an interview he had had with Albert Speer, the German armaments minister. Speer indicated that in the period since the Hamburg raid the amount of damage to arms factories per bomb dropped had gone down by 60 or 70 percent. Allied claims that they had contributed to a 30 percent drop in arms output were fundamentally in error. Speer suggested that the pattern of bombing first one city and then moving on to another was actually a great advantage to German production, since it allowed for a restoration of output in each city in turn. Munitions production in Hamburg, for example, was now 140 percent of what it had been before the raids of July 1943. Speer did indicate that Allied attacks on German oil installations were of quite a different character and that such "scientific raiding" might deal a fatal blow to Germany if pursued.[22]

In weighing what Allied leaders knew about Germany's war position, there is (ironically) no better example of their being in possession of quite certain information than was the case with German oil production. Needless to say, oil was the virtual mother's milk of the German (and Allied) war machine, and, at least in the latter stages of the war, the Allies possessed definite indicators as to the German fuel situation. Largely because of Ultra, and also due to extensive photographic reconnaissance (PR), the drastic decline in German petroleum reserves as a result of Allied bombing was amply documented. The flood of information from decrypts and other sources led the Allied Joint Intelligence Committee to conclude on July 14, 1944, that in view of German oil shortages it was hard to see how Germany could avoid complete collapse before the end of the year, provided intensive bombing of refineries and synthetic petroleum facilities continued. Hard data suggested that German fuel production in fact had fallen, in the preceding four months, to a level that provided only about 50 percent of the minimum needed for German combat operations. This was an especially striking finding since, given the need to provide tactical support for the D-Day invasion, Allied bombing of German oil targets had previously received only limited emphasis—and even then was undertaken more by the Americans than the British.

Despite the above assessments, throughout the fall of 1944 Bomber Command devoted the majority of its effort to area bombing of German cities. As one historian has summarized the situation, Harris "in his capacity as head of Bomber Command . . . resisted the call to focus his strength against Germany's oil resources, preferring to put his faith, which all Allied intelligence including Ultra had shown to be misplaced, in the creation of fire-storms and rubble."[23] It was not until the beginning of 1945 that British airmen turned to a major effort against petroleum. In the process, together with the American air force, they succeeded in reducing German oil production to a trickle. An important point is that Bomber Command's reversion to the area offensive after September 1944 eased the pressure on the German oil infrastructure (despite continued American attacks) and allowed them to increase production significantly, a fact again amply documented by the available intelligence.

To summarize, then: there was considerable evidence in the later stages of the war, from a variety of intelligence sources, that the area offensive was having a relatively inconclusive effect on German morale and even less of an effect on German arms production. At the same time, there was lots of evidence that a concentrated assault on German oil, together with other precision attacks against such targets as aircraft factories and the German transportation system, would prove decisive. All this, says one leading student of British intelligence, was passed on to relevant authority. Yet the area offensive continued as before, since "the truth of Ultra did not suit the champions of heavy bombing."[24]

In returning to the theme of proportionality, and to the question of what did British officials know and when did they know it, the answer seems relatively clear: they had reason to know a lot (about the ineffectiveness of the area offensive) and to know it as early as 1943; they had even more reason to know it in the latter stages of the war. Thus an ethical critique of the area offensive can't be dismissed simply as retroactive moralizing. Relevant officials had the necessary information *at the time* to make the appropriate moral (and practical) judgment, which was that no claims of military utility could possibly justify the mass slaughter of German civilians being undertaken.

It has been rightly suggested that "awareness of the consequences of one's actions seems a necessary if not sufficient condition for moral conduct. . . . the principle seems [especially] beyond dispute for public officials deciding important policy issues."[25] What seems particularly incomprehensible in this regard is the way in which Arthur Harris and his supporters preferred to cling to their illusions about the effectiveness of area bombing when all around them was evidence that they were living in a world of illusions. Just as difficult to accept, however, was the performance of those in the top leadership outside the cocoon of High Wycombe, who were seemingly capable of more reasoned analysis of the data and indeed were persuaded by it that area bombing was basically ineffective. This greater realism did not lead them to demand that Harris abandon his fantasies and adopt a course of action that would have been both pragmatically and ethically more appropriate.

DOING GOOD AND DOING WELL

In offering a practical—and, in consequence, a moral—critique of the area bombing offensive, we could perhaps content ourselves with suggesting that area bombing had much less military effect than was claimed and thus was morally indefensible in terms of standards of proportionality. Yet the moral argument gains in force if it can be shown that there were viable alternatives to what was done and that these alternatives would have been far preferable in terms of military efficiency, not to mention a more suitable standard of moral conduct. As one Bomber Command veteran suggests, "Whether the methods by which victory in war is sought are morally permissible or not . . . is [determined] by the range of available alternatives, for the amount of destruction must be the minimum compatible with the achievement of the aim."[26]

By way of introduction a point made in the last chapter deserves elaboration. Within the government, the stress on airpower generally as the key to victory never enjoyed anything like a full consensus; indeed from the earliest days, there were prominent voices suggesting other possibilities. The fact that alternatives to concentrating on the strategic air offensive were always available (at least in theory) was attested to by the Lord Privy Seal, Sir Stafford Cripps, in a speech to the House of Commons shortly after Cripps had joined the War Cabinet in February 1942. Cripps seemed to take account of the vastly changed strategic situation occasioned by the entry, first of the Soviet Union and later of the United States, into the war:

> I would remind the House that this policy [the strategic air offensive] was
> initiated at a time when we were fighting alone against the combined forces of

Germany and Italy and it then seemed that it was the most effective way in which
we, acting alone, could take the initiative against the enemy. Since that time we
have had an enormous access of support from the Russian armies . . . and also
from the great potential strength of the United States of America. Naturally, in
such circumstances the original policy has come under review. . . . I can assure
the House that the Government are fully aware of the other uses to which our
resources could be put, and the moment they arrive at a decision that the
circumstances warrant a change, a change in policy will be made.[27]

Cripps's comments were not received very kindly at High Wycombe and
for obvious reasons. In any case it is important to recognize what an
extraordinary share of British wartime production was devoted to her air
force. As of 1942, the RAF's bill for capital works alone was equal to about
one-sixth of the total national budget for all purposes, civilian and military,
in a typical prewar year. One estimate is that Britain assigned anywhere from
40 to 50 percent of her military output to the RAF, which meant that only
50 to 60 percent was left for the navy and army combined. A rather significant
admission of this basic commitment was provided by Sir James Grigg,
Secretary of State for War, in a statement to the House of Commons in March
1944. Grigg indicated that the "RAF programme is already employing more
workpeople than the Army programme, and I daresay that there are, in fact,
as many engaged on making heavy bombers as on the whole Army programme."[28] Professor A. V. Hill of Cambridge, a distinguished scientist and
former official at Whitehall, put the issue in stark terms as early as February
1942: "The disaster of this policy [emphasizing heavy bombers] is not only
that it is futile but that it is extremely wasteful, and will become increasingly
wasteful as time goes on."[29] In terms of pure cost effectiveness, the resources
the Germans gave to air defense and to reconstructing damaged factories and
railways were on balance distinctly less than the resources given to Bomber
Command to inflict the damage in the first place. A macabre statistic is that,
on average, it took almost three tons of British bombs to kill one German
civilian. Over the whole war, the average result of a single British bomber
sortie was less than three dead Germans, of whom perhaps one was a
production worker.[30]

The grip that Bomber Command had on British output of materiel, and the
subsequent feeding of Arthur Harris's belief that Bomber Command held the
key to success in the war against the Nazis, may perhaps be seen in Harris's
memorandum of December 7, 1943, to the Air Ministry. Harris argued that there
was "little doubt" that the Germans would capitulate once 40 to 50 percent of
their principal towns were destroyed. He went on to estimate that given an

expected loss rate of 5 percent in Bomber Command sorties over the next four months, matched against an anticipated production of 212 Lancasters each month, "it appears that the Lancaster force alone should be sufficient but only just sufficient to produce in Germany by April 1st, 1944, a state of devastation in which surrender is inevitable." All this would be possible, however, only if Bomber Command was given "priority in labour and materials over all conflicting claims."[31] This proposal was in effect a suggestion that the Royal Air Force be permitted to take over the British war economy.

It is more than a little interesting to ponder the consequences of a larger share of British arms production being given to the other services rather than to Bomber Command. What if, for example, additional effort had been given to the building of landing craft for amphibious operations, the scarcity of which was a major deterrent to an earlier invasion of France? We have already observed that as a consequence of giving first priority to supplying the RAF (and particularly Bomber Command) with its supposed needs, Britain was forced to purchase almost all of its transport aircraft, as well as a high percentage of its tanks and huge amounts of ammunition, from the United States. The basic fact is that there was no actual compulsion upon the British government to go all out in building up the strategic bomber force; there were ample opportunities in other areas of the war effort for (perhaps better) use of such resources.

Airpower Options

One way in which to approach the question of alternatives available to the British government is to suggest that there needn't have been so much emphasis on the bombers in the first place. Putting it this way serves as a rebuttal to one of the standard arguments of those favoring the area offensive, which was that the campaign against German cities was a military necessity. There is an equally powerful case to be made against the idea of military necessity if we can demonstrate that, even given the British emphasis on airpower, the capabilities of Bomber Command were badly misused. The evidence, in fact, does strongly suggest that not only did Bomber Command absorb a disproportionate share of British resources but that this outlay of personnel and materiel could have been employed far more effectively. In the earlier period of the war, to cite only two examples, a greater commitment to the anti–U-Boat campaign in the North Atlantic would have paid significant dividends as would have a more substantial effort in North Africa (conceivably resulting in the defeat of Rommel's Afrika Korps some months before its actual demise).

The issue of operational alternatives becomes particularly acute, however, in the last ten months of the war. A military historian and former RAF navigator summarizes the case this way:

> [The] strategic bomber forces had the possibility of bringing the German war machine to a dead halt, and it seems reasonable to suppose that they could have done so within 1944. By April 1945 they had done so. Their operations were decisive. They could have been decisive earlier. . . . After the middle of 1944 there was often, though not always, a choice between area attacks on towns and precise attacks on oil plants, railway targets and other installations. Owing to deep disagreements, the effort was divided to a greater extent than it need have been and it seems virtually certain that Germany's downfall could have been accelerated if a greater concentration had been achieved. Operationally it could have been achieved. If it had been, some months might have been taken off the duration of the war.[32]

This is really quite an extraordinary argument and one that is heavy with moral implications. *If* airpower could have brought the war to an earlier conclusion, the savings in life and treasure—and not just German life— would have been enormous, particularly given the fact that the heaviest bloodletting of World War II occurred in the last ten months of the struggle.

It is important to note, in this regard, that the opposition to Arthur Harris and his supporters didn't just come from those who were morally discomfited by the logic of the area offensive. Indeed it is striking how, almost from the beginning of that offensive, there were a number of expert and quite unsentimental voices outside High Wycombe who offered at times quiet and at other times more vocal opposition to the logic of devoting almost all of Bomber Command's resources to the destruction of German cities. The fact that this was so seems to make the moral defensibility of the area offensive all the more problematical. That is to say, if the overwhelming weight of professional opinion was in support of the rationale of city attacks, we might more easily dismiss the ethical cavils of the pacifists and the priests. Since the experts were far from unified on the pragmatic wisdom of the area offensive, the criticisms of the latter have to be viewed in a rather different light.

To be sure, little of the doubt expressed by the professionals was offered in ethical terms although it was not for that reason less strongly felt. A number of these individuals conceded as well that in view of the technical and resource difficulties confronting Bomber Command in 1942, it might be inevitable that the aircrew should for the short term concentrate on the relatively simple task of devastating German industrial cities. The assumption, however, was that once

these technical and resource difficulties were resolved (e.g., more heavy bombers, more navigational aids), it would be logical to revert to a strategy that
promised more concrete returns than simply killing lots of German civilians.

The governmental opposition to Harris's area offensive strategy could be
found in various places. Notable was the resistance within the Air Ministry
itself, and in particular within the Directorate of Bomber Operations. By the
end of 1943, there was an increasing disillusionment with Harris's claims
concerning the achievements of Bomber Command. His assertions were
frequently refuted by specific facts and figures assembled by the Air Staff,
and given the development of the Pathfinder Force and navigational aids
such as OBOE and H2S, the hope of many was that the new equipment and
improved training and tactics would lead the way toward more precise night
attacks on targets in Germany.[33]

The staff of the Directorate of Bomber Operations were the personal advisers
to Sir Charles Portal on all matters relating to bombing policy. Group-Captain
S. O. Bufton, an experienced Bomber Command pilot, became head of the
directorate in 1942 and immediately expressed his doubts about the wisdom of
the area offensive. Bufton became famous (or notorious, depending on one's
point of view) for his adherence to the concept of precision bombing. He regarded
area bombing as only a temporary expedient until precision attacks on German
targets could be achieved. It was Bufton, for example, who led the way in the
creation of the Pathfinder Force, which he saw as a critical step in the British
ability to undertake genuinely selective bombing.

As the war progressed, Bufton became increasingly frustrated by Harris's
seeming ability to defy the growing consensus within the Air Ministry that
Bomber Command was capable of a general campaign of precision bombing
of Germany that would produce far better results than indiscriminate attacks
on German cities. For example, in responding to Harris's boast that his
Lancasters could force Germany to surrender by the spring of 1944 without
the necessity of a land campaign in Western Europe, Bufton wrote Portal
along the following lines:

> The C-in-C [Harris] states that there can be little doubt that the enemy would be
> caused to capitulate by the destruction of between 40 and 50 per cent of the principal
> German towns, and that the Lancaster force alone should be sufficient, but only just
> sufficient, to produce in Germany by 1 April 1944 a state of devastation in which
> surrender is inevitable. I am of the opinion that it would be sounder for Bomber
> Command to subordinate as far as may be necessary their efforts to achieve a quick
> victory in favour of helping the Americans to deploy their strength so that the
> Combined Bomber forces (and *Overlord*) may together achieve a certain victory.[34]

In somewhat more direct language, Bufton assessed Harris's strategy as being that of "a gambler doubling up on each losing throw" (this with specific reference to the Battle of Berlin). Following the successful D-Day invasion, Bufton threw his weight behind those attempting to convince Harris that attacks on German synthetic oil installations offered the most promising short-cut to victory.[35]

Aside from Bufton, perhaps the other most prominent voice within the Air Ministry calling into question the area offensive was that of Sir Norman Bottomley, deputy chief of the Air Staff. Actually, Bottomley's attitude toward Harris's strategy was not quite as clear-cut as that of Bufton. When Bottomley was a staff officer at Bomber Command in 1940, for example, he opined that the aim of the bombers must be "primarily to destroy the enemy's will to win the war, leaving the destruction of his means to win the war an incidental or indirect task." His seeming commitment to morale as the main objective of the bombing offensive, which of course implied area bombing, evidently remained with Bottomley for a time until his reading of the results of the area offensive converted him into an open skeptic.

By the fall of 1943, he had become a tacit and sometimes open ally of Bufton in querying Bomber Command's strategy. He had become especially concerned about the need to reduce German fighter strength. At the beginning of 1944 he wrote Harris to the effect that it was imperative that he "attack, as far as practicable, those industrial centres associated with the German fighter air-frame and ball-bearing industry."[36] On September 14, 1944, he sent a further directive to Harris stating that the sole first priority of the bombing offensive should be oil, with transportation links and tank and vehicle production as second priority. Bottomley had become one of Harris's dreaded panacea merchants.

The fact seems to be that as the war progressed, and certainly by the middle of 1943, support within the ranks of the Air Ministry for Harris's area offensive had generally eroded, and his adherents were steadily reduced to a relatively small group of acolytes at High Wycombe. Again, this was not necessarily because of moral qualms about the devastation of German cities. Nevertheless the revolt against Harris's strategy is quite notable, including as it did a number of professional airmen with previous operational experience with Bomber Command. The skepticism of these men was matched by a general disillusionment among the civilian staff of the Air Ministry, especially those offering expert scientific advice in the operational research division of the Ministry.

Sir Arthur Harris's attitude toward these dissenters was a mix of contempt and airy dismissal. He commented bitterly in a letter to Portal in January

1945 that "I note no inclination on your part, or anywhere else in the Air Ministry for that matter, to discuss with me, or even to consult me beforehand upon such matters as the strategic policy applicable to my force, or to take me into confidence or consultation thereafter." That earlier attempts to do so had been basically exercises in frustration was a point that Harris (perhaps unwittingly) omitted. He described Bufton as "an ex-Station Commander of my Command who has always been persona non grata to me and my staff." Harris let the cat out of the bag in a follow-up communication to Portal when he said that his problem with Bufton was that he appeared to ignore a "major and essential part of his job, namely, to press forward the interests, urgent requirements and doctrines of Bomber Command . . . while spending much of his time trying to run my command."

Harris seemed to have somewhat more forgiving views on Bottomley, but he crisply reminded Portal that Bottomley was his "junior in the Service" and claimed that he had tried to work loyally with the deputy chief of the Air Staff after Bottomley had assumed executive control of Bomber Command after September 1944, "yet little I now do appears to meet with approval."[37] That there was widespread disapproval of Harris's continuation of the area offensive among various officials in the Air Ministry was certainly true. On the other hand, given the disinclination of Harris's superiors to force him to take their advice, such complaints could hardly be taken as particularly threatening, certainly not to the extent of persuading him to consider any real change in his bombing policy.

A DIFFERENT STRATEGY FOR BOMBER COMMAND

It is necessary now to summarize what options were open to Bomber Command aside from the area offensive and to do so in at least some detail. We begin with a fairly elementary but rather important point: the majority of German military industry (as in all industrial countries) was located on the outskirts of the cities. Bomber Command's essential strategy during the area offensive was to hit the center of cities. The continuing result was that the most vital part of the German war-making machine was left relatively untouched by city bombing. This was particularly evident, for example, in the two most notorious Bomber Command attacks of World War II, those on Hamburg and Dresden. In each case, the supposed military objectives of these raids, i.e., the submarine facilities in Hamburg and the rail marshalling yards in Dresden, emerged almost unscathed.

Now it may be objected that for a good period of the war the only thing that Bomber Command could be reasonably confident of hitting was the center of German cities. To put it slightly differently, by using these centers as the primary aiming points, the British could be reasonably confident that their bombs would strike at least some theoretically relevant targets rather than simply being wasted in a vain attempt to hit the industries located on the perimeter of the city. This is not a small objection, but it is also not one that is completely self-evident if Harris and his supporters had put their focus earlier in the war on developing greater precision in night (and even day) attacks. Indeed there is considerable evidence that such an effort would have been amply rewarded.

Aside from improved navigational techniques and new guides to bombing accuracy, an obvious requirement for precision bombing over Germany, and most especially in daylight, was the use of long-range fighter escorts. It was the introduction of such aircraft, in the form of the P-51 Mustang, that gave the Americans the capability for sustained daylight bombing in the far reaches of the Reich. Ironically, the Mustang had a distinctly British accent. It originated in a request from the Royal Air Force to North American Aviation, who built the first prototype in 1940. Some 600 had been provided to the RAF by 1941, but at this point they lacked a sufficiently powerful engine. Five of the aircraft were subsequently fitted with Merlin 61 engines, and the production line in America was modified to accommodate American-built Packard Merlins. By adding additional fuel tanks, the Mustang was converted into a plane that could outperform all the standard German fighters.[38] Yet, by some strange circumstance, the RAF failed to benefit from this technological breakthrough while the Americans employed large numbers of the redesigned Mustangs in their own operations.

One conclusion is that Arthur Harris resisted the introduction of great numbers of the Mustangs to Bomber Command since this would have had the effect of negating his insistence on nighttime area bombing as the only feasible strategy for his aircrew. A. J. P. Taylor summarizes the point by saying that "no senior RAF leader sought the answer of long-range fighters, just as no senior British general of the First World War sought the answer of tanks to the problem of trench warfare."[39] The implication was that in both instances the adoption of the new technology would have contradicted (or rendered irrelevant) long-cherished beliefs in a particular military doctrine.

This point receives even greater support from the saga of the Mosquito fighter-bomber. The development of the Mosquito presented another range of possibilities for Arthur Harris that could well have changed the entire direction of the air offensive. The De Havilland Mosquito was able accurately to mark bombing targets from extremely high altitudes (around 28,000 feet). The height at which it flew made it possible to use navigational systems such as Oboe to maximum effect. Moreover, the Mosquito could fly at around 350 MPH, which enabled it to deliver a 4,000-pound bomb to the farthest corners of Germany with enemy fighters having only the flimsiest chance of catching it. Mosquito casualties over Germany were indeed a fraction of those suffered by the Lancasters.[40] Strictly from the point of view of resources, the Mosquito featured a crew of two compared to the five or six in a four-engined bomber. The fact seems to be then that adoption of the Mosquito as Britain's standard bomber would have saved a great deal of money, not to mention manpower.

Why, then, was the Mosquito not chosen as the primary vehicle for Bomber Command's offensive against Germany? The reasons for this surprising omission may have had more to do with Bomber Command's own professional interests than with a concern about hitting more precise military targets in Germany. As one of the principal historians of Bomber Command has put it, the promise of increased accuracy from a fleet of Mosquitos was viewed more as a threat than a promise: "It was the very inflexibility of [Harris's] Main Force and its alleged unsuitability for operations demanding great accuracy and co-operation with other elements which partly enabled its Commander to pursue so independent a strategy. A bombing weapon as delicate and subtle as 300-400 Mosquitoes would, in all probability, have been coveted by Tedder, if not by Spaatz [head of the US Strategic Air Force]."[41] The point, then, is that the very crudity of Harris's forces was a major protection against their being taken over by other command authorities.

Attacking German Chokepoints

Leaving aside the missed opportunities in developing fighter escorts or in selecting the Mosquito as a primary instrument for Bomber Command, there is a legitimate debate about when Harris's aircrew did finally reach a point where they had a real choice between precision and area bombing. One of the principal British scientists working on problems of bombing accuracy states that as of late 1943 "had we realized the improvement in our bombing technique we might have abandoned area bombing earlier, or at least have put more effort into precision attacks at night. . . . But we had become so indoctrinated with the area policy that few of us realized that Portal's original oil bombing policy could now have been revived with a hope of success."[42] This is a rather significant admission to make, but in any case by the summer of 1944 it *was* recognized by virtually one and all that Bomber Command had now developed a genuine capacity for fairly precise bombing of German targets. Even Arthur Harris seemed to admit to this fact. He suggests (without apparent irony) that "it was not until the last year of the war that we had the technical equipment for such attacks [i.e., against key factories]." Another RAF veteran comments that when that stage was reached, it was actually possible, with vastly improved navigational and aiming devices, to place a heavier concentration of bombs on precision targets by non-visual than by visual methods.

The question then becomes how Bomber Command could have been employed in the last ten months of the war and, not incidentally, in a way that would have hastened victory and avoided unnecessary civilian suffering. The answer has been suggested already in our earlier discussion and needs only summary here. A concerted British and American attack on German oil installations (especially the synthetic petroleum plants) would have almost certainly produced decisive and immediate results. A special oil panel of the USSBS concluded after the war, for example, that "even a small part of the bombs dropped on cities would have sufficed to completely knock out oil targets at an early date."[43] As early as May 30, 1944, Albert Speer wrote to Hitler that "with the attacks on the hydrogenation plants, systematic bombing raids on economic targets have started at the most dangerous point. The only hope is that the enemy, too, had got an air staff. Only if it has as little comprehension of economic targets as ours would there be some hope that after a few attacks on this decisive economic target it would turn its attention elsewhere."[44] The success that Bomber Command enjoyed in attacking oil installations prior to the D-Day invasion, even though this constituted only a minor part of their operations, was only one example of what ordinary aircrew could now achieve when led to the target by experienced Pathfinders. In the immediate aftermath of the Normandy invasion there was a further Allied air effort against German oil facilities, undertaken almost entirely by the USAAF. Even though Spaatz's bombers devoted just 17 percent of their efforts to oil in July and August, the results were dramatic. Petroleum available to Germany fell from 715,000 tons in May to 472,000 tons in July. The Luftwaffe's supply of aviation fuel fell from 180,000 tons in April to only 10,000 tons by August.

Speer was hardly less concerned about the effect of Allied bombing raids on the German transportation system. He commented in November 1944 that a "successful continuation of these attacks would be capable of resulting in a production catastrophe of decisive significance for the further conduct of the war." A month later, he observed that "we were fortunate that the enemy did not put this far-reaching plan into effect until about six or nine months ago."[45] In the event, the assault on the German transportation system did eventually produce rather dramatic results. Basically the system had remained relatively intact until the spring of 1944, but after that it declined precipitously until it came virtually to a halt in early 1945. The Allied Strategic Air Targets Committee stressed how the attacks on transportation had a symbiotic relationship to German oil production. The output of oil products could not be distributed effectively, and shipments of coal, out of which much of the oil was produced, could not be delivered. In effect, there was a stranglehold at both ends of the petroleum production process.[46]

The Overall Report of the British Bombing Survey Unit offered a summary assessment of the elements leading to the collapse of the Nazi war machine:

> Three major factors were associated in Germany's defeat. The first and most obvious was the over-running of her territory by the armies of the Allies. The second was the breakdown of her war industry, which was mainly a consequence of the bombing of her communications system. The third was the drying-up of her resources of liquid fuel, and the disruption of her chemical industry, which resulted from the bombing of synthetic-oil plants and refineries.[47]

The specialists may quibble over whether the attacks on oil or transportation were most decisive, but what is striking about this analysis is the absence of any reference to the effect of general city bombing, which Bomber Command continued to emphasize right up to the last days of the war.

In an interrogation of Albert Speer in July 1948, the German armaments minister rated six different targeting systems in terms of their effect on the German military position. The area bombing of cities he ranked fifth in importance (barely ahead of attacks on naval installations, shipping activity, and airfields). In his own view, it was the "American attacks, which followed a definite system of assault on industrial targets, [which] were by far the most dangerous. It was in fact these attacks which caused the breakdown of the German armaments industry."[48] This is not to say that Bomber Command played no part in the assault on the German oil and transportation systems, nor that the Americans did not occasionally engage in general area attacks themselves (notably at Dresden). It is to say that Harris's insistence on continuing his area offensive almost certainly delayed the day of victory because of the lack of a unified Allied air campaign against the truly vulnerable linchpins in the German war effort.

The Removal of Arthur Harris

In considering the alternatives available to British decision-makers with respect to bombing strategy in the last year of the war, the question of removing Arthur Harris as head of Bomber Command inevitably reasserts itself. Enough has been said already to indicate that Harris would hardly have gone along with a new scheme of focusing on precise (or at least non-area) targets in Germany. Sacking Harris, of course, would not have been an easy decision to make for any of the principals involved, including Churchill, Portal, and Sinclair. We have already considered in some detail the factors that persuaded these men against the dismissal of Harris, particularly in the crucial summer and fall months of 1944. Yet the fact that Harris's ouster, or perhaps some kind of euphemistic "reassignment" to other duties, would have been an awkward step to take does not mean that it was beyond the realm of possibility.

The fact is that getting rid of Harris was a lot more conceivable in 1944 than it would have been earlier. There were several qualified candidates available to take his place who had developed a great deal of experience in Bomber Command's operations. Notable among these was Ralph Cochrane, perhaps the most imaginative of Harris's group commanders, who had developed advanced precision marking techniques as leader of 5 Group. Another possible replacement was Air Vice Marshal Donald Bennett, a man with extensive operational experience in Bomber Command, and whom Harris himself had described as "one of the most efficient and finest youngsters I have ever come across in the Service." Even Harris's own Deputy, Robert Saundby, might have stepped into the breach. Saundby seemed to be a fervent supporter of his chief in the area offensive, but his personal qualities were far different than Harris's, and he could be expected at least to consider alternatives to Bomber Command's strategy without the arrogant dismissal of any debate on the matter characteristic of Harris.

It was Harris's failure to make good on his boast of winning the war singlehandedly in the Battle of Berlin that could well have provided a logical point for relieving him of his duties. As of March 1944, it was clear that his area strategy had not only failed significantly to effect the German war-making capacity but had also been enormously costly in terms of resources, not to mention the lives of aircrew. In addition, a number of people at the Air Ministry, including Portal himself, had by this point grown rather weary of Harris's general obduracy and unwillingness (or inability) to discuss alternative bombing strategies. Since Harris had so few reservoirs of good will outside his immediate circle at High Wycombe, his removal from command would hardly have been an occasion for general lamentation among those who had dealt with him for the last two years.

There is evidence that Portal at least considered moving against Harris at the beginning of 1944. He is reported to have asked Bufton, "What do you think about the C-in-C then, Bufton? Do you think it might be good to have a change?" The exasperation of the Americans, the Ministry of Economic Warfare, and various departments of the Air Ministry were combining to make Harris's status at this point somewhat problematical. Yet aside from the essentially political factors involved in so dramatic a step as the sacking of Harris, it appears that a quite separate element existed in protecting the career of the head of Bomber Command. The fact is that Harris's superiors were uncertain at the beginning of the year as to whether any real alternative strategy in the air offensive against Germany would pay greater dividends than Harris's area bombing. The success of the American precision bombing campaign at this point was rather problematical, and the indecision about viable alternatives to the area offensive went a long way toward saving Harris.

The position later in 1944 was, of course, entirely different, and the failure of Harris's superiors to rein in him or in fact to relieve him of command is difficult to understand and even more difficult to excuse. All the circumstances now allowed a virtually unfettered Allied air campaign of relatively precise bombing of German oil and transportation targets. Moreover, there was manifold evidence that this effort could prove (and indeed was proving) to be decisive in the war against the Nazis. Nevertheless, Harris went blithely ahead, and was allowed to go blithely ahead, in smashing one German city after another in a virtual paroxysm of irrelevant destruction.

7

Final Reflections

> "The good that I would do, I do not,
> and the evil that I would not do, that I do!"
>
> —St. Paul (Romans 7.19)

The main burden of the moral argument here has been that whatever rationales may be offered for the British area bombing offensive against Germany prior to the spring of 1944, after that date it was quite without ethical justification. If this assertion is accepted, it is a matter of some importance to consider why the area offensive, after a brief pause, resumed in September 1944 and maintained its intensity almost to the last days of the war. In many ways there is no issue more critical to the central purpose of this book. When both practical military considerations (the new capability for, and obvious effectiveness of, precision bombing) as well as the dictates of reasonable proportionality in British military strategy are combined, it seems almost incomprehensible that Bomber Command should have continued—and been allowed to continue—its assault on German civilian life in the final months of World War II. It is well to recall, in this regard, that about 80 percent of all the bomb tonnage dropped on Germany by the Allied air forces came during the last ten months of the war.

THE REASONS WHY

To be sure we have already touched on some of the possible explanations for what happened, in particular the obsession of Arthur Harris with city attacks and the inability or unwillingness of his superiors to rein him in. Yet we need to probe deeper, for there are some more fundamental aspects of the situation that seem to go beyond simply command arrangements or arguments about the utility of different strategies. As with a lot of other aspects of the war effort, it may be seriously misleading to assume that in this instance the British government adopted or maintained a course of action only after rational calculation of precise costs and benefits. As Michael Sherry has written, the development of the area offensive (and other bombing in World War II) "certainly resulted from choices but not from a moment of choice. . . . If anything characterized [this] era, it was the capacity of leaders to avoid the appearance of choice."[1]

The Force of Momentum

One factor in the resumption of the area offensive seems particularly apropos to Sherry's argument. It is somewhat difficult to discuss because it implies that the most violent period of Bomber Command's operations against German cities was an essentially mindless exercise unconnected to any real military analysis, not to mention any reasonable moral sensitivity to the suffering of civilians. Nevertheless, it would appear to have been an important impetus to the second phase of the city bombing campaign undertaken by the British.

By early fall 1944, the effect of earlier decisions taken by the British government concerning the allocation of military resources began to be fully realized. The production of aircraft for Bomber Command had "acquired a remorseless momentum of its own". In 1940 there were only 41 four-engined heavy bombers delivered to the RAF, and in 1941 there were some 500. This increased the following year to about 2,000, and for 1943 and 1944 the figures were 4,600 and 5,500 respectively. At its peak, the Ministry of Aircraft Production was employing about 1,700,000 people.[2]

Bomber Command had more than 1,000 heavy bombers in its squadrons as of the summer of 1944 and frequently more aircrew at its disposal than there were planes to fly. By April 1945, there were some 1,600 available to the RAF, and during the last four months of the war the average daily strength of heavy aircraft was over 1,400.[3] As noted, there were so many aircrew coming out of final training that many were designated as "surplus to requirements" for actual operational duty, creating a situation in which there were a number of young men anxious to show their stuff but with decreasing opportunities to do so. In the face of this enormous surge in the number of aircraft as well as aircrew available to Bomber Command, it became a question of how to employ the vast array of planes and personnel at the disposal of Arthur Harris. It seemed hardly thinkable to allow this armada to even partially stand down since so much political and military authority had previously been committed to the buildup of Bomber Command as a decisive weapon against Germany. Moreover, in line with the past belief in the merits of the area offensive, most aircrew had basically been trained in the techniques of the nighttime destruction of cities. Very few pilots wanted to become "beginners" again by being instructed in quite a different set of bombing tactics.[4]

The latter comments may seem contradictory to what we have written before about the capacity of Bomber Command for daylight precision bombing after the summer of 1944. It has been argued that Bomber Command should have been forced to abandon the area offensive in favor of selective attacks on German oil and transportation targets. The contradiction is, however, more apparent than real. There was a significant segment of Bomber Command (e.g., 5 Group, famous for its accurate marking techniques under the leadership of Leonard Cheshire) who were available for a precision bombing campaign. A concerted effort to train (or retrain) at least a good number of other aircrew in precision bombing, using the new navigational and aiming devices now available, was also a possibility open to Harris and his colleagues. What this would have required, however, was a (most unlikely) conversion of Harris to the merits of precision bombing along with a corresponding willingness to overcome the resistance of many of his present pilots to the new emphasis in targeting. Realistically, such a change in strategy would have implied that a number of Harris's bombers would have simply refrained from city attacks during this reorientation period. Since Harris had so little belief in precision bombing, he was hardly interested in persuading his aircrew that there was merit in adopting new methods of operation. Moreover, he recoiled before the idea of leaving any of his aircraft on the ground no matter what the justification for doing so.

The above circumstances help to explain an attack such as that delivered on Würzberg in March 1945. Würzberg was a city of considerable historic although little military importance, but that was precisely the point. Essentially all the targets in Germany that were of military significance had been reduced to rubble. Even Harris admits that by this time it had become much more difficult to identify any further genuinely strategic targets. At the same time, his philosophy continued to be that bombing anything in Germany was better than bombing nothing. Hence Würzberg became a logical victim for Bomber Command simply because it had been relatively untouched—and, above all, because it was there.

Under all the circumstances detailed above, then, there was an almost overwhelming impetus to continue the area offensive virtually to the last days of the war. There were the vested interests of those in Bomber Command who had staked their professional reputations on the military logic of attacking German cities. There was a vast array of equipment and people who had to be kept occupied and who were basically trained for indiscriminate bombing. The British government had committed itself to providing ever-expanding resources for carrying out the area offensive. The momentum created by their earlier decisions proved impossible to resist.

Pride of Place

In accounting further for the reversion of Bomber Command to the area offensive in the last year of the war—as well as its stubborn insistence on the wisdom of city attacks prior to this time—it is easy enough to focus on the unusual independence of Arthur Harris and his ability to deflect or defy the supposed desire of higher authority to adopt a different strategy. Any reasonable assessment would seem to suggest, however, that his superiors, while often exasperated by his pigheadedness and obvious distortion of the record, nevertheless retained a sneaking admiration for the fact that Bomber Command was the one service that seemed to defy the growing American domination of Allied military planning and, indeed, stood out as the one genuinely independent British contribution to the war effort. From the Prime Minister on down, there was an acute and painful realization that Britain's relative position in the world was rapidly being superceded by the much greater power of the United States. Bomber Command's stubborn insistence on going its own way was thus a reminder of an earlier period in which the British writ ruled supreme around the globe.

There are a number of interrelated and rather subtle factors that need to be examined in developing this point. The first involves the ambiguous and, at times, contradictory relationship between Bomber Command and the USSAF (United States Strategic Air Forces). There was a considerable community of interests between these two groups throughout the war in that both were intent on convincing their political masters that airpower was the key to victory. This led to frequent situations in which representatives of the two groups would present a united front against the competing claims for resources made by their respective counterparts in the army and navy. The classic example came at the Casablanca Conference in early 1943. Sir Arthur Harris and his opposite numbers in the USSAF may have disagreed on targeting policy for their bombers, but they were quite together on the necessity of giving the strategic bombing forces priority consideration. In adopting this common stance, they were able to maximize their influence and heavily sway the final decisions taken at Casablanca. Still later, in the spring of 1944, both the British and American bomber commanders argued against redirecting their efforts toward tactical support of the coming D-Day invasion, even if they disagreed once again on the best strategy for attacking targets in Germany itself.

This appearance of a (at least partial) united front was, however, never more than a marriage of convenience and was subject to all the strains and suspicions characteristic of such a relationship. To return to the Casablanca Conference, the leadership of Bomber Command had two quite different objectives: to gain an overall imprimatur for the strategic air offensive and, at the same time, to insure that Bomber Command would not somehow become subordinate to the growing power of the USSAF. The nightmare of Arthur Harris, and it is not too strong a phrase, was that his forces would either directly or indirectly be subsumed to the American bombing effort, not only in terms of doctrine but even in terms of overall operational control. Harris caught an early glimpse of this danger prior to becoming head of Bomber Command, when he spent a year in Washington as head of an RAF delegation examining various American airframe designs. It was apparent to him that if the United States joined Britain in the fight against Germany, the Americans would inevitably want (and expect) to become the senior partners in the anti-Nazi enterprise.

By the summer of 1943, the number of bombers in the USSAF exceeded those in Bomber Command, and even more alarming was the evident American penchant for highly centralized control of air policy. At a conference in Cairo in November 1943, for example, the Americans announced that they planned to put the Eighth and Fifteenth Air Forces under a single commander and ultimately under the control of the American Supreme Commander of the coming invasion of Europe. The British suspected that this would be only a forerunner to Bomber Command's itself coming under American control. The vice chief of the Air Staff, Sir Douglas Evill, sent a secret cable to London arguing that "everything possible" should be done to resist the American proposal for unification of command of the Eighth and Fifteenth Air Forces, and in particular for their being placed under direct operational control by the Supreme Commander for D-Day. "Such centralization," he warned, "would logically suggest inclusion of the RAF strategic night-bomber force, and there are insuperable operational and political objections to this."[5]

There are copious examples attesting to Harris's extreme sensitivity concerning invidious comparisons between the achievements of Bomber Command and those of the USSAF, sensitivities that, as noted above, found at least a fairly sympathetic ear at the Air Ministry and in Whitehall. One example of this came after Bomber Command had been diverted to transportation targets in France and the Low Countries prior to the Normandy invasion. His aircrew proved far more successful in their attacks on rail targets than Harris had anticipated, and the head of Bomber Command resented the fact that they did not seem to be receiving appropriate credit for their achievement. Harris wrote to Portal on July 1, 1944, along the following lines: "I think you should be aware of the full depth of feeling that is being aroused by the lack of adequate, or even reasonable credit to the Royal Air Force . . . for their efforts in the invasion. . . . I for one cannot forbear a most emphatic protest against the grave injustice which is being done to my crews."[6] Portal was receptive to Harris's concern, and convened a meeting at the Air Ministry to consider how Bomber Command's reputation might be reinforced in the press and public opinion. In this final stage of the war, Portal worried, RAF operations ran the risk of being overshadowed by the Americans. "There was accordingly a genuine danger that the part which it had played in the earlier part of the war would be forgotten."[7]

This obsession with image and reputation to be sure was hardly confined to the British side. General Carl Spaatz, for example, was (against all the evidence) convinced that Bomber Command's area offensive might just succeed and bear out Harris's wildly optimistic claims about winning the war singlehandedly. Even after the failures in the Battle of Berlin, Spaatz fretted that Bomber Command would be allowed to "go on bombing Germany and will be given a chance of defeating her before the invasion."[8]

It was the question of area or precision bombing that was obviously critical in the whole relationship between Bomber Command and the USSAF. The Americans were on record as favoring the latter whereas the British were committed to the former. Had Bomber Command somehow accepted precision bombing as basic doctrine, they would in effect have been accepting the American way of war. Given the USSAF's background and training in precision bombing, Bomber Command would have been submitting itself to the tutelage of the Americans in shaping a new targeting policy. Since Bomber Command had been basically trained for area bombing, Arthur Harris—in the interests of his own service's independence—had a vested interest in proving that the area offensive was the superior air strategy. Doing so was a way of marking out a quite distinct role for Bomber Command in the war effort. The British representatives at the Casablanca Conference seemed fairly sensitive to this fact, which led to the final ambiguity in the instructions for Operation Pointblank, with its apparent emphasis on attacking precision targets but also leaving room open for general area attacks as well.

There is a fairly unpleasant implication to this analysis that has to be squarely faced. The argument suggests that Harris would have pursued—and perhaps did pursue—area bombing regardless of the accumulating evidence about its lack of effectiveness and certainly without any moral compunction about its effect on German civilians simply because this was the most effective way of maintaining his Command's independence of the Americans. Even more, the British government allowed him to pursue this course because it too was desirous of sustaining at least some vestige of independent action in the war effort for reasons having to do basically with British prestige and self-image. This is indeed a somewhat unattractive argument to make. On the basis of the available evidence, it also seems to be an accurate one.

It goes a long way toward explaining, for instance, why Arthur Harris was not replaced as head of Bomber Command in 1944. We have earlier summarized the factors that might have been cited to justify such a dismissal, including the failures in the Battle of Berlin and especially Harris's open defiance of Portal later that year. The fact is, however, that Arthur Harris *was* Bomber Command, at least in the minds of the general public, not to mention the Americans. He had been carefully built up earlier in the war as one of Britain's most daring and decisive military figures, and, more to the point, was "one of the very few senior British officers who seemed able to ignore, let alone defy the American predominance in the conduct of grand strategy."[9] To dismiss him would be in effect to dismiss Bomber Command itself, or at the least to call into question all of its achievements since 1942.

Such achievements as there were, of course, depended on the presumption that area bombing was an effective strategy. Even though the Air Ministry, by the fall of 1944, had generally been converted to precision bombing of Germany, Bomber Command was identified by everybody with area bombing, and Arthur Harris was the prime apostle of area bombing. To sack Harris, or absolutely to insist on Bomber Command's devoting itself solely to precision bombing, would be an implicit repudiation of the whole strategy pursued in the preceding years. The results for the image of Bomber Command, which, it must be emphasized, stood out as the most important remaining symbol of British independence of action, would have been at the least highly deleterious. Under the circumstances, Harris's superiors, while often resentful of his insubordination and increasingly doubtful about the merits of area bombing, grudgingly decided to let events take their course, to pursue the path of least resistance.

Sir Archibald Sinclair, Secretary of State for Air, even offered a sympathetic assessment of the emotional difficulties that Harris must then be feeling (and which, by implication, others in the government perhaps shared). When Portal showed Sinclair copies of his acerbic correspondence with Harris in late fall 1944, commenting that the head of Bomber Command was "evidently under considerable emotional stress," Sinclair became the amateur psychologist. "I see what troubles his soul: our failure to go nap on the policy of obliteration and that the laurels which he is receiving are for successes—e.g., the pathfinders [and] the oil plan—which are not of his own design."[10] A mordant letter from Barry Sullivan to his brother-in-law Basil Liddell Hart perhaps best summarized the whole situation. Sullivan was serving in the RAF on Malta but was depressed by the seemingly uncontrolled destruction being meted out by Bomber Command. He feared that the government had "become Frankenstein, dominated by its own creation—the monster of Bomber Command."[11]

The Spirit of the People

The official rationale for the initiation of the area offensive against Germany in 1942 made much of its supposed effect on German civilian morale. In retrospect, however, British bombing of Germany seems to have had at least as much to do with bolstering English spirits as depressing those of the enemy. This was (ironically) a factor of its own in the area offensive's being maintained until the last days of the war, and it is one that we have already briefly addressed.

The concern about Bomber Command's remaining as a symbol of an independent British contribution to the war effort was especially felt at the higher levels of the British government, which had to deal with the increasingly assertive Americans on a daily basis. The subtleties of wartime coalition politics presumably were a good deal less central in the life of the average British citizen. At the same time, the man in the street and the Prime Minister did share one thing in common, and that was an admiration for the courage and resoluteness of the aircrew of Bomber Command. Indeed a primary theme of wartime government propaganda in Britain was that these aircrew represented, in many ways, the quintessential example of British steadfastness and devotion to duty.

Early in the war, for example, a 50-minute feature film entitled "Target for Tonight" was released by the government, and audiences everywhere thrilled to the exploits of the real-life crew of "F For Freddie" (who were suitably modest under the gaze of the cameras). The special mission that formed the centerpiece of this cinema exercise was an attack against a target in the Ruhr (described, not surprisingly, as an important military objective). Shortly after, the booklet *Bomber Command* was issued, which provided 128 pages of text, photographs, and diagrams and exulted that the bombing of Germany was a "policy well in keeping with our national character. Blended in it are courage and caution. [The aircrew] are of the same breed as the men who each evening notched their dragon prows into the sun's red rim on the first voyage to Labrador, who braced the yards of the *Golden Hind* to round Cape Horn and who stumbled with Scott from the South Pole."[12] Assuming that these sentiments found a responsive audience among the British people, any implied, not to mention overt, criticism or repudiation of Bomber Command's past activities was calculated to have a serious impact on the public's perception that Britain, as represented by Bomber Command, could lay claim to some very special qualities of bravery and military accomplishment.

What is critical in this consideration of British morale, of course, was the notion constantly pushed by High Wycombe, the Ministry of Information, and others that Bomber Command's area offensive was doing serious damage to the German capacity to make war. What was at stake here was what might be called "the Singapore syndrome." The fall of the British bastion at Singapore to the Japanese in February 1942 was a blow to the nation's sense of its military valor and competence. Singapore before the war had been widely considered to be virtually impregnable, yet it was taken after only a few weeks' campaign by the enemy. Moreover, some 80,000 British military personnel were taken prisoner by the Japanese, which suggested something other than a fight to the last man.[13] When combined with other British military reversals, for example, the fall of Tobruk in North Africa and the disasters in Norway and France, the British public was subject to a considerable crisis of confidence. It was almost exactly at the time of the fall of Singapore, however, that Sir Arthur Harris was appointed head of Bomber Command and launched his aggressive campaign of direct assault on the Nazi regime, beginning with the raids on Lübeck, Rostock, and Cologne. The government's elaborate description of the success of these operations proved to be a tonic to many in British society and assuaged the lingering fears about the capacity of British arms to face the aggressor.

A somewhat different morale factor came to the fore after the invasion of Normandy. There was no question by July 1944 but that the Germans were headed for defeat. At the same time, the enormous buildup of American ground, naval, and air forces was apparent to all, and there was a reluctant recognition (and not just within governmental circles) that the United States was now the decisive factor in the balance of forces against the enemy. The somewhat bitter acceptance of this new fact was reflected in the sardonic comment, widespread at the time, that the main problem with the flood of American soldiers coming to Britain was that they were "over-paid, over-sexed and over here." Yet there appeared to be one exception to this increasingly unequal relationship. Bomber Command was theoretically continuing to do devastating damage to Germany. If the publicity about its exploits could be believed, it was actually performing a role as important as, if not more important than, the role of the Americans in the air campaign.

Whatever the reality of these assertions, giving continued support to the efforts of Bomber Command—and to the notion that the area offensive was Germany's greatest burden—was viewed by many in government as critical to sustaining public support for the war effort after five long years. Arthur Harris, of course, had been built up as an almost mythical figure, and few in British society had either the specialized background or the inclination to doubt that he and his aircrew were indeed playing a great role in bringing the Germans to heel. It was only after the war, when a great deal of new information become available on the actual operations of Bomber Command, that widespread questioning developed about British air policy. At the time, the area offensive was seen by a great many as a symbol not only of the British genius in introducing new forms of military technology but also of British resoluteness in war-making itself.

An Eye for an Eye

Earlier in this essay we discussed whether British area bombing of Germany might not have been motivated, at least in part, by a straightforward desire for revenge—given German air attacks on Great Britain and, in particular, raids on British cities. One conclusion was that, to a surprising degree, the revenge motive seemed to be lacking among important segments of British public opinion, especially among those (ironically) in the most heavily bombed British towns and cities. Polls taken by the Gallup organization never showed more than 50 percent in favor of outright reprisal raids on Germany.[14] For his part, Sir Arthur Harris denied that revenge was ever a significant factor in the decision to initiate and to continue city bombing of Germany.

This is hardly the whole story, however. There may have been some truth to Harris's assertion but it would be a mistake to take it at face value. Harris himself admits saying (during a German attack on London), "Well, they are sowing the wind, and they will reap the whirlwind." Indeed, there is convincing evidence that, over the entire period of the area offensive, the desire to do unto the enemy as they had done unto Britain was at least one impulse to bombing policy among some in the Government and in the general public as well. In a press conference on May 25, 1943, Churchill touched on the theme of retribution and of the moral lesson of the Germans being hoist with their own petard, receiving in full measure the sort of devastation that they had so coldly meted out to others. The air weapon, he said,

> was the weapon these people chose to subjugate the world. This was the weapon with which they struck at Pearl Harbour. This was the weapon with which they boasted—the Germans boasted—they would terrorize all the countries of the world. And it is an example of *poetic justice* that this should be the weapon in which they should find themselves most out-matched and first out-matched in the ensuing struggle.[15]

By the summer of 1944, one might have expected that such thirst for retribution as existed would have been considerably slaked. Bomber Command, after all, as well as the USAAF, had been laying waste to Germany from one end to the other for two full years. The terrible disproportionality between the original offense and the subsequent punishment would seemingly have satisfied even the most hardened souls: for every ton of bombs dropped on Britain during the war, the Germans received 315 tons in return. Churchill himself conceded that the original "debt" incurred by German air attacks against Britain was "repaid tenfold, twentyfold, in the frightful routine bombardment of German cities. . . . Certainly the enemy got it all back in good measure, pressed down and running over. Alas for poor humanity!"[16] As it happened, however, two new events occurred at this point that seem to have given fresh spur to the demand (at least by some) for retaliation against the incorrigible Germans.

The first of these involved the initiation of German rocket attacks against British cities. Hitler placed much hope in the *Vergeltungswaffen* (the "weapons of retaliation") as a means of reversing his steadily declining military fortunes. As it turned out, the V-1s and V-2s had little effect in delaying his final defeat, but the character and nature of this new weapon of war seemed to confirm (or reconfirm) in the minds of many that the Germans were quite beyond the pale of civilized conduct. The V-1 was a cruise missile powered by a jet engine and carried about a ton of high explosive. It could fly as fast as 450 MPH and had a range of some 200 miles. When its engine exhausted its fuel, the rocket simply went down wherever it happened to be, killing and destroying without discrimination. The first V-1 missiles were launched at England two weeks after the Normandy invasion; eventually, 7,400 were sent from France and another 800 from Holland. Many were destroyed in flight, but the ones that did arrive killed or injured about 25,000 British civilians.

The V-2 was a ballistic missile that soared 60 miles above the earth as its fuel was consumed in a 60-second burst. It then plummeted toward the ground at speeds as high as 3,500 MPH. The V-2 was a particularly fearsome weapon not only because of its indiscriminate character but also because there was no effective defense against it once it was launched. Some 1,500 V-2s were directed at Britain, killing or injuring a further 10,000 citizens.[17] The rage that was felt within Britain at this new departure in warfare, extending from the Prime Minister to the average citizen, certainly tended to blunt whatever remorse may have started to develop by the summer of 1944 concerning the suffering of German civilians. As Churchill said to the House of Commons on July 6, "The flying bomb is a weapon literally and essentially indiscriminate in its nature, purpose and effect. [Its] introduction obviously raises some grave questions."[18] One way in which Churchill proposed to answer these "questions" was to consider large-scale gas attacks on German cities as a retaliation for the rockets raining down on Britain. He asked his advisers to provide him with a "cold-blooded" assessment as to "how it would pay us to use poison gas. . . . We could drench the cities of the Ruhr and many other cities in Germany in such a way that most of the population would be requiring constant medical treatment."[19]

The other event in 1944 that may well have refueled the rather primitive impulse toward retribution being visited on the German people was the Battle of the Bulge, which began on December 16 of that year. The German offensive in the Ardennes Forest was particularly galling to a British people who had anticipated, after five long years of war, that an end to the hostilities might be at hand. The initial successes of the Germans in the Ardennes suggested that the conflict might actually go on for an indeterminate period. This in itself mitigated against any restraint in the air war against Germany and aroused once again all the anger concerning German responsibility for initiating the war in the first place. It is significant, in this regard, that the fateful attack on Dresden took place less than a month after the conclusion of the Ardennes offensive.

To suggest that the area offensive continued up until virtually the last days of the war at least in part because Great Britain was intent on meting out just punishment to the Germans is a fairly controversial—and, to some, perhaps offensive—argument. Moreover, it is one that obviously is not as easy to substantiate as other aspects of British bombing policy, particularly since, after the war, most involved in that policy hastened to deny that they had ever been moved by so ignoble an impulse as a sheer desire for retribution. It also needs emphasizing that bombing as a tool for revenge (quite aside from its supposed military utility) was hardly a one-sided phenomenon in the war. The Germans for their part undertook overtly terrorist raids on Britain, the purpose of which was clearly not military but rather retributional. In addition to the indiscriminate German rocket attacks in 1944, there were the so-called "Baedekker raids" in the spring of 1941. Hitler and Goering announced that in order to punish the British for their supposed outrages in bombing Germany, the Luftwaffe would undertake a series of raids on British cities of particular historical and cultural significance. Such targets were identified by them as those rating three stars in the famous Baedekker tourist guide. Subsequently Canterbury, Exeter, Bath, York, and other equally famous sites were subjected to massive air raids. Hitler summarized the rationale for these raids by stating that "if they [the British] announce that they will attack our cities on a large scale, then we shall wipe their cities out."[20]

As far as Britain itself is concerned, the subsequent denials of their being a revenge motive in the area offensive are hard to square with the evidence that such an impulse did exist, both for those who had a direct role in the area offensive and for some segments of the general public as well. Not surprisingly, the real truth in this matter is often best found in private reflections offered at the time rather than in the more public postwar justifications of the area offensive. One of Churchill's personal aides seemed to touch on some of the actual motivations for the bombing of Germany when he recorded in his diary on March 20, 1940, that "news of our gigantic air-raid on Sylt, as a reprisal for a raid on Scapa Flow the other day, very well received by the public. . . . It looks as if this may be the beginning of a more active phase of the war, since the Germans will now probably undertake another raid by way of reprisal, and so things will go on until somebody goes so far as to bomb civilians."[21] In the event, both sides did go so far as to attack civilians.

Do Unto Others If They Can't Do Unto You

There was a final element in the initiation, but especially the continuation, of the area offensive until the very end of the war. Despite all the apocalyptic predictions in Britain before 1939 about Germany's ability to deliver a devastating air strike on the United Kingdom in the first days of a conflict, it gradually became apparent that the Germans actually had little capacity for massive strategic bombing. To be sure, the Blitz from the fall of 1940 to the spring of 1941 did some considerable damage in lives and materiel, but hardly on the order of what had been fearfully anticipated before the conflict. Once Hitler invaded the Soviet Union, moreover, the resources of the Luftwaffe were almost entirely redirected to the East, and air attacks on the British islands were no more than a minor annoyance for the remainder of the war, save for the V-1 and V-2 assaults in 1944. Given the fact that the Luftwaffe could not (or did not) retaliate in kind for British attacks on German cities, there was little incentive on the part of the British government to stay their hand with respect to German civilians.

In a curious sense what we had here was an early confirmation of the basic notion of deterrence as it later came to influence the debate over the West's nuclear strategy toward the Soviet Union. Deterrence in its essentials was a doctrine not for the *use* of air power (in this case nuclear missiles and nuclear bomb-carrying aircraft) but for persuading one's enemy not to initiate this particular form of air warfare. The premise behind an effective deterrent strategy was that if one could inflict an equal or greater degree of damage on a potential instigator of nuclear warfare, that country would be deterred from beginning a nuclear exchange, assuming it was capable of some fairly basic cost-benefit calculations. Also crucial to the notion of deterrence was the idea of credibility, that is, that one would actually carry out the threatened retaliation if attacked.[22]

The Germans seem to have attempted various forms of deterrence against British strategic bombing almost from the first days of the war. This derived not out of any unusual sensitivities to civilian suffering but rather from a belief that Germany might well be more vulnerable to an unrestricted strategic air war than her enemies. Thus the Nazi leaders in 1939 made much of their pledge not to initiate air attacks on cities should their opponents desist from doing so as well. More specifically, they publicly agreed to President Roosevelt's call for a mutual forbearance in air attacks on cities, which the American leader issued in the first week of the war. As noted, Berlin had done relatively little to develop a genuine strategic bombing force, and she obviously hoped to constrain London's use of Bomber Command by suggesting the moral opprobrium that would be attached to the British government by the international community if Great Britain should openly initiate attacks on civilian targets.

As the war progressed, the Germans engaged in rather different attempts at deterrence. George Quester suggests, for example, that the Baedekker raids were actually a last-gasp attempt by the Germans to maintain the earlier mutual restraint as far as the bombing of cities was concerned. In other words, the devastation inflicted on Canterbury, Exeter, and other cities might persuade the British to forgo a general area bombing offensive of Germany.[23] Hitler and other Nazi spokesmen also constantly referred to the development of new terror weapons that would cause the British to regret that they had ever started indiscriminate air warfare (or were continuing it). The V-1 and V-2 offensive against Britain might also be seen as an effort to deter further devastation of German cities, although the simple push for revenge seems to have been as prominent in this case as the idea of persuading Britain to curtail her own air offensive.

If there were efforts by the Germans to employ the concept of deterrence, it is self-evident that they badly failed in their objective. Indeed, several of them actually seem to have steeled the British in their determination to continue the area offensive unabated. The decisive point about these German attempts to dissuade London from a generalized assault on their cities was the lack of the essential ingredient of credibility in their deterrence strategy once Britain came to realize that the capacity of Germany for serious aerial retaliation against the British islands was limited. This does not mean that the suffering inflicted by the Blitz was not deeply felt, nor that the effect of the German rocket campaign in 1944 was lightly discarded. It is simply to say that London recognized that there was little, if any, real balance between the amount of destruction that Germany could visit on Britain compared to that which Bomber Command was able to inflict on the Germans. Under the circumstances—and in accord with one of the basic principles of deterrence—there was little incentive on the part of Churchill and his advisers to restrain the area offensive.

A SUMMING UP

When Air Marshal Sir Arthur Harris died in April 1984 at the age of 91, the *London Observer* suggested in its obituary that Winston Churchill and others had made Harris a scapegoat for the area bombing offensive against Germany. Even so, it admitted, "moral questions remain. Fairly or otherwise, 'Bomber' Harris will always be the symbol for a part of the British war effort about which many people have very mixed feelings."[24] A little-noticed irony attended Harris's death: he passed away at his home on Goring-on-Thames West of London. A certain German field marshal by that (approximate) name spent a good deal of time directing his bombers over the Thames, and his efforts played a considerable part in spurring Harris's subsequent campaign of destroying German cities.

To quote young Peterkin again, when all is said and done, what did it all mean? What did it mean for the war effort? What did it mean for the decision-makers, for the boffins, for the aircrew, for the hardy band of dissenters? What did it mean for British society generally? Above all, what did it mean in terms of the conduct of war, that most characteristic and lamentable of human activities, in the 20th century? In these final pages I propose to step back from all the warp and woof of the area offensive—the details of aircraft and bombs, the arguments over strategy, the character of the raids over Germany—and attempt an overview of what was done and what it ultimately may have signified.

It must be admitted at the outset that one of the reasons the British bombing of German cities has remained morally controversial is that it failed in its proclaimed purposes, a cynical but perhaps understandable phenomenon. Successful captains in wartime tend to be spared quibbles about the doubtful elements in their success; it is enough that they have achieved victory. One recalls President John F. Kennedy's mordant comment after the Bay of Pigs fiasco that "victory has a hundred fathers but defeat is an orphan." If Bomber Command had been able to force a German surrender prior to the D-Day invasion—which Arthur Harris held out as a possibility—the air campaign over Germany would likely be regarded as a masterpiece of military strategy, and the moral queries of the critics would have been consigned to obscurity. As it turned out, the area offensive did seem to be both a crime *and* a mistake. The fact of the latter made many considerably less tolerant of the former.

Such toleration was also no doubt lessened by the consistent exaggeration, one might say arrogance, with which the spokesmen for Bomber Command presented their strategic theories. As Max Hastings says, "If the airmen had pitched their demands for resources, their own hopes and their subsequent claims more modestly, history might have judged them more kindly."[25] Even after all the evidence was in, Arthur Harris, for one, continued to drum away on the same tired theme. In his memoirs, he argues that "it is an obvious and most certain conclusion that if we had had the force we used in 1944 a year earlier, and if we had then been allowed to use it together with the whole American bomber force, and without interruption, Germany would have been defeated outright by bombing. . . . We were only prevented from having that force by the fact that the Allied war leaders did not have enough faith in strategic bombing."[26] It is easy enough to suggest here that Bomber Command in reality commanded an enormous share of the available military resources and still failed in its avowed purpose. The real point is that such obstinacy removed any inclination to give Harris and his supporters the benefit of the doubt after the war. Since they were so obviously wrong in their strategic calculations, it was tempting to lay a heavy moral indictment on their methods as well.

It is always interesting in evaluating a particular historical event—and at times rather essential to our understanding of it—to gauge whether the action taken may have been basically "accidental" or, on the contrary, the logical outcome of previous trends. As we have discussed earlier, one of the main themes in the defense of area bombing was that it was the result of essentially unexpected problems in navigation and protection of aircraft in daylight raids over Germany. Yet the evidence available is hardly supportive of this particular demurral concerning the morality of British bombing policy. The fact is that of all the belligerents in World War II, only Great Britain and the United States had made a strong commitment to the strategic air offensive before the conflict began, and only they decided to mount and sustain such an offensive once the war began.

More to the point, in the whole interwar development of the RAF under the guidance of Trenchard and his disciples, the possibility of area bombing could be logically deduced from the thinking of British air power theorists. The official history suggests as much: "Operations between October 1944 and May 1945 were the climax of the strategic air offensive. The Bomber Command part in them represented the realization of most of the hopes and ambitions which had inspired the British Air Staff for a quarter of a century."[27] If, as has been argued, this final phase of Bomber Command's operations was the most morally problematical, it will not do to say that Harris and others were essentially forced into them by unanticipated operational difficulties. This culminating period in the area offensive may indeed be traced to the "hopes and ambitions" dating back to the formation of the RAF in 1918.

The postwar trials of the major German war criminals at Nuremberg provide another reference point concerning the British bombing of German cities. There was a studious effort on the part of the Allies to avoid placing the issue of area bombing on the agenda of the Tribunal. The chief American prosecutor at the trials, Telford Taylor, later recalled that "aerial bombardment had been used so extensively and ruthlessly on the Allied as well as the Axis side that neither at Nuremberg nor Tokyo was the issue made a part of the trials."[28] It was obviously felt that such indelicate references might compromise the case being made against the crimes of the defendants.

In the event, several of those in the dock declined to make so subtle a distinction between the killing of thousands of civilians in air raids and their own dubious activities. The events at Hamburg and Dresden—and

Hiroshima—were used as important pieces of evidence in their defense, the burden of their argument being that their accusers had in fact committed crimes just as great as those that they were charged with. Moreover, the German defendants made the same use of doubtful precedents in international law that the British employed to justify their own actions. Thus Field Marshall Kesselring defended the German bombing of Warsaw in 1939 by saying that "in the German view, Warsaw was a fortress, and moreover it had strong air defenses. Thus, it fell under the stipulations of the Hague Convention for land warfare, which can analogously be applied to air warfare."[29] It was precisely the 1907 Hague Convention (as we have seen) that was used by the British to justify their aerial attacks on "defended" German cities during World War II.

That so loathsome a collection of individuals as those under indictment at Nuremberg should have tried to use British conduct to justify their own might simply be dismissed as a rather desperate attempt to escape the hangman's noose. Yet there is something deeply troubling about the fact that they should have been able to make even a superficial connection between their activities and those of Bomber Command. Kant's famous Categorical Imperative asserted that the basis of all morality was that one should "act only on that maxim whereby thou canst at the same time will that it should become a universal law." The fact that the area offensive was so morally problematical made it vulnerable to those of quite dubious persuasions pleading "reciprocity." Moreover, it has continued to be so employed. Various terrorist groups have from time to time defended their indiscriminate killing of civilians by saying that they were only following the precedent established by the British in World War II. Such an argument has had at least a certain credibility with a great many people who view the area offensive itself simply as an exercise in terror rather than military strategy.[30] This is what might be called the "nemesis effect" of violating the war convention, even in a worthy cause: such a departure often returns to haunt those originally responsible for it. Others pursuing a far less just end now find it convenient—and possible—to wrap themselves in the mantle of legitimacy when they employ these new techniques of violence, which often are directed at the very society that originally introduced them.[31]

The Drive Toward Total War

To say that Bomber Command was basically an instrument of terror is a harsh indictment and, to some, an unfair one as well. What is beyond dispute is that the area offensive was a watershed event in the development of the concept of total war, or, perhaps more precisely, in the re-introduction of this concept in the contemporary period. Total war—as earlier defined—involves not just the complete mobilization of the resources of the state for military purposes but also the blurring, if not evaporation, of any distinction between the home front and the battle front. In total war, both sectors are fused to create an essentially unbroken and universal field of conflict, and military operations in all parts of this landscape are regarded as not only necessary but legitimate. A paper presented by the British Naval Staff in 1921 to the Committee of Imperial Defence addressed this melancholy development:

> Nothing can be clearer than the fact that modern war resolves itself into an attempt to throttle the national life. Waged by the whole power of the nation, its ultimate object is to bring pressure on the mass of the enemy people, distressing them by every possible means, so as to compel the enemy's government to submit to terms.[32]

It need hardly be said that the phenomenon of total war has been one of the more grievous assaults on the human condition in this century. It is also self-evident that it was the development of airpower that provided a powerful impetus to its emergence, since the new technology made it possible to wage war not just on the enemy's soldiers but on the society supporting them. As one leading authority on the development of war has put it, the introduction of the strategic bomber led to "a crisis in the law of war, and a process of barbarization such as had not been seen in Europe since the second half of the seventeenth century."[33]

This reference to the barbarization of the means of war is fairly common in analyses of the area offensive and deserves a little elaboration. We have said that the British bombing of Germany actually represented not an introduction but more exactly a re-introduction of the concept of total war. A comparison is often made in this context between World War II and the Thirty Years War. The essential argument is that the latter represented a particularly horrific example of total war in operation, and its calamities were such that the European state system resolved henceforward to establish at least some restraint on the methods of warfare. Certainly the Thirty Years War (1618-1648) provided a most sobering example of what unlimited war could produce. There was, for example, the sack of Magdeburg in 1631 by the army of Tilly, in which some 30,000 citizens of the town were systematically put to the sword. It is estimated that overall one-third of the German population succumbed during the fighting.

After this disaster one can observe at least an attempt by the European powers to limit warfare in the interests of all concerned. Naturally, this was hardly an even and unbroken process, and during the Napoleonic period in particular there were horrors (e.g., in the Peninsular campaign in Spain) that echoed those of an earlier era. Nevertheless, the overall effort seemed to be in the direction of establishing certain guidelines that would prevent the catastrophe of unrestrained conflict. The struggle of 1914-1918 put a severe strain on this enterprise, but even then there was a reluctance—at least among some of the participants—to open the Pandora's box of totally unlimited warfare. As late as June 1917, for example, when Lord Curzon put before the British War Cabinet a proposal for bombing raids on German cities, there was opposition on the grounds that this meant imitating the German policy of "frightfulness."[34]

World War II, however, according to this argument, represented the final abandonment of the concept of limits in modern war, and it was the introduction of massive strategic bombing that was primarily responsible. One of the earliest critiques of the area offensive to appear in Great Britain after the war made much of this notion. The author referred ironically to the green light given to Bomber Command in May 1940 to attack a full range of targets in Germany as "the splendid decision." He then went on to state that "the fundamental principle of civilized warfare was repudiated on May 11th, 1940 [sic]. . . and with the keystone removed the whole structure of civilized warfare as it had been gradually built up in Europe the preceding two centuries collapsed in ruins."[35]

This is pretty strong stuff. *Was* Dresden, as the above author (and a number of others) suggests, simply a reprise of the destruction of Magdeburg? If it be so regarded, the logical conclusion would be that mankind had advanced not at all in 300 years, that its capacity for cruelty and arbitrary destruction was essentially the same as before. Such a conclusion seems such a denial of any reasonable hope for the progress of civilization that it is tempting to try to set it aside. Yet the comparison of Dresden and Magdeburg has a melancholy logic to it. Consider this comment in the *official* history of the Royal Air Force: "The destruction in Germany was by then [the time of the attack on Dresden] on a scale which might have appalled Attila or Genghis Khan."[36] Perhaps the only difference between the two was that Magdeburg was laid waste by individuals who could directly observe the consequences of their actions, whereas the destruction of Dresden was an impersonal act carried out with studied technical efficiency by aircrew who could have little direct sense of the effect of their bombs on the people below.

The re-emergence of the concept of total war, as partly represented by the area offensive against Germany (we should not ignore the Nazis' own contribution here), clearly has had an enormous effect on the postwar world. Indeed, it has been this lingering residue of the area offensive that perhaps constitutes one of the most dolorous aspects of strategic bombing in World War II. To be sure, there has been no repetition of total war on the scale of World War II, and for that much we can be grateful. Yet many of the essential mindsets that led to (and made possible) strategic bombing have been much in evidence since 1945. One of these has been what might be called the "score card" approach to war, in which sheer numbers of bombers, tons of bombs dropped, number of killed and injured, and square miles of destruction achieved have been used as the basic indicator of military progress. This predilection for abstract quantification was very prevalent at High Wycombe, but we have seen it more recently as well, particularly in the Vietnam war.

That struggle drew on the precedent of the area offensive in yet another way. A basic operating principle in Vietnam seemed to be that since the "people" were the basic source of strength for the enemy's armed forces, then the "people" themselves became a legitimate military target. The truth of this observation might be seen in a bizarre conversation the American journalist Neil Sheehan had with the commander of American forces in Vietnam, General William Westmoreland. Sheehan asked Westmoreland "if he was worried about the large number of civilian casualties from the air strikes and the shelling." The general looked at him carefully and then replied, "Yes, Neil, it is a problem, but it does deprive the enemy of the population, doesn't it?"[37] Westmoreland's appalling comment was really only a restatement of Lord Cherwell's argument about the beneficial effects of dehousing German workers in World War II (not to mention the more general theory of attacking German morale). In some ways, one can even admire Westmoreland's lack of pretense. He was bold enough to argue that simply killing lots of civilians had its own military rationale. That premise was also implicit in Lord Cherwell's defense of area bombing, but he chose to mask the logic of his analysis by resorting to euphemisms about workers temporarily without shelter.

The most obvious connection between the phenomenon of strategic bombing in World War II and military doctrine in the postwar world, however, has had to do with nuclear weapons and in particular theories of nuclear deterrence. It is not too much to say that much nuclear targeting policy was simply area bombing writ large. For a number of years American, and presumably British, policy was to deter the Soviet Union by the threat of massive devastation of Soviet cities. There did come to be a greater emphasis in the latter stages of the Cold War on so-called counter-force strategy, in which nuclear weapons would be directed toward relatively traditional military targets such as airfields, command-and-control centers, missile silos, and so forth. Even here, however, the degree of collateral damage (that is, destruction of civilians) that would have been occasioned by even a limited nuclear strike threatened to be enormous.

Daniel Ellsberg recalls how appalled he was by his experience working on nuclear targeting policy at the Pentagon in the early 1960s. At that time, the plans of the Joint Chiefs of Staff basically envisaged the total devastation of the Soviet Union with an all-out strike designed to kill millions of civilians. Ellsberg, in his typically flamboyant language, attributed such thinking to a "mad dog" mentality within the military leadership, especially the Air Force generals, "who subscribed to the Douhet theory . . . of waging total war from the air."[38] Now Ellsberg is a rather controversial figure, and there are many who may question his *bona fides* in criticizing a strategy that, after all, he himself was involved in developing at the time. The point remains that the very conceivability of destroying a large city (or number of cities) in a matter of a half-hour in the interests of "national security" and in pursuance of a "just cause"—defeating Nazi or Soviet aggression— has to be regarded as having its roots in the systematic devastation of German cities in World War II. Before that war began, such a policy was generally regarded as inconceivable. Later it turned out to be quite conceivable indeed. This change in the realm of the thinkable made it all the more easy to devise even more apocalyptic military polices that, in an earlier age, would have been dismissed as beyond the pale of what democratic societies could legitimately do in war. The echos of area bombing have indeed resonated loud and long.[39]

The Failure of Imagination

When the young British climber Andrew Irving was asked in the 1920s why he wanted to scale Mount Everest, his immortal reply was, "Because it's there." Just so with the introduction of long-range bombers. In the period between 1939 and 1945, the scientists and the technicians developed ever more sophisticated means of applying violence, and in some sense the machines took over control of the war. Because the technology was there, it proved well-nigh irresistible to employ it. As Thomas Murray comments, "No one ever has ever made the argument that war ought to be made total, as a matter of reason and right. War simply became and more and more total, as a matter of fact and possibility."[40] Of course, as a new method of war, strategic bombing raised a whole host of interrelated political, social, economic, and ethical problems. These were far more difficult problems to solve, particularly in the heat of wartime, than essentially technical matters of bombload and navigational systems. It is a truism that man's social wisdom lags behind his technological wisdom, and the development of atomic weapons has often been cited as an example. The phenomenon of strategic bombing in World War II also stands in testimony to the point.

Clearly, one of the reasons for the inability of the decision-makers to place strategic bombing in a broader and more appropriate context is the tendency in war, and particularly in total war, of military operations escalating to the use of all conceivable means. Clausewitz called this the "first principle of war," and it was evident in striking fashion in World War II. Now this does not mean that wars must inevitably degenerate into indiscriminate savagery—earlier we argued that the Shermanesque thesis was basically false—but the point is that a *tendency* in that direction is ever present, and it takes a concerted effort to deal with it. When a relatively novel, new technique of war becomes available, such an effort is made all the more difficult.

This is particularly the case since it is a rare event for those in authority to feel that they are at something of a crossroads, that they are faced with a truly fundamental decision about adopting an entirely new line of military policy. On the contrary, the standard feeling is one of incrementalism, that is to say, that what is now being suggested is simply a logical, and seemingly marginal, continuation of what has already been done. This point certainly applies to the evolution of British bombing of Germany. It started out as an attempt to hit precise targets and with little or no unintended damage to civilians. Then there was an ambiguous period dating from May 1940 to February 1942, in which the definition of legitimate targets was expanded. Much emphasis continued to be on precision attacks on traditional military objectives, but there was an increasing tendency to include a broader category of potential targets as well, including German cities. Finally, the decision was made simply to concentrate (at least for the time being) on large urban areas. In this two-and-one-half-year period, there never seems to have been one critical point in which the central issue of city bombing was directly faced. Such a strategy simply evolved out of a series of smaller, more detailed steps.

If this is a fair characterization of British bombing strategy, we need to take note not only of the incremental way in which the area offensive was eventually adopted but also of something else that was integral to it, what might be called a fatal lack of imagination. The "donkeys" was a common pejorative directed at the British generals of World War I. The term suggested that those in high command were essentially impervious to reality, stubbornly determined to press on with patently false strategic premises, and quite insensitive to the human cost of their illusions in the bargain.[41] A comparison is often made in this respect between Sir Arthur Harris and Sir Douglas Haig, the British commander on the Western Front. The latter, as head of all British ground forces, was noted for his unswerving commitment to frontal assaults against the German lines in France and Belgium in a vain attempt to achieve a decisive breakthrough that would lead to victory. The Passchendaele campaign in 1917, as one example of Haig's strategy, cost the British 400,000 casualties in return for the capture of five miles of muddy terrain.

There is something to be said for the comparison between Harris and Haig, although there were differences between the two men as well. It is instructive to recall Haig's opinion that "from the point of view of morality and public opinion" he was opposed to any effort at the "devastation of enemy lands and destruction of industrial and populous centres on a vast scale."[42] This judgment was presumably facilitated by the fact that Haig was jealous of the emerging glamour of the air service and assured one and all that airpower would always remain secondary and subordinate to the army and the navy. Harris, for his part, must be credited with displaying a concern for his own men perhaps greater than Haig ever demonstrated. He was always intent on giving his aircrew the best possible opportunity for survival by providing them with superior equipment and training. Nevertheless, if the leaders of Bomber Command cannot be dismissed as simply donkeys, it remains that those at High Wycombe—and their political masters as well—demonstrated a rather striking degree of detachment about the many and varied criticisms that were levied at their activities.[43] They plowed ahead with the area offensive in a seeming inability to conceive of or at least insist on alternatives, although several lay at hand.

There is more here as well, and it is reflected in a rather extraordinary reminiscence from Air Marshall Sir Robert Saundby, deputy to Arthur Harris. In discussing the attack on Dresden, he mused that the destruction of the city

> was one of those terrible things that sometimes happen in wartime, brought about by an unfortunate combination of circumstances. Those who approved it were neither wicked nor cruel, though it may well be that they were too remote from the harsh realities of war to understand fully the appalling destructive power of air bombardment in the spring of 1945.[44]

Two things command attention in this statement: the suggestion that nobody was really at fault for the attack on Dresden (which resulted from "an unfortunate combination of circumstances"), and the comment that those who nevertheless approved it may have been too "remote" from reality in 1945 to understand what 1,000 Lancasters over Dresden could do. This after three years of the area offensive. If taken at face value, such ignorance of the effects of area bombing really shows a rather remarkable inattention to detail. What it may show even more is how the pristine atmosphere at High Wycombe and in Whitehall tended to shield the decision-makers from having to face the real human consequences of what they were ordering. Of course, they could have explored these consequences if they so desired, but it evidently never occurred to them to do so. Perhaps they even doubted the relevance of attempting to do so.

War and Democracy

There is a long-held theory that democracies are slow to anger but, once aroused, notably violent and ruthless in their waging of war. The underlying logic is that democratic regimes depend on popular support for prosecution of a war effort—unlike, perhaps, more authoritarian regimes—and thus they attempt to arouse the more primitive instincts of their people for the righteous smiting of the heathen. Once such emotions are set loose, it is hard to control them, and thus the predilection, ironically, for democratic nations to wage war without restraint.

Consider this comment from a Union officer in the American Civil War, who, in his postwar reminiscences of fighting Confederate guerillas in Missouri, delivered himself of the following:

> There exists in the breasts of people of educated and Christian communities wild and ferocious passions . . . which may be aroused and kindled by . . . war and injustice, and become more cruel and destructive than any that live in the breasts of savage and barbarous nations.[45]

The contemporary British military historian Basil Liddell Hart seemed to agree. He suggested that normally Britain was on a higher plane of decency and humanity than most other nations, but that "our methods of war . . . tend to be more inhuman than those of battle-minded Continental countries." More specifically, he argued that British military tactics in World War II tended "to be less human than that of the Germans . . . their inhumanity being manifested rather in the political consolidation of military results."[46]

There are many who will be made uneasy—or made angry—by this disquisition on the comparative "humanity" of German versus British military operations in World War II, and certainly the *Wehrmacht* was guilty of quite horrendous violations of the war convention on numerous occasions. Nevertheless, it is a fact that the Germans never came close to matching the British area bombing offensive of Germany in their own air attacks on Britain, although it can easily be argued that this was more because of operational limitations than concerns about limits in war. Even so, this may miss the point that Britain was fighting for a particular vision of the future of humanity. That vision was intimately related to the value system that had been so laboriously constructed in Britain itself over several hundred years, in particular respect for the dignity and integrity of the individual and the value of a single human life. The troubling question remains whether, in defeating the larger threat, Britain did not in some ways diminish the very cause for which she was fighting.

It has been observed about World War I that, in the course of conquering German imperialism, there was "meted out heavy punishment to that broad humane liberalism which for two centuries had been one of the most vital elements in British politics."[47] If such was the case, the same seems to apply in even greater degree to the British experience in World War II. Lord Acton's famous axiom that power tends to corrupt and absolute power to corrupt absolutely may be quoted to good effect here. In the last year of the war, the Allies generally, and Bomber Command specifically, had virtually absolute power of aerial destruction over Germany, and that this had a corrupting effect on British standards of humanity seems inescapable. In an observation on the American Civil War, Bruce Catton caught the essential dilemma facing free societies at war. He observed that in the search for victory democracies may be driven to "perform acts that alter the very soil in which society's roots are nourished."[48]

Even if this is so, one is drawn back to a particular group of individuals who were at the heart of the area offensive and perhaps deserve the final word: the aircrew themselves. It is well to recall Winston Churchill's tribute to his predecessor Neville Chamberlain in the House of Commons upon the latter's death in November 1940.

> History with its flickering lamp stumbles along the trail of the past, trying to reconstruct its scenes, to revive its echoes, and kindle with pale gleams the passion of former days. What is the worth of all this? The only guide to a man is his conscience. The only shield to his memory is the rectitude and sincerity of his actions. It is very imprudent to walk through life without this shield, because

we are so often mocked by the failure of our hopes and the upsetting of our calculations; but with this shield, however the fates may play, we march always in the ranks of honour.[49]

None of what has been written here denies that the aircrew of Bomber Command had a shield of sincere belief in the rectitude of what they were doing: helping to vanquish an unparalleled evil. The tragedy was that not only were they mocked by the failure of many of the calculations provided by others concerning the area offensive, but that they paid such a grievous price for the pursuit of an illusion. If moral blame needs to be assigned for the devastation of German cities, the aircrew should stand last in the ranks of the accused. They were ultimately only the messengers, not the authors of the message.

NOTES

Notes to Preface

1. Martin Middlebrook and Chris Everitt, *The Bomber Command War Diaries* (London: Viking, 1985), 682.
2. Gavin Lyall, *The War in the Air* (New York: William Morrow and Company, 1968), 379.
3. Gwynne Dyer, *War* (Homewood, Illinois: Dorsey Press, 1985), 93.
4. William Tuohy, "New Statue to Bomber Chief Raises German Ire," *Los Angeles Times* (October 25, 1991), A5; *Financial Times* (June 1, 1992).
5. Ronald Schaffer, *Wings of Judgment* (New York: Oxford University Press, 1985).
6. *Ibid.*, 92.
7. James Cate and Wesley Craven, *The Army Air Forces in World War II* (Chicago: University of Chicago Press, 1948-1958), Volume III, 732.

Notes to Chapter 1

1. Donald Cameron Watt, "Restraints on War In The Air Before 1945," in *Restraints on War*, ed. Michael Howard (Oxford: Oxford University Press, 1979), 60-61; Robin Higham, *Air Power* (New York: St. Martin's Press, 1972), 21.
2. John Pimlott, "The Theory and Practice of Strategic Bombing," in *Warfare in the Twentieth Century*, ed. Collin McInnes and G. D. Sheffield (London: Unwin Hyman, 1988), 121.
3. Cited in Geoffrey Best, *Humanity in Warfare* (New York: Columbia University Press, 1980), 269.
4. Martin Creveld, *Technology and War* (New York: Free Press, 1989), 188.
5. Basil Liddell Hart, *Paris, or the Future of War* (London: K. Pau., Trench, Trubner, Ltds., 1925), 50. Ironically, Liddell Hart developed into one of the severest critics of the British strategic bombing offensive in World War II, not only on pragmatic but also on moral grounds. A more detailed discussion of his position is offered in Chapter IV.
6. *Ibid.*, 37.
7. Giulio Douhet, *The Command of the Air*, trans. Dino Ferrari (New York: Coward-McCann, 1942), 57-58.

8. *Ibid.,* 54-55.

9. The full text of the memorandum may be found in Noble Frankland and Charles Webster, *The Strategic Air Offensive Against Germany* 1939-1945 (London: Her Majesty's Stationery Office, 1961), IV, 74 (hereafter cited as *SAOG*).

10. Tom Harrison, *Living Through the Blitz* (London: Collins, 1962), 33.

11. *SAOG,* Volume I, 89ff.

12. F. M. Sallager, *The Road to Total War* (Santa Monica, CA: The Rand Corporation, 1969), 18.

13. *SAOG,* Volume I, 99.

14. Martin Middlebrook and Chris Everitt, *The Bomber Command War Diaries* (London: Viking, 1985), 21.

15. John Colville, *The Fringes of Power* (New York: W. W. Norton and Company, 1985), 52-53.

16. George Quester, *Deterrence Before Hiroshima* (New York: John Wiley and Sons, 1966), 106.

17. Hugh Trevor-Roper, ed., *Hitler's War Directives* (London: Sidgwick and Jackson, 1964), 6-7.

18. Max Hastings, *Bomber Command* (New York: Simon and Schuster, 1987), 84-86.

19. R. V. Jones, *Most Secret War* (London: Hamish Hamilton, 1978), 183.

20. Charles Messenger, *"Bomber" Harris* (New York: St. Martin's Press, 1984), 40.

21. Colville, *The Fringes of Power,* 311.

22. *SAOG,* Volume I, 323-4.

23. J. M. Spaight, *Bombing Vindicated* (London: Geoffrey Bles, 1944), 45.

24. *SAOG,* Volume I, 178.

25. *Ibid.,* 331-336.

26. Arthur Harris, *Bomber Offensive* (London: Collins, 1947), 74-75, 113.

27. *Ibid.,* 107.

28. Winston S. Churchill, *The Grand Alliance* (Boston: Houghton Mifflin Company, 1951), 507-509.

29. Harris, *Bomber Offensive,* 112-113.

30. Ronald Clark, *The Rise of the Boffins* (London: Phoenix House, 1962), 182-208.

31. Michael Bowyer, *Mosquito* (London: Faber and Faber, 1967).

32. United States, *Strategic Bombing Survey* (Washington, D.C.: Government Printing Office, 1945). Area Studies Division Report No. 31, 4.

33. Anthony Verrier, *The Bomber Offensive* (New York: The Macmillan Company, 1969), 167.

34. The standard treatment of the attack on Hamburg remains Martin Middlebrook's *The Battle of Hamburg* (London: Allan Lane, 1980).

35. Martin Caidin, *The Night Hamburg Died* (New York: Ballantine Books, 1960), 9. Caidin reports without comment that the British employed phosphorus bombs in considerable quantities over Hamburg because of their "demonstrated ability to depress the morale of the Germans."

36. H. R. Allen, *The Legacy of Lord Trenchard* (London: Cassell, 1972), 149-151.

37. *SAOG,* Volume II, 47-48.

38. Noble Frankland, *The Bombing Offensive Against Germany* (London: Faber and Faber, 1965), 74.

39. John Keegan, *The Second World War* (New York: Viking, 1989), 416.

40. Harris, *Bomber Offensive,* 220-223.

41. Basil Liddell Hart, *History of the Second World War* (New York: G. P. Putnam's Sons, 1970), 609.

42. David Irving, *The Destruction of Dresden* (New York: Holt, Rinehart and Winston, 1963).

43. *SAOG,* Volume III, 109.

44. *Ibid.,* 112 (emphasis added).

45. Middlebrook and Everitt, *The Bomber Command War Diaries,* 683, 695.

46. Robin Cross, *The Bombers* (New York: Macmillan Publishing Company, 1987), 160; Hilary St. George Saunders, *Royal Air Force 1939-1945* (London: Her Majesty's Stationery Office, 1954), Volume III, 392.

Notes to Chapter 2

1. Richard H. Wyman, "The First Rules of Air Wafare," *Air University Review* (March-April 1984), 95.

2. Lee Kennett, *A History of Strategic Bombing* (New York: Scribner's, 1982), 63-64.

3. "General Report of the Commission of Jurists at the Hague," *American Journal of International Law* XVII (October 1923), Supplement, 249.

4. "The Hague Rules of 1923," *ibid.,* 250-251.

5. L. Oppenheim, *International Law,* ed. H. Lauterpacht (New York: Longmans, Green, 1952), 7th edition, Volume 2, 519.

6. Kennett, *A History of Strategic Bombing,* 70.

7. Hans Rumpf, *The Bombing of Germany* (New York: Holt, Rinehart and Winston, 1963), 17-18.

8. Michael Walzer, *Just and Unjust Wars* (New York: Basic Books, 1977), 44.

9. Sir John Slessor, *The Central Blue* (London: Cassell and Company, 1956), 214. Slessor anticipated the later attitude of the Air Staff when he commented on the "difficult and depressing negotiations about the legality of bombing which took up so much of our time in 1938 and 1939. . . . It was all an unhappy, tedious and really rather meaningless business. In reality, speaking for myself (and I think for the rest of the Air Staff), I regarded it all as a matter not of legality but of expediency. . . . We never had the least doubt that sooner or later the gloves would come off."

10. Great Britain, *5 Parliamentary Debates* (Commons), Volume 337 (June 21, 1938), 936.

11. Great Britain, *5 Parliamentary Debates* (Commons), Volume 351 (September 14, 1939), 750.

12. Angus Calder, *The People's War* (New York: Pantheon Books, 1969), 491.

13. Martin Middlebrook, *The Battle of Hamburg* (London: Allen Lane, 1980), 343-344.

14. Russell Grenfell, *Unconditional Hatred?* (New York: Devin-Adair, 1954), 173.

15. F. J. P. Veale, *Advance to Barbarism* (London: Thompson and Smith, 1948),129.

16. Great Britain, *5 Parliamentary Debates* (Commons), Volume 379 (May 6, 1942), 1364.

17. Great Britain, *5 Parliamentary Debates* (Commons), Volume 388 (March 31, 1943), 155.

18. Great Britain, *5 Parliamentary Debates* (Lords), Volume 130 (February 9, 1944), 750.

19. Max Hastings, *Bomber Command* (New York: Simon and Schuster, 1987), 172-173.

20. *Ibid.* Emphasis in original.

21. Sir Arthur Harris, *Bomber Offensive* (London: Collins, 1947), 58.

22. Ian McLaine, *Ministry of Morale* (London: George Allen and Unwin, 1979), 161-162.

23. Important sources of such information were the personal observations of British military personnel who entered into Germany toward the end of the war, as well as of those who comprised the British occupying force in that country once hostilities had ended. The claims by Bomber Command that they had aimed only at "military" targets were belied by the evidence of widespread devastation of virtually every major German city.

24. Noble Frankland and Charles Webster, *The Strategic Air Offensive Against Germany 1939-1945* (London: Her Majesty's Stationery Office, 1961), Volume III, 115 (hereafter cited as *SAOG*).

25. Dudley Saward, *Bomber Harris* (Garden City, N.Y.: Doubleday, 1985), 665.

26. Great Britain, *5 Parliamentary Debates* (Commons), Volume 420 (March 12, 1946), 965-966.

27. Harris, *Bomber Offensive,* 268.

28. *The Guardian* (April 7, 1984).

29. John Colville, *The Fringes of Power* (New York: W. W. Norton and Company, 1985), 644.

30. Charles Messenger, *"Bomber" Harris* (New York: St. Martin's Press, 1984), 210, 212-213.

31. It should be recognized that another reason for the snubbing of Harris at the end of the war had to do with the arrogance he had displayed in his relationship with the Air Staff and many others during the war. The denial of a Peerage for him in 1945 represented, in some sense, belated revenge on the part of many who had earlier suffered his slings and arrows in (mostly) aggrieved silence.

32. *SAOG*, Volume III, 80.

33. H. R. Allen, *The Legacy of Lord Trenchard* (London: Cassell, 1972), 103.

34. Harris, *Bomber Offensive,* 28-60, 121, 162.
35. *New York Times* (April 7, 1984), 32.
36. Harris, *Bomber Offensive,* 277.
37. Norman Longmate, *The Bombers* (London: Hutchinson, 1983), 145.
38. Hastings, *Bomber Command,* 245.
39. Harris, *Bomber Offensive,* 10, 22-23.
40. *Ibid.,* 176-177. Harris argued as well that there was no set body of international law governing the use of aircraft against urban targets, a point that we have dealt with earlier in this chapter.
41. *Ibid.,* 242.
42. Robert C. Earhart and Alfred F. Hurley, eds., *Air Power and Warfare* (Washington, D.C.: Office of Air Force History, 1979), 200-201.
43. Basil Liddell Hart, "The Military Strategist," in *Churchill Revised,* ed. A. J. P. Taylor et al. (New York: The Dial Press, 1969), 175.
44. Winston S. Churchill, *The Gathering Storm* (Boston: Houghton Mifflin Company, 1948), 149.
45. Harold Nicolson, *The War Years 1939-1945* (New York: Atheneum, 1967), 121-122.
46. Sir John Colville, as quoted in Ronald Lewin's *Churchill as Warlord* (New York: Stein and Day, 1973), 7.
47. Barton Bernstein, "Why We Didn't Use Poison Gas in World War II," *American Heritage* (August-September 1985), 42.
48. Hastings, *Bomber Command,* 107.
49. A. J. P. Taylor, "The Statesman," in *Churchill Revised,* ed. A. J. P. Taylor et al. (New York: The Dial Press, 1969), 48-49.
50. H. A. Jones, *The War in the Air* (London: Oxford University Press, 1937), 79.
51. R. V. Jones, *Most Secret War* (London: Hamish and Hamilton, 1978), 183.
52. Winston S. Churchill, *The Grand Alliance* (Boston: Houghton Mifflin Company, 1951), 507-509 (emphasis in original).
53. *SAOG,* Volume I, 342-343.
54. Charles Messenger, *"Bomber" Harris,* 231.
55. Winston Churchill, *The Hinge of Fate* (Boston: Houghton Mifflin Company, 1950), 281.
56. Martin Gilbert, *The Second World War* (New York: Henry Holt and Company, 1989), 308, 352. Churchill went out of his way to provide Stalin with suitably graphic evidence of what Bomber Command was doing to Germany. In April 1943 he sent Stalin a film revealing the results of the British bombing of Essen. Stalin responded by saying he would show the film to the entire Soviet army and population.
57. Taylor, "The Statesman," 48.
58. *SAOG,* Volume II, 12-13.
59. *Ibid.,* 14 (emphasis supplied).
60. Hastings, *Bomber Command,* 188.
61. Harris, *Bomber Offensive,* 145.

62. Anthony Verrier, *The Bomber Offensive* (New York: The Macmillan Company, 1969), 183.
63. *SAOG*, Volume II, 84.
64. Denis Richards, *Portal of Hungerford* (London: Heinemann, 1978).
65. Harris, *Bomber Offensive*, 106-107.
66. R. W. Thompson, *Churchill and Morton* (London: Hodder and Stoughton, 1976), 44, 48.
67. Alex Danchev, "The Central Direction of War," in *Sword and Mace*, ed. John Sweetman (London: Brassey's Defence Publishers, 1986), 68.
68. Longmate, *The Bombers*, 345-346.
69. Verrier, *The Bomber Offensive*, 183, 251.
70. *SAOG*, Volume I, 154.
71. Hastings, *Bomber Command*, 184.
72. *SAOG*, Volume III, 52-54.
73. Longmate, *The Bombers*, 151.
74. Colville, *The Fringes of Power*, 37, 165.

Notes to Chapter 3

1. Freeman Dyson, *Weapons and Hope* (New York: Harper and Row, 1984), viii.
2. *Ibid.,* 120.
3. Solly Zuckerman et al., *Science in War* (London: Penguin Books, 1940), 34.
4. Arthur Compton, *Atomic Quest* (New York: Oxford University Press, 1956), 41-42.
5. Herbert F. York, "Making Weapons, Talking Peace," *Bulletin of the Atomic Scientists* (May 1988), 27.
6. Ronald Clark, *Tizard* (London: Methuen, 1965), 234.
7. Quoted in Ronald W. Clark, *The Rise of the Boffins* (London: Phoenix House, 1962).
8. The Earl of Birkenhead, *The Professor and the Prime Minister* (Boston: Houghton Mifflin Company, 1962), 263.
9. Sir Solly Zuckerman offers some interesting evidence on the Cherwell-Tizard dispute. It was Zuckerman, along with J. D. Bernal, who had undertaken a study of the effects of bombing on Hull and Birmingham that Cherwell supposedly used to buttress his argument about "dehousing." Zuckerman notes, however, that his final report actually refuted Cherwell's whole thesis. Collapse of morale, he found, was never a major threat in either British city. At the same time, Zuckerman dismisses the notion that the Cherwell-Tizard dispute was one between darkness and light. He argues that Tizard was himself in favor of some area bombing, and that the argument between the two "was a technical one." Solly Zuckerman, *From Apes to Warlords* (New York: Harper and Row, 1978), 139-148.

10. Anthony Verrier, *The Bomber Offensive* (New York: The Macmillan Company, 1969), 89.
11. C. P. Snow, *Science and Government* (Cambridge, Massachusetts: Harvard University Press, 1961), 49.
12. *Ibid.,* 50.
13. Clark, *The Rise of the Boffins,* 227.
14. For a discussion of the debate over the Transportation Plan, see Walt W. Rostow, *Pre-Invasion Bombing Strategy* (Austin, Texas: University of Texas Press, 1981).
15. Hilary St. George Saunders, *The Fight Is Won* (London: Her Majesty's Stationary Office, 1954), 85.
16. Solly Zuckerman, *Nuclear Illusion and Reality* (New York: Vintage Press, 1983), 56, 240.
17. *Ibid.,* 15, 29.
18. Solly Zuckerman, "Bombs and Morals," *The New Republic* (November 17, 1986), 37-42. Review of Ronald Schaffer's *Wings of Judgment* (New York: Oxford University Press, 1985).
19. Solly Zuckerman, *Scientists and War* (New York: Harper and Row, 1966), 131,138.
20. *Ibid.,* 47-48.
21. Clark, *The Rise of the Boffins,* 69.
22. P. M. S. Blackett, *Studies of War* (New York: Hill and Wang, 1962), 73.
23. Paul Johnson, *Modern Times* (New York: Harper and Row, 1983), 402.
24. P. M. S. Blackett, *Military and Political Consequences of Atomic Energy* (London: Turnstile Press, 1948), 116.
25. Clark, *The Rise of the Boffins,* 223.
26. R. V. Jones, *Most Secret War* (London: Hamish Hamilton, 1978), 210.
27. *Ibid.,* 210-211.
28. Arthur Harris, *Bomber Offensive* (London: Collins, 1947), 131.
29. Quoted in Zuckerman, *Scientists and War,* 126.
30. One classic study of the factors in German military morale during World War II is Edward A. Shils and Morris Janowitz, "Cohesion and Disintegration in the Wehrmacht in World War II," *Public Opinion Quarterly* XII (Summer 1948).
31. R. V. Jones, *Most Secret War,* 385.
32. Gavin Lyall, ed., *The War in the Air* (New York: William Morrow and Company, 1968), 295.
33. Norman Longmate, *The Bombers* (London: Hutchinson, 1983), 35.
34. Neil Sheehan, *A Bright Shining Lie* (New York: Vantage Books, 1989), 107-109. Vann, it should be noted, frowned on such tactics in both moral and practical terms, since it encouraged people to join the Viet Cong. It should also be observed that Vann later became somewhat less discriminating. By 1972, when he held effective military command in the Central Coast and the Highlands, he was known as "Mr. B-52" for his willingness to call in air

strikes against the enemy. This shift seems to reflect the behavior of those in Bomber Command who lost their initial squeamishness about attacking German civilians.

35. J. M. Spaight, *Bombing Vindicated* (London: Geoffrey Bles, 1944), 122.

36. J. Glenn Gray, *The Warriors* (New York: Harper and Row, 1959), 135.

37. John Colville, *The Fringes of Power* (New York: W. W. Norton and Company, 1985), 453-454.

38. Paul Fussell, *Wartime* (New York: Oxford University Press, 1989), 50, 58. Sir John Slessor, who led Bomber Command's 5 Group from May 1941 to March 1942 and was later was head of Coastal Command as well as a principal figure in the RAF Air Staff during the war, recalled that he ordered that the dropping of beer bottles be accepted seriously, since it led to higher aircrew morale. "The beer bottle remained a highly-regarded piece of operational equipment." Sir John Slessor, *The Central Blue* (London: Cassell and Company, 1956), 374.

39. An interesting analysis of aircrew's actual reaction to the first dropping of the atomic bomb is William Bradford Huie's *Hiroshima Pilot* (New York: Putnam, 1964).

40. The feelings of Esmond Romilly as cited in *Friends Apart* by Philip Toynbee (London: McGibbon and Kee, 1954), 68.

41. Dieter Georgi, "The Bombing of Dresden," *Harvard Magazine* (March-April 1985), 56-64.

42. Lyall, *The War in the Air*, 266-267.

43. Colville, *The Fringes of Power*, 496-497.

44. Guenter Lewy, "Superior Orders, Nuclear Warfare, and the Dictates of Conscience," in *War and Morality*, ed. Richard A. Wasserstrom (Belmont, California: Wadsworth Publishing Company, 1970), 118. Goebbel's thesis was later used at the Nuremberg trails to bring charges against certain members of the Luftwaffe for their own activities.

45. John U. Nef, *War and Human Progress* (Cambridge, Massachusetts: Harvard University Press, 1950), 372.

46. Verrier, *The Bomber Offensive*, 208.

47. Longmate, *The Bombers*, 378.

48. David Irving, *The Destruction of Dresden* (New York: Holt, Rinehart and Winston, 1963), 116.

49. Longmate, *The Bombers*, 269.

50. Martin Middlebrook, *The Battle of Hamburg* (London: Allen Lane, 1980), 349.

51. Irving, *The Destruction of Dresden*, 138, 142.

52. Max Hastings, *Bomber Command* (New York: Simon and Schuster, 1987), 112.

53. Paul Johnson, *Modern Times*, 404.

54. Colville, *The Fringes of Power*, 549.

55. Spaight, *Bombing Vindicated*, 115.

56. H. R. Allen, *The Legacy of Lord Trenchard* (London: Cassell, 1972), ix.

57. Hastings, *Bomber Command*, 352.

Notes to Chapter 4

1. Brian Bond, *Liddell Hart* (London: Cassell, 1979), 154.

2. Ian McLaine, *Ministry of Morale* (London: George Allen and Unwin, 1979), 160.

3. Ronald Schaeffer, *Wings of Judgment* (New York: Oxford University Press, 1985), xiii.

4. Angus Calder, *The People's War* (New York: Pantheon Books, 1969), 491.

5. See, for example, Bernard Cohen's *The Public's Impact on Foreign Policy* (Boston: Little Brown and Company, 1973). An earlier study that still remains of interest is James Rosenau's *Public Opinion and Foreign Policy* (New York: Random House, 1961).

6. Typical of the evidence available was this headline from the *Sunday Express* on September 5, 1943, which proclaimed that the RAF had "Coventrated" 43 cities in the Reich. Two months later the *Sunday Times* proclaimed that a third "of Berlin [had been] laid in Ruins. City to be reduced area by area." The story that followed allowed as how a third of all of Germany's major cities had been devastated as well. Norman Longmate, *The Bombers* (London: Hutchinson, 1983), 370.

7. Howard Cowan, "Allies Decide on New Policy of Terror Raids," *St. Louis Post Dispatch* (February 18, 1945), 1.

8. Noble Frankland and Charles Webster, *The Strategic Air Offensive Against Germany 1939-1945* (London: Her Majesty's Stationery Office, 1961), Volume III, 13 (hereafter cited as *SAOG*).

9. Longmate, *The Bombers*, 368.

10. Max Hastings, *Bomber Command* (New York: Simon and Schuster, 1987), 125.

11. Robert H. Ahrenfeldt, *Psychiatry in the British Army* (New York: Columbia University Press, 1958), 13-28.

12. Sir Robert Vansittart, *The Black Record* (London: Hamish Hamilton, 1941), viii, 4-5, 18-20.

13. T. D. Burridge, *British Labour and Hitler's War* (London: Deutsch, 1976), 54, 60-64.

14. In his earlier writings, especially *Air Power and War Rights* (London: Longmans, Green, 1924), Spaight fretted that aerial warfare might revert to "strong cave-man stuff." One deterrent to indiscriminate destruction, he suggested, might be to have an officer in control of each airplane. With true gentlemen at the plane's controls, the temptation to resort to crude tactics might be mitigated, especially since a good deal of chivalry had been demonstrated by pilots in World War I. Curiously, in view of his later stance, Spaight expressed distinct doubts about the moral justification of bombing cities. In 1930, for example, he called them "bad work for civilization" and openly opposed such measures. See J. M. Spaight, *Air Power and the Cities* (London: Longmans, Green, 1930), 234.

15. J. M. Spaight, *Bombing Vindicated* (London: Geoffrey Bles, 1944), 7-23, 119-122.

16. Hastings, *Bomber Command*, 174.

17. Calder, *The People's War*, 229.
18. Tom Harrisson, *Living Through the Blitz* (London: Collins, 1976), 318.
19. Hastings, *Bomber Command*, 174.
20. Ronald Jasper, *George Bell* (London: Oxford University Press, 1967), 249. "The Sword of the Spirit" received a good deal of private support from the government, a fact that the latter was generally anxious to conceal.
21. Calder, *The People's War*, 478.
22. John Collins, *Faith Under Fire* (London: Frewin, 1966), 69.
23. Calder, *The People's War*, 485.
24. F. A. Iremonger, *William Temple* (London: Oxford University Press, 1948), 545.
25. *Ibid.*, 232, 542.
26. Charles Smyth, *Cyril Forster Garbett* (London: Hodder and Stoughton, 1959), 291.
27. Vera Brittain, *Testament of Experience* (London: Victor Gollancz, 1957), 335. The distinguished British diplomatist Harold Nicolson can hardly have had much in common with Vera Brittain, but his views on the Church's role in wartime were curiously rather supportive of this particular point. As a member of the BBC Board of Directors, Nicolson had to decide on whether the clergy should be allowed to preach forgiveness of enemies. "I say I prefer that to the clergy who seek to pretend that the bombing of Cologne was a Christian act." The essential Nicolson is also reflected, however, in his further comment that "I wish the clergy would keep their mouths shut about the war. It is none of their business." Harold Nicolson, *The War Years 1939-1945* (New York: Atheneum, 1967), 228.
28. Gordon C. Zahn, "Social Science and the Theology of War," in *Morality and Modern Warfare*, ed. William J. Nagle (Baltimore: Helicon Press, 1960), 118.
29. Calder, *The People's War*, 495-497.
30. Great Britain, *5 Parliamentary Debates* (Commons), Volume 393 (October 28, 1943), 364.
31. Calder, *The People's War*, 490; Hastings, *Bomber Command*, 174.
32. Paul Fussell, *Wartime* (New York: Oxford University Press, 1989), 148-149.
33. Basil Liddell Hart, *Paris, of the Future of War* (London: K Paul, Trench, Trubner, 1925), 45.
34. Basil Liddell Hart, *The Liddell Hart Memoirs*, Volume I (New York: G. P. Putnam's Sons, 1965), 98-99, 142.
35. Bond, *Liddell Hart*, 145.
36. For a more detailed expression of Liddell Hart's views on British wartime strategy, see, for example, *This Expanding War* (London: Faber, 1942) and *Thoughts on War* (London: Faber, 1944).
37. Basil Liddell Hart, *The Liddell Hart Memoirs*, Volume II, 245.
38. Bond, *Liddell Hart*, 143, 146.
39. John Colville, *The Fringes of Power* (New York: W. W. Norton and Company, 1985), 306.
40. Bond, *Liddell Hart*, 149.
41. Anthony Trythall, *'Boney' Fuller* (London: Cassell, 1977), 226.

42. Bond, *Liddell Hart,* 153.

43. John J. Mearsheimer, *Liddell Hart and the Weight of History* (Ithaca: Cornell University Press, 1988), 99-126, 154.

44. Great Britain, *5 Parliamentary Debates* (Lords), Volume 121 (January 27, 1942), 480.

45. George Bell, *The Church and Humanity* (New York: Green and Company, 1946), 50.

46. Great Britain, *5 Parliamentary Debates* (Lords), Volume 125 (February 11, 1943), 1080.

47. Bell, *The Church and Humanity,* 23, 26-27.

48. Geoffrey Best, "The Bishop and the Bomber," *History Today* 33 (September 1983), 31.

49. Longmate, *The Bombers,* 374.

50. Woolton did go on to say that "I also want to tell you that there isn't a soul who doesn't know that the only reason why you make it is because you believe it is your duty to make it as a Christian priest." Woolton claimed (perhaps more out of friendship than realism) that the House held Bell in the "greatest respect," even while completely disagreeing with him. Jasper, *George Bell,* 277.

51. Great Britain, *5 Parliamentary Debates* (Lords), Volume 130 (February 9, 1944), 738-746.

52. *The Daily Telegraph* (June 15, 1959).

53. Fenner Brockway, *Bermondsey Story* (London: George Allen and Unwin, 1949), 219-229.

54. *Ibid.,* 232.

55. *Ibid.,* 230.

56. Great Britain, *5 Parliamentary Debates* (Commons), Volume 395 (December 1, 1943), 338.

57. Great Britain *5 Parliamentary Debates* (Commons), Volume 408 (March 6, 1945), 1901.

58. Great Britain, *5 Parliamentary Debates* (Commons), Volume 408 (March 6, 1945), 1902-1903.

59. Hilary Bailey, *Vera Brittain* (Harmondsworth, Middlesex: Penguin Books, 1987), 17.

60. Brittain, *Testament of Experience,* 38, 109.

61. *Ibid.,* 326, 334-335.

62. *Ibid.,* 358.

63. Vera Brittain, *Humiliation with Honor* (London: Andrew Dakers, 1942), 86, 89.

64. Brittain, *Testament of Experience,* 292.

65. Vera Brittain, "Massacre by Bombing," *Fellowship* 10 (March 1944). This episode was one of the few examples of public protest against area bombing in the United States during the war. See "Obliteration Raids On German Cities Protested in U.S.," *New York Times* (March 6, 1944) and "Patterson Assails Anti-Bombing Plea," *New York Times* (March 11, 1944).

66. Brittain, *Humiliation with Honor,* 27, 41.

67. Brittain, *Testament of Experience,* 289.
68. *Ibid.,* 351, 367.
69. *Ibid.,* 374, 398.

Notes to Chapter 5

1. Sissela Bok offers a very apt description of what she calls the "moralizers" in international affairs, especially those who are "high-handed in the face of human complexity." For other examples of the moralistic temptation, see her *A Strategy for Peace* (New York: Pantheon Books, 1989), 118-125.
2. Donald Warwick, "The Ethics of Administrative Discretion," in *Public Duties: The Moral Obligations of Government Officials,* Joel Fleishman et al., eds. (Cambridge, Massachusetts: Harvard University Press, 1981), 93.
3. Karl Von Clausewitz, *On War,* trans. Michael Howard and Peter Paret (Princeton: Princeton University Press, 1976), 75-76.
4. Michael Walzer, *Just and Unjust Wars* (New York: Basic Books, 1977), 32.
5. Arthur Tedder, *With Prejudice* (Boston: Little, Brown and Company, 1966), 19.
6. David Irving, *The Destruction of Dresden* (New York: Holt, Rinehart and Winston, 1963), 10.
7. Michael Howard, "Temperamenta Belli: Can War Be Controlled?" in *Restraints on War,* ed. Michael Howard (Oxford: Oxford University Press, 1979), 3-4. Clausewitz actually seems to agree with Howard on this point, and in so doing demonstrates that he was hardly consistent in his treatment of the environment of war. He allows as how "war is simply the continuation of political intercourse. . . . War cannot be divorced from political life; and whenever this occurs in our thinking about war, the main links that connect the two elements are destroyed and we are left with something pointless and devoid of sense." Assuming that "political life" can in some sense be equated with the moral values of the nation (as we argue here), this appears to contradict his other comments on the uncontrollability of war, not to mention the irrelevance of ethical considerations in conflict. Clausewitz, *On War,* 605.
8. Sir Harold Nicolson, *The War Years 1939-1945* (New York: Atheneum, 1967), 429.
9. Herbert Feis, *Churchill, Roosevelt, Stalin* (Princeton: Princeton University Press, 1957), 273-274.
10. Rushworth Kidder, "The Three Great Domains of Human Action," *Christian Science Monitor* (January 29, 1990), 13. For Lord Moulton's original essay, see "Law and Manners," *Atlantic Monthly* (July 1924), 1-5.
11. For the text of the Hague Convention of 1907, see A. Pearce Higgins, *The Hague Peace Conference and Other International Conferences Concerning the Laws and Usages of War* (Cambridge: Cambridge University Press, 1909). See also Sheldon Cohen, *Arms and Judgment* (Boulder, Colorado: Westview Press, 1989), 117-124.

12. James F. Childress, "Just-War Theories," in *War, Morality and the Military Profession,* ed. Malham M. Wakin, 2nd edition (Boulder, Colorado: Westview Press, 1986), 256-276.
13. Douglas Botting, *From the Ruins of the Reich: Germany 1945-1949* (New York: Crown, 1985), 130. Churchill himself, on a visit to Germany in the late spring of 1945, seems to have been shaken by what he saw of all this. He was "moved and upset" by the conditions he observed, and in particular thought the faces of the children were "very strained." John Colville, *The Fringes of Power* (New York: W. W. Norton and Company, 1985), 579.
14. Walzer, *Just and Unjust Wars,* 153.
15. Norman Longmate, *The Bombers* (London: Hutchinson, 1983), 345-346.
16. John C. Ford, "The Morality of Obliteration Bombing," *Theological Studies* 5 (1944), 280-305.
17. John Rawls, *A Theory of Justice* (Cambridge, Massachusetts: Harvard University Press, 1971), 379.
18. Noble Frankland, *The Bombing Offensive Against Germany* (London: Faber and Faber, 1965), 113-114.
19. Max Hastings, *Bomber Command* (New York: Simon and Schuster, 1987), 124.
20. J. E. Hare and Carey B. Joynt, *Ethics and International Affairs* (New York: St. Martin's Press, 1982), 70.
21. Peter Fleming, *Operation Sea Lion* (New York: Simon and Schuster, 1957), 260-264. It is true that for a time after the fall of France Hitler seemed willing to make peace with Britain if she would allow German hegemony on the Continent. Hitler even spoke of allowing the British to retain their empire. The implication was that Great Britain would be allowed a continued independent, if subordinate, existence. Given the record of Hitler's adherence to his "solemn vows," however, this offer has to be viewed with considerable skepticism.
22. Winston S. Churchill, *The Grand Alliance* (Boston: Houghton Mifflin Company, 1951), 606-607.
23. Longmate, *The Bombers,* 354.
24. Frankland, *Bombing Offensive,* 96.
25. *Ibid.,* 61-62.
26. Winston Churchill, *The Hinge of Fate* (Boston: Houghton Mifflin Company, 1950), 770.
27. Dwight D. Eisenhower, *Crusade in Europe* (New York: Doubleday, 1949), 419.
28. Dudley Saward, *Bomber Harris* (Garden City, New York: Doubleday, 1985), 601.
29. See, for example, *Foundations of the Metaphysics of Morals,* trans. Lewis White Beck (Indianapolis: Bobbs Merrill, 1959), 39ff, and *The Doctrine of Virtue,* trans. Mary J. Gregor (New York: Harper and Row, 1964), 134-135.
30. W. W. Rostow, *Pre-Invasion Bombing Strategy* (Austin: University of Texas Press, 1981), 51.
31. Winston S. Churchill, *Closing the Ring* (Boston: Houghton Mifflin Company, 1951), 529.
32. John Finnis, Joseph Boyle, and Germain Grisez, *Nuclear Deterrence, Morality and Realism* (Oxford: Clarendon Press, 1987), 40.

33. Ronald Lewin, *Churchill as Warlord* (New York: Stein and Day, 1973), 110.

34. Gavin Lyall, ed., *The War in the Air* (New York: William Morrow and Company, 1968), 360-363.

35. Churchill, *Closing the Ring*, 529-530.

36. G. Elfstrom and N. Fotion, *Military Ethics* (London: Routledge and Kegan Paul, 1986), 17.

37. Neil Sheehan, *A Bright Shining Lie* (New York: Vantage Books, 1989), 108.

38. In discussing the matter of obligations, one might count as an imperfect duty the responsibility of free societies to extend the benefits of freedom to those suffering under an oppressive regime. The question for present purposes becomes whether area bombing had at least some degree of proportionality in that it helped, even in a marginal way, in the defeat of the Nazis and thus released the German people from their bondage to an abhorrent regime. Such an argument, while logically of some interest, is almost never found in the literature supportive of British bombing policy in World War II.

Notes to Chapter 6

1. J. E. Hare and Carey B. Joynt, *Ethics and International Affairs* (New York: St. Martin's Press, 1982), 4-5.

2. Norman Longmate, *The Bombers* (London: Hutchinson, 1983), 356.

3. United States, *Strategic Bombing Survey, Overall Report, European War* (Washington, D.C.: Government Printing Office, 1945), 108 (hereafter cited as USSBS).

4. Earl R. Beck, "The Allied Bombing of Germany, 1942-1945, and the German Response: Dilemmas of Judgment," *German Studies Review* V (October 1982), 334.

5. Joseph Goebbels, *The Goebbels Diaries, 1942-1943*, trans. Louis Lochner (Garden City, New York: Doubleday, 1948), 102.

6. *Ibid.*, 252.

7. Walter Goerlitz, *The History of the German General Staff: 1657-1945*, trans. Brian Battershaw (New York: Praeger, 1953), 434.

8. Robin Cross, *The Bombers* (New York: Macmillan Publishing Company, 1987), 144.

9. John Kenneth Galbraith, *The Affluent Society* (Boston: Houghton Mifflin, 1958), 163.

10. John Keegan puts the total number of men and women diverted from other sectors of the German armed forces to air defense at about two million. He goes on to say that this was the one and only military justification that might be given for the area offensive. *The Seond World War* (New York: Viking, 1989), 430.

11. P. M. S. Blackett, *Military and Political Consequences of Atomic Energy* (London: Turnstile Press, 1948), 195.

12. Sir Arthur Tedder, *With Prejudice* (Boston: Little Brown and Company, 1966), 103.

13. Albert Speer, *Inside the Third Reich,* trans., Richard and Clara Winston (New York: The Macmillan Company, 1970), 214.

14. Adolf Galland, one of the leading figures in the German Luftwaffe, addressed this point as far as German airpower was concerned when he suggested that "less changing from one target category to another, and adequate repetition of attack, would have broken the backbone of the Luftwaffe and of its strategic potential more quickly, with less expenditure of manpower and materiel, and more conclusively." "Defeat of the Luftwaffe," in *The Impact of Air Power,* ed. E. M. Emme (New York: Van Nostrand, 1959), 258.

15. USSBS, *Over-All Report, European War* (September 30, 1945), 18.

16. Goebbels, *The Goebbels Diaries,* 1942-1943, 438.

17. F. W. Winterbotham, *The Ultra Secret* (London: Weidenfeld and Nicolson, 1974). Ultra was the term used for all the information gathered from the "Enigma" machine, which was the basic German encrypting device, and which the British had come into possession of shortly before the war began.

18. Christopher Andrew, "Churchill and Intelligence," in *Leaders and Intelligence,* ed. Michael I. Handel (London: Frank Cass, 1989), 181.

19. F. H. Hinsley, *British Intelligence in the Second World War,* Volume III, Part I (New York: Cambridge University Press, 1984), 304. This multi-volume series is the official history of British intelligence activity in the war and its influence on strategy and operations.

20. *Ibid.,* 307, 516.

21. *Ibid.,* 296-298.

22. *Ibid.,* 925.

23. Martin Gilbert, *The Second World War* (New York: Henry Holt and Company, 1989), 639.

24. Peter Calvocoressi, "Ne Plus Ultra World War," *The Times* (London), May 3, 1984.

25. Mark Moore, "Realms of Obligation and Virtue," in *Public Duties: The Moral Obligations of Government Officials,* ed. Joel L. Fleishman, Lance Liebman, and Mark Moore (Cambridge, Massachusetts: Harvard University Press, 1981), 10.

26. Noble Frankland, *The Bombing Offensive Against Germany* (London: Faber and Faber, 1965), 113-114.

27. Great Britain, *5 Parliamentary Debates* (Commons), Volume 378 (February 25, 1942), 316-317.

28. Great Britain, *5 Parliamentary Debates* (Commons) Volume 397 (March 2, 1944), 1602.

29. John Ellis, *Brute Force* (New York: Viking, 1990), 177.

30. Archer Jones, *The Art of War in the Western World* (New York: Oxford University Press, 1987), 582. Sir Arthur Harris at one point even boasted about the exorbitant costs of training his aircrew. He noted that the education of a Bomber Command pilot was the most expensive of all the world's air forces, amounting to about 10,000 pounds for each person, "enough to send ten men to Oxford or Cambridge for three years." Harris, *Bomber Offensive* (London: Collins, 1947), 98.

31. Noble Frankland and Charles Webster, *The Strategic Air Offensive Against Germany 1939-1945* (London: Her Majesty's Stationery Office, 1961), Volume II, 54-57 (hereafter cited as *SAOG*).

32. Frankland, *The Bombing Offensive Against Germany,* 88, 103.

33. James Stokesbury, *A Short History of Air Power* (New York: William Morrow and Company, 1986), 229.

34. Max Hastings, *Bomber Command* (New York: Simon and Schuster, 1987), 266.

35. It is important to accept that few if any of the major figures involved in the British strategic air offensive were models of consistency. Bufton, for example, certainly favored precision bombing as a general rule, but even late in the war he sometimes varied from this theme. He was a major supporter of the Thunderclap Plan, for example. In defending this scheme, Bufton adopted the mantle of the airpower clinician: "If we assume that the day-time population of the area attacked is 300,000, we may expect 220,000 casualties. 50 percent of these, or 110,000 may expect to be killed. . . . Such an attack, resulting in so many deaths . . . cannot help but have a shattering effect on political and civilian morale all over Germany." *SAOG,* Volume III, 98-105.

36. *SAOG,* Volume IV, 298.

37. Charles Messenger, *"Bomber" Harris* (New York: St. Martin's Press, 1984), 180-181.

38. *Ibid.,* 390.

39. A. J. P. Taylor, *The Second World War* (New York: Paragon Books, 1975), 78.

40. Hastings, *Bomber Command,* 194.

41. Anthony Verrier, *The Bomber Offensive* (New York: The Macmillan Company, 1969), 244. To be fair, there is some question as to whether there were sufficient resources in Great Britain to construct a huge force of Mosquitos. These aircraft were mostly made of wood, and whether there were sufficient carpenters in England physically to build the critical mass of Mosquitos needed remains a disputed question.

42. R. V. Jones, *Most Secret War* (London: Hamish Hamilton, 1968), 304.

43. H. R. Allen, *The Legacy of Lord Trenchard* (London: Cassell, 1972), 181.

44. Tedder, *With Prejudice,* 117.

45. Hastings, *Bomber Command,* 117-119.

46. Solly Zuckerman, "Strategic Bombing and the Defeat of Germany," *Journal of the Royal United Services Institute* 130 (June 1985), 69.

47. Longmate, *The Bombers,* 360.

48. Allen, *The Legacy of Lord Trenchard,* 185, 214.

Notes to Chapter 7

1. Michael Sherry, *The Rise of American Air Power* (New Haven: Yale University Press, 1987), 363.

2. Norman Longmate, *The Bombers* (London: Hutchinson, 1983), 166, 169-173.

3. John Campbell, *The Experience of World War II* (New York: Oxford University Press, 1989), 112.

4. I am grateful to Mr. Don Kerr, a career (and now retired) RAF navigator at the International Institute of Strategic Studies in London, for suggesting these particular points during a personal interview.

5. Max Hastings, *Bomber Command* (New York: Simon and Schuster, 1987), 272.

6. Paul Fussell, *Wartime* (New York, Oxford University Press, 1989), 156-157.

7. Hastings, *Bomber Command*, 300.

8. Walt W. Rostow, *Pre-Invasion Bombing Strategy* (Austin: University of Texas Press, 1981), 45.

9. Robin Cross, *The Bombers* (New York: Macmillan Publishing Company, 1987), 158.

10. Longmate, *The Bombers*, 329.

11. Brian Bond, *Liddell Hart* (London: Cassell, 1979), 148.

12. Longmate, *The Bombers*, 124-125. There was some unintentional irony here: Scott's expedition to the South Pole is now regarded as a prime example of bad planning and faulty execution.

13. Noel Barber, *A Sinister Twilight: The Fall of Singapore* (New York: Houghton Mifflin, 1968). On the effects of the debacle at Singapore, see also J. R. M. Butler, *Grand Strategy*, Volume III, Part II (London: Her Majesty's Stationery Office, 1964), 403-421.

14. Tony Carty, "The Origins of the Doctrine of Deterrence," in *Ethics and Defence*, ed. Howard Davis (Oxford: Basil Blackwell, 1986), 119.

15. Martin Gilbert, *The Second World War* (New York: Henry Holt and Company, 1989), 433. Emphasis supplied.

16. Winston S. Churchill, *Their Finest Hour* (Boston: Houghton Mifflin Company, 1949), 349.

17. Larry Addington, *The Patterns of War Since the Eighteenth Century* (Bloomington: Indiana University Press, 1984), 211.

18. Winston S. Churchill, *Triumph and Tragedy* (Boston: Houghton Mifflin Company, 1953), 44.

19. Barton Bernstein, "Why We Didn't Use Poison Gas in World War II," *American Heritage* (August-September 1985), 42.

20. Lee Kennett, *A History of Strategic Bombing* (New York: Scribner's, 1982), 117-124.

21. John Colville, *The Fringes of Power* (New York: W. W. Norton and Company, 1985), 78.

22. For a good general discussion of deterrence theory, see Patrick Morgan, *Deterrence* (Beverly Hills, California: Sage Publications, 1977) as well as Anthony Kenny, *The Logic of Deterrence* (Cambridge: Cambridge University Press, 1985).

23. George Quester, *Deterrence Before Hiroshima* (New York: John Wiley and Sons, 1966), 152.

24. *The London Observer* (April 8, 1984).

25. Hastings, *Bomber Command,* 352.
26. Arthur Harris, *Bomber Offensive* (London: Collins, 1947), 263.
27. Noble Frankland and Charles Webster, *The Strategic Air Offensive Against Germany 1939-1945* (London: Her Majesty's Stationery Office, 1961), Volume III, 118 (hereafter cited as *SAOG*).
28. Telford Taylor, *Nuremberg and Viet Nam* (Chicago: Quadrangle Books, 1970), 89.
29. Kennett, *A History of Strategic Bombing,* 108.
30. Geoffrey Best, "The Bishop and the Bomber," *History Today* 33 (September 1983), 32.
31. Geoffrey Best, *Humanity in Warfare* (New York: Columbia University Press, 1980), 285.
32. Michael Howard, "*Temperamenta Belli*: Can War Be Controlled?" in *Restraints on War,* ed. Michael Howard (Oxford: Oxford University Press, 1979), 10.
33. Martin Creveld, *Technology and War* (New York: The Free Press, 1989), 196.
34. Arthur Marwick, *Britain in the Century of Total War* (Boston: Little, Brown and Company, 1968), 113.
35. A. Jurist (F. J. P. Veale), *Advance to Barbarism* (London: Thompson and Smith, 1948), 127.
36. Hilary St. George Saunders, *The Fight is Won* (London: Her Majesty's Stationery Office, 1954), 271.
37. Neil Sheehan, *A Bright Shining Lie* (New York: Vantage Books, 1989), 621.
38. *Ibid.,* 592.
39. Raymond Aron's *The Century of Total War* (Boston: The Beacon Press, 1960) still remains as one of the most perceptive analyses of the issues discussed here.
40. Thomas E. Murray, "Morality and Security: The Forgotten Equation," in *Morality and Modern Warfare,* ed. William J. Nagle (Baltimore: Helicon Press, 1960), 59.
41. See, for example, Alan Clark's *The Donkeys* (London: Hutchinson, 1961).
42. H. A. Jones, *The War in the Air* (Oxford: Clarendon Press, 1937), Appendices, 15.
43. Perhaps in contrast to the views of British infantrymen in World War I, veterans of Bomber Command have not taken kindly to the notion that they were led by donkeys. Thus Noble Frankland muses how "strange [it is] that those who developed this doctrine [of strategic bombing] and tried later to put it into practice are now in danger of being labelled as the 'donkeys' and the exponents of inhumanity of the second war." Frankland, *The Bombing Offensive Against Germany* (London: Faber and Faber, 1965), 26.
44. David Irving, *The Destruction of Dresden* (New York: Holt, Rinehart and Winston, 1963), 9.
45. Michael Fellman, *Inside War: The Guerilla Conflict in Missouri During the American Civil War* (New York: Oxford University Press, 1989), as quoted in James M. McPherson, "Wartime," *New York Review of Books* (April 12, 1990).
46. Bond, *Liddell Hart,* 155.

47. Marwick, *Britain in the Century of Total War*, 113.
48. Bruce Catton, *The Civil War* (New York: American Heritage Press, 1971), 185. The truth (or warning) in Catton's analysis may be seen in some unexpected situations. There is, for example, the reaction of Israeli soldiers on the West Bank engaged in suppressing the *Intifada*. When Israeli Prime Minister Yitzhak Shamir visited a military unit in the area in January 1989, he was barraged with complaints from the soldiers that their humanity was being undermined by their brutalizing of the Palestinians. One captain stated that "the basic values we grew up on changed, whether we like it or not, during our service here." *San Francisco Chronicle* (January 18, 1989).
49. Colville, *The Fringes of Power*, 292.

BIBLIOGRAPHY

Addington, Larry H. *The Patterns of War Since the Eighteenth Century.* Bloomington, Indiana: Indiana University Press, 1984.

Ahrenfeldt, Robert H. *Psychiatry in the British Army in the Second World War.* New York: Columbia University Press, 1958.

Allen, Wing Commander H. R. *The Legacy of Lord Trenchard.* London: Cassell, 1972.

Andrews, Allen. *The Air Marshals.* New York: William Morrow and Company, 1970.

Bailey, Hilary. *Vera Brittain.* Harmondsworth, Middlesex: Penguin Books, 1987.

Bailey, Sydney. *War and Conscience in the Nuclear Age.* New York: St. Martin's Press, 1987.

Batchelder, Robert. *The Irreversible Decision, 1939-1950.* Boston: Houghton Mifflin, 1961.

Beck, Earl R. "The Allied Bombing of Germany, 1942-1945, and the German Response: Dilemmas of Judgment." *German Studies Review* V (October 1982).

Bell, George. *Christianity and World Order.* New York: Penguin Books, 1940.

―――. *The Church and Humanity.* New York: Green and Company, 1946.

Bernstein, Barton. "Why We Didn't Use Poison Gas in World War II." *American Heritage* (August-September 1985).

Best, Geoffrey. "The Bishop and the Bomber." *History Today* (September 1983).

―――. *Humanity in Warfare.* New York: Columbia University Press, 1980.

Bidinian, Larry. *The Combined Allied Bombing Offensive Against the German Civilian 1942-1945.* Lawrence, Kansas: Coronado Press, 1976.

Birkenhead, Lord (Frederick Winston Smith). *The Professor and the Prime Minister*. Boston: Houghton Mifflin Company, 1962.

Blackett, P. M. S. *Military and Political Consequences of Atomic Energy*. London: Turnstile Press, 1948.

————. *Studies of War*. New York: Hill and Wang, 1962.

Blix, Hans. "Area Bombardment: Rules and Reasons." *The British Yearbook of International Law 1978*. Oxford: Clarendon Press, 1979.

Bok, Sissela. *A Strategy for Peace*. New York: Pantheon Books, 1989.

Bond, Brian. *Liddell Hart*. London: Cassell, 1979.

Botting, Douglas. *From the Ruins of the Reich: Germany 1945-1949*. New York: Crown, 1985.

Bowyer, Michael. *Mosquito*. London: Faber and Faber, 1967.

Boyle, Andrew. *Trenchard*. London: Collins, 1962.

Boyle, Joseph, Finnis, John, and Grisez, Germain. *Nuclear Deterrence, Morality and Realism*. Oxford: Clarendon Press, 1987.

Brittain, Vera. *Humiliation With Honor*. London: Andrew Dakers Limited, 1942.

————. "Massacre by Bombing." *Fellowship* 10 (March 1944).

————. *Testament of Experience*. London: Victor Gollancz, 1957.

Brockway, Fenner. *Bermondsey Story*. London: George Allen and Unwin, 1949.

Brodie, Bernard. *War and Politics*. New York: The Macmillan Company, 1973.

Burridge, T. D. *British Labour and Hitler's War*. London: Deutsch, 1976.

Caidin, Martin. *The Night Hamburg Died*. New York: Ballantine Books, 1960.

Calder, Angus. *The People's War*. New York: Pantheon Books, 1969.

Calvocoressi, Peter. "Ne Plus Ultra World War." *The Times* (London). May 3, 1984.

Campbell, John. *The Experience of World War II*. New York: Oxford University Press, 1989.

Casey, Lord Richard. *Personal Experience 1939-1945*. London: Constable, 1962.

Cate, James and Craven, Wesley. *The Army Air Forces in World War II*. Seven volumes. Chicago: University of Chicago Press, 1948-1958.

Catton, Bruce. *The Civil War*. New York: American Heritage Press, 1971.

Chesire, Leonard. *Bomber Pilot*. London: Hutchinson, 1943.

Churchill, Winston S. *The Second World War*. Five Volumes. Boston: Houghton Mifflin Company, 1948-1953.

Clark, Alan. *The Donkeys*. London: Hutchinson, 1961.

Clark, Ronald. *The Rise of the Boffins*. London: Phoenix House, 1962.

————. *Tizard*. London: Methuen, 1965.

Cohen, Sheldon. *Arms and Judgment*. Boulder, Colorado: Westview Press, 1989.

Collins, John, *Faith Under Fire*. London: Frewin, 1966.

Colville, John. *The Fringes of Power*. New York: W. W. Norton and Company, 1985.

Compton, Arthur. *Atomic Quest*. New York: Oxford University Press, 1956.

Costello, John. *The Pacific War*. New York: Rawson, Wade, 1981.

Creveld, Martin. *Technology and War*. New York: Free Press, 1989.

Cross, Robin. *The Bombers*. New York: Macmillan Publishing Company, 1987.

Davis, Howard, ed. *Ethics and Defence*. Oxford: Basil Blackwell, 1986.

Dupuy, R. Ernest and Dupuy, Trevor N. *The Encyclopedia of Military History*. Second edition. New York: Harper and Row, 1986.

Dockrill, Michael and Paskins, Barrie. *The Ethics of War*. Minneapolis: University of Minnesota Press, 1979.

Douhet, Giulio. *The Command of the Air*. Trans. Dino Ferrari. New York: Coward-McCann, 1942.

Dyer, Gwynne. *War*. Homewood, Illinois: Dorsey Press, 1985.

Dyson, Freeman. *Weapons and Hope*. New York: Harper and Row, 1984.

Dzwonchyk, Wayne. "Fateful Pathway Clearly Marked." *World War II* (January 1988).

Earhart, Robert C. and Hurley, Alfred F., eds. *Air Power and Warfare.* Washington, D.C.: Office of Air Force History, 1979.

Eisenhower, Dwight D. *Crusade in Europe.* New York: Doubleday, 1949.

Elfstrom, G. and Fotion, N. *Military Ethics.* London: Routledge and Kegan Paul, 1986.

Ellis, John. *Brute Force.* New York: Viking, 1990.

Emme, E. M., ed. *The Impact of Air Power.* New York: Van Nostrand, 1958.

Feis, Herbert. *Churchill, Roosevelt, Stalin.* Princeton: Princeton University Press, 1957.

Fleishman, Joel, Liebman, Lance, and Moore, Mark, eds. *Public Duties: The Moral Obligations of Government Officials.* Cambridge, Massachusetts: Harvard University Press, 1981.

Fleming, Peter. *Operation Sea Lion.* New York: Simon and Schuster, 1957.

Frankland, Noble. *The Bombing Offensive Against Germany.* London: Faber and Faber, 1965.

Frankland, Noble and Webster, Charles. *The Strategic Air Offensive Against Germany 1939-1945.* Four Volumes. London: Her Majesty's Stationery Office, 1961.

Fuller, J. F. C. *The Second World War 1939-1945.* New York: Duell, Sloan and Pearce, 1949.

Fussell, Paul. *Wartime.* New York: Oxford University Press, 1989.

Galbraith, John. *The Affluent Society.* Boston: Houghton Mifflin, 1958.

Galland, Adolf. *The First and the Last.* Trans. Mervyn Sawill. New York: Holt, 1954.

"General Report of the Commission of Jurists at the Hague." *American Journal of International Law* XVII (October 1923).

Georgi, Dieter. "The Bombing of Dresden." *Harvard Magazine* (March-April 1985).

Gibson, Guy. *Enemy Coast Ahead.* London: Michael Joseph Ltds., 1946.

Gilbert, Martin. *The Second World War.* New York: Henry Holt and Company, 1989.

Gray, J. Glenn. *The Warriors.* New York: Harper and Row, 1959.

Goebbels, Joseph. *The Goebbels Diaries, 1942-1943.* Trans. Louis Lochner. Garden City, New York: Doubleday, 1948.

Goerlitz, Walter. *The History of the German General Staff: 1657-1954.* Trans. Brian Battershaw. New York: Praeger, 1953.

Great Britain, *5 Parliamentary Debates* (Commons). Volumes 337-408.

———. *5 Parliamentary Debates* (Lords). Volumes 121-130.

Grenfell, Russell. *Unconditional Hatred?* New York: Devin-Adair, 1954.

Handel, Michael, ed. *Leaders and Intelligence.* London: Frank Cass, 1989.

Hare, J. E. and Joynt, Carey B. *Ethics and International Affairs.* New York: St. Martin's Press, 1982.

Harris, Arthur. *Bomber Offensive.* London: Collins, 1947.

Harrison, Tom. *Living Through the Blitz.* London: Collins, 1976.

Hartle, Anthony. *Moral Issues in Military Decision Making.* Lawrence: University Press of Kansas, 1989.

Hastings, Max. *Bomber Command.* New York: Simon and Schuster, 1987.

Held, Virginia, Morgenbesser, Sidney, and Nagel, Thomas. *Philosophy, Morality and International Affairs.* New York: Oxford University Press, 1974.

Higham, Robin. *Air Power.* New York: St. Martin's Press, 1972.

Hinsley, F. H. *British Intelligence in the Second World War.* Three volumes. New York: Cambridge University Press, 1984.

Hoffmann, Stanley. *Duties Beyond Borders.* Syracuse: Syracuse University Press, 1981.

Howard, Michael, ed. *Restraints on War.* Oxford: Oxford University Press, 1979.

———. *War and the Liberal Conscience.* New Brunswick, New Jersey: Rutgers University Press, 1978.

Huie, William Bradford. *The Hiroshima Pilot.* New York: Putnam, 1964.

Hurley, Alfred F. *Billy Mitchell: Crusader for Air Power.* Bloomington, Indiana: Indiana University Press, 1975.

Iremonger, F. A. *William Temple*. London: Oxford University Press, 1948.

Irving, David. *The Destruction of Dresden*. New York: Holt, Rinehart and Winston, 1963.

Isaacson, Walter and Thomas, Evan. *The Wise Men*. New York: Simon and Schuster, 1986.

Janowitz, Morris and Shils, Edward A. "Cohesion and Disintegration in the Wehrmacht in World War II." *Public Opinion Quarterly* XII (Summer 1948).

Jasper, Ronald. *George Bell*. London: Oxford University Press, 1967.

Johnson, Brian. *The Secret War*. London: BBC Publications, 1978.

Johnson, Paul. *Modern Times*. New York: Harper and Row, 1983.

Jones, Archer. *The Art of War in the Western World*. New York: Oxford University Press, 1987.

Jones, H. A. *The War in the Air*. Oxford: Clarendon Press, 1937.

Jones, Neville. *The Origins of Strategic Bombing*. London: Kimber, 1973.

Jones, R. V. *Most Secret War*. London: Hamish Hamilton, 1978.

Keegan, John. *The Second World War*. New York: Viking, 1989.

Kennett, Lee. *A History of Strategic Bombing*. New York: Scribner's, 1982.

Kenny, Anthony. *The Logic of Deterrence*. Cambridge: Cambridge University Press, 1985.

Knightley, Phillip. *The Second Oldest Profession*. New York: Penguin Books, 1988.

Liddell Hart, Basil. *History of the Second World War*. New York: G. P. Putnam's Sons, 1970.

———. *The Memoirs of Captain Liddell Hart*. Two volumes. London: Cassell, 1965.

———. *Paris, or the Future of War*. London: K Paul, Trench, Trubner: 1925.

———. *Revolution in Warfare*. London: Faber, 1946.

———. *This Expanding War*. London: Faber, 1942.

———. *Thoughts on War*. London: Faber, 1944.

Longmate, Norman. *The Bombers*. London: Hutchinson, 1983.

Lyall, Gavin. *The War in the Air*. New York: William Morrow and Company, 1968.

Marwick, Arthur. *Britain in the Century of Total War*. Boston: Little, Brown and Company, 1968.

Maxwell, Mary. *Morality Among Nations*. Albany: State University of New York Press, 1989.

McInnes, Colin and Sheffield, G. D., eds. *Warfare in the Twentieth Century*. London: Unwin Hyman, 1988.

MacIsaac, David. *Strategic Bombing in World War Two*. New York: Garland Publishing Co., 1976.

McLaine, Ian. *Ministry of Morale*. London: George Allen and Unwin, 1979.

McPherson, James M. "Wartime." *New York Review of Books* (April 12, 1990).

Mearsheimer, John. *Liddell Hart and the Weight of History*. Ithaca, New York: Cornell University Press, 1988.

Messenger, Charles. *"Bomber" Harris*. New York: St. Martin's Press, 1984.

Middlebrook, Martin. *The Battle of Hamburg*. London: Allen Lane, 1980.

Middlebrook, Martin and Everitt, Chris. *The Bomber Command War Diaries*. London: Viking, 1985.

Morgan, Patrick. *Deterrence*. Beverly Hills, California: Sage Publications, 1977.

Morrison, Wilbur. *Fortress Without a Roof*. London: W. H. Allen, 1982.

Nagle, William J., ed. *Morality and Modern Warfare*. Baltimore: Helicon, 1968.

Nef, John. *War and Human Progress*. Cambridge, Massachusetts: Harvard University Press, 1950.

Nicolson, Harold. *The War Years 1939-1945*. New York: Atheneum, 1967.

Nye, Joseph. *Nuclear Ethics*. New York: The Free Press, 1986.

O'Connell, Robert. *Of Arms and Men*. New York: Oxford University Press, 1989.

Oppenheim, L. *International Law*. Ed. by H. Lauterpacht. 7th edition. New York: Longmans, Green, 1952.

Overy, R. J. *The Air War 1939-1945*. New York: Stein and Day, 1980.

Palmer, R. R. *A History of the Modern World*. 2nd edition. New York: Alfred A. Knopf, 1964.

Paret, Peter, ed. *Makers of Modern Strategy*. Princeton: Princeton University Press, 1986.

Quester, George. *Deterrence Before Hiroshima*. New York: John Wiley and Sons, 1966.

Rawls, John. *A Theory of Justice*. Cambridge, Massachusetts: Harvard University Press, 1971.

Revie, Alastair. *The Lost Command*. London: David Bruce and Watson, 1971.

Rich, Norman. *Hitler's War Aims*. New York: W. W. Norton and Company, 1973.

Richards, Denis. *Portal of Hungerford*. London: Heinemann, 1978.

———. *Royal Air Force 1939-1945*. Three volumes. London: Her Majesty's Stationery Office, 1953-1954.

Robinson, Bruce. *Lancaster—The Story of a Famous Bomber*. Hemel Hempstead: Harleyford, 1974.

Rostow, Walt W. *Pre-Invasion Bombing Strategy: General Eisenhower's Decision of March 25, 1944*. Austin, Texas: University of Texas Press, 1981.

Rumpf, Hans. *The Bombing of Germany*. New York: Holt, Rinehart and Winston, 1963.

Sallager, F. M. *The Road to Total War*. Santa Monica, California: The Rand Corporation, 1969.

Saundby, Air Marshall Sir Robert. *Air Bombardment*. London: Chatto and Windus, 1961.

Saunders, Hilary St. George. *Royal Air Force. Volume III: The Fight is Won*. London: Her Majesty's Stationery Office, 1954.

Saward, Dudley. *Bomber Harris*. Garden City, New York: Doubleday, 1985.

Schaffer, Ronald. "American Military Ethics in World War II: The Bombing of German Civilians." *Journal of American History* 67 (September 1980).

———. *Wings of Judgment*. New York: Oxford University Press, 1985.

Schindler, Dietrich and Toman, Jiri, eds. *The Laws of Armed Conflicts*. Third revised edition. Geneva: Henry Dunant Institute, 1988.

Sheehan, Neil. *A Bright Shining Lie*. New York: Vantage Books, 1989.

Sherman, William C. *Air Warfare*. New York: The Ronald Press, 1926.

Sherry, Michael. *The Rise of American Air Power*. New Haven: Yale University Press, 1987.

———. "The Slide to Total War." *The New Republic* (December 16, 1981).

Slessor, Sir John. *The Central Blue*. London: Cassell, 1956.

Smoke, Richard. *National Security and the Nuclear Dilemma*. New York: Random House, 1987.

Smyth, Charles. *Cyril Forster Garbett*. London: Hodder and Stoughton, 1959.

Snow, C. P. *Science and Government*. Cambridge, Massachusetts: Harvard University Press, 1961.

Sorge, Martin K. *The Other Price of Hitler's War*. New York: Greenwood Press, 1986.

Spaemann, Robert. *Basic Moral Concepts*. Trans. T. J. Armstrong. London: Routledge, 1989.

Spaight, J. M. *Air Power and the Cities*. London: Longmans, Green, 1930.

———. *Air Power and War Rights*. London: Longmans, Green, 1924.

———. *Bombing Vindicated*. London: Geoffrey Bles, 1944.

Speer, Albert. *Inside the Third Reich*. Trans. Richard and Clara Winston. New York: The Macmillan Company, 1970.

Stokesbury, James. *A Short History of Air Power*. New York: William Morrow and Company, 1986.

Sweetman, John, ed. *Sword and Mace*. London: Brassey's Defence Publishers, 1986.

Taylor, A. J. P., ed. *Churchill Revised*. New York: The Dial Press, 1969.

———. *The Second World War*. New York: Paragon Books, 1975.

Taylor, Telford. *Nuremberg and Viet Nam*. Chicago: Quadrangle Books, 1970.

Tedder, Lord Arthur. *Air Power in War*. London: Hodder and Stoughton, 1948.

———. *With Prejudice*. Boston: Little Brown and Company, 1966.

Thompson, R. W. *Churchill and Morton*. London: Hodder and Stoughton, 1976.

Toynbee, Philip. *Friends Apart*. London: McGibbon and Kee, 1954.

Trever-Roper, Hugh, ed. *Hitler's War Directives*. London: Sidgwick and Jackson, 1964.

Trythall, Anthony. *"Boney" Fuller*. London: Cassell, 1977.

United States, *Strategic Bombing Survey*. 64 Reports. Washington, D.C.: Government Printing Office, 1945.

Vansittart, Sir Robert. *The Black Record*. London: Hamish Hamilton, 1941.

Veale, F. J. P. *Advance to Barbarism*. London: Thompson and Smith, 1948.

Verrier, Anthony. *The Bomber Offensive*. New York: The Macmillan Company, 1969.

Von Clausewitz, Karl. *On War*. Trans. Michael Howard and Peter Paret. Princeton: Princeton University Press, 1976.

Wakin, Malham M., ed. *War, Morality and the Military Profession*. 2nd edition. Boulder, Colorado: Westview Press, 1986.

Walzer, Michael. *Just and Unjust Wars*. New York: Basic Books, 1977.

Wasserstrom, Richard, ed. *War and Morality*. Belmont, California: Wadsworth Publishing Company, 1970.

Winterbotham, F. W. *The Ultra Secret*. London: Weidenfield and Nicolson, 1974.

Wyman, Richard H. "The First Rules of Air Warfare." *Air University Review* (March-April 1984).

York, Herbert. "Making Weapons, Talking Peace." *Bulletin of the Atomic Scientists* (May 1988).

Zuckerman, Solly. "Bombs and Morals." *The New Republic* (November 17, 1986).

———. *From Apes to Warlords.* New York: Harper and Row, 1978.

———. *Nuclear Illusion and Reality.* New York: Vintage Press, 1983.

———. *Science in War.* London: Penguin Books, 1940.

———. *Scientists and War.* New York: Harper and Row, 1966.

———. "Strategic Bombing and the Defeat of Germany." *Journal of the Royal United Services Institute* 130 (June 1985).

INDEX

suggests possibility of attacking German cities with poison gas, 194

suggests that suffering of German people was poetic justice, 193

support of for city bombing in 1940, 46-7

tribute to Neville Chamberlain on latter's death, 208-9

upset at conditions in German cities at end of World War II, 223

see also airpower strategy (British) in World War II; area bombing offensive against Germany

Civil War (American), 133, 207-8

Clarion, Operation, xiii

Clausewitz, Karl von, 81, 149

and numbing effect of modern technology on sensitivities of soldiers, 81

and relationship between ethics and warfare, 132-3

inconsistencies in arguments of concerning level of violence in wartime, 222

on the "first principle of warfare", 205

Cochrane, Sir Ralph, 180

Collins, Reverend John (Chaplain of Bomber Command), 97

denounces immorality of area offensive, 97

Cologne, bombing of on May 31, 1942, 15

Colville, Sir John, 42

combatants and non-combatants in wartime, xii, 5, 9-10, 154-6

difficulty in definition of, 140-1

principle of double effect and, 139-40

treatment of governed by concept of proportionality, 142-4

see also ethics and warfare

Copenhagen

and Bomber Command attack on, 154

Coventry

German attack on, 11, 103

Cripps, Sir Stafford, 83

suggests alternatives to reliance on the area offensive, 169-70

urges Bomber Command aircrew to be morally sensitive, 83-4

Curzon, Lord, 202

deterrence, concept of, 195-7

and nuclear deterrence as reflection of area bombing strategy in World War II, 203-4

definition of, 196

fails to prevent area offensive against Germany, 197

German concern with, 196-7

Directorate of Bomber Operations, and opposition within to Arthur Harris, 173

dissent against area bombing, 101-27

among military historians, 105-10

and diverse tactics and arguments among dissenters, 104

and ostracism of dissenters by British society and government, 109

and pressures against expression of dissent, 101

range and type of, 101

relatively greater toleration for in World War II, 101-2

within Parliament, 115-20

see also George Bell; Vera Brittain; J.F.C. Fuller; Basil Liddell Hart; Alfred Salter; Richard Stokes

Douhet, General Giulio, 6

and air warfare as more humane than other military methods, 6

Dresden, attack on, 20

and reaction of Arthur Harris to Churchill memorandum concerning, 58

AP newspaper dispatch describing effects of, 89-90

Arthur Harris's moral reflection on, 41-2

British aircrew objections to, 83

Churchill memorandum after, 20

compared to sack of Magdeburg (1631), 202

reasons for and effects of, 20

remoteness from reality of those ordering, 207

Dunkirk, 147

Dyson, Freeman, xv

background of, 64-5

moral condemnation of area offensive, 64

first major defeat incurred by at Moscow, 148

German government monitors state of popular opinion in, 159-60

launches terror bombing raids against Britain, 195

little strategic bombing of Britain by after 1941, 196

military advances of in 1942, 149

proposes ban in 1936 on bombing of cities, 28

see also Joseph Goebbels; Adolf Hitler; oil production (German); Albert Speer

Goebbels, Joseph, 80

and effects of unconditional surrender formula on German public opinion, 160

denounces immorality of Allied air campaign, 80

takes satisfaction in Allied exaggeration of effects of bombing, 164

Grigg, Sir James

and level of resources assigned to the Royal Air Force, 170

Guernica, German attack on (1937), 7

Hague Convention (1907)

and restrictions on aerial warfare, 25-6, 200

Germans base legal defense of bombing of Warsaw on, 137-8

Hague Draft Rules of Aerial Warfare (1923), 26-7

Britain indicates acceptance of, 28

Hague Peace Conference (1899), 25

Haig, Sir Douglas, 206

compared to Arthur Harris, 206

Hamburg, attack on, xii, 17, 41-2, 82, 175

lack of effect of on German arms production in city, 162

use of phosphorus bombs in, 212

Harris, Sir Arthur, 11, 14-15, 35-6, 38-43, 47, 52-61, 153, 166

ability of to defy pressure from his superiors, 52-6

admits that Bomber Command had precision bombing capability as of 1944, 178

and relationship between destruction of German cities and lives of British soldiers, 152

and vulnerability to dismissal from command in 1944, 180-1

argues for resumption of area offensive in September, 1944, 19

asserts that Bomber Command could win war by itself, 170-1

as symbol of independent British role in the war, 189

attempts to gain support for Bomber Command in 1942, 15

boasts about expense of training his aircrew, 225

built up by British government as heroic figure, 189

challenges competence of other military and civilian officials in Britain, 138-9

claims that bombing of Berlin could end the war, 17

compared to World War I general Douglas Haig, 206

comments on attack on Dresden, 42

concerned about Bomber Command aircrew developing moral doubts about area offensive, 83

confidence expressed in by members of Bomber Command, 76

controversy over memorial to, xiii

defies attempts by superiors to end area offensive after September, 1944, 54-6

denounces disguising of the real purpose of British bombing, 32-3

doubtful professional judgment of, 43

ignores intent of Casablanca Conference, 53-4

lack of honors extended to after the war, 36-7

moral responsibility for area offensive, 40-3

obituary on death of, 197

objects to air strategy before D-Day, 69

Official Dispatch of never published, 37

on bombing to preserve lives of Allied soldiers, 143